What Does DOS Mean? MODEM?

DOS is an acronym for **D**isk **O**perating **S**ystem. A specialized, disk-oriented program that provides an easy-to-use link between the user and a computer's disk drive. Modem is an acronym for **Mo**dulator/**Dem**odular, a device that translates digital pulses from a computer into analog signals for telephone transmission, and analog signals from the telephone into digital pulses the computer can understand. The modem provides communications capabilities between computer equipment over common telephone facilities.

These are only two of the more than 4,500 clear, complete, nontechnical definitions *Webster's New World Dictionary of Computer Terms, Third Edition,* gives you. Whether you're brand new to the world of computers, in the process of study, or already a confident user— here is a source of help that clarifies the unknown and puts language power behind your computer vocabulary!

It's The Reliable Backup You'll Use Every Day!

Webster's
New World
DICTIONARY
OF
COMPUTER
TERMS
Third Edition

Webster's New World
New York

Third Edition

**WEBSTER'S
NEW WORLD**

Simon & Schuster, Inc.
15 Columbus Circle
New York, NY 10023

DISTRIBUTED BY PRENTICE HALL TRADE SALES

Manufactured in the United States of America

6 7 8 9 10

Library of Congress Cataloging-in-Publication Data

Webster's New World dictionary of computer terms.

 Rev. ed. of: Webster's New World dictionary of computer terms / compiled by Laura Darcy and Louise Boston. c1983.
 1. Computers—Dictionaries.   2. Electronic data processing—Dictionaries.   I. Darcy, Laura. Webster's New World dictionary of computer terms.
QA76.15.W36 1988   004'.03   8888-14279
ISBN 0-13-949231-3 (pbk.)

INTRODUCTION

Today the use of computers, especially micro-computers, is one of the fastest-growing and most important developments of our time. These machines are being used by more and more people to do everything from solving complex business problems to composing music. A major problem with any revolutionary development is the nomenclature. In a fast-moving field such as computer technology, many new terms and concepts develop with the technology. It is important that these terms and concepts be defined and constantly updated and refined.

Webster's New World Dictionary of Computer Terms, Third Edition is a collection of more than 4,500 computer terms that focus on those topics of interest to computer users. These terms have been selected as those most likely to confront the beginning computer user. The book is written in terms a layperson can understand. Wherever possible, technical terms have been avoided so that the definitions might be easily read and understood. Where a proper understanding of a term depends upon the comprehension of another term, the reader is directed to it by a cross reference.

All terms are entered in a strict alphabetical listing, so that spaces and dashes are to be ignored in looking up a particular word or phrase. A term that begins with a number is entered in the position it would occupy if the number had been spelled out; for example, RS-232C appears in the position for "RS-two thirty-two C."

The most common meaning has been provided for most words. Frequently, the same word will have other, more specific meanings when used in specialized fields within the computer industry. If a term has more than one commonly accepted meaning, or is used as more than one part of speech, each sense is preceded by a number. Wherever possible, the more general sense of the word appears first. Because many of the terms have been recently introduced, absolute standardization of meaning has not yet taken place, and one term may have several similar, yet slightly different meanings.

The use of computers will continue to grow. People in all walks of life will become increasingly dependent upon them. A common understanding, among lay and professional users, of the basic terms of the technology will need to be achieved. This dictionary is designed as a tool to help bring that understanding about.

A

AAAI An abbreviation for **AMERICAN ASSOCIATION FOR ARTIFICIAL INTELLIGENCE**, a professional organization concerned with advancing artificial intelligence.

abbreviated addressing A modification of the Direct Address mode that uses only part of the full address and provides a faster means of processing data due to shortened code.

abend An acronym for **ABNORMAL ENDING**. An early termination of a program due to an error condition, such as division by zero or trying to add a number and a letter.

abort The procedure for terminating a program when a mistake, malfunction, or error occurs.

absolute address An address that is permanently assigned by the machine designer to a particular storage location. For example, the addresses 0000, 0001, 0002, and 0003 might be assigned to the first four locations in a computer's storage. Also called **MACHINE ADDRESS**.

absolute coding Coding that uses machine instructions and absolute addresses; therefore, it can be directly executed by a computer without prior translation to a different form. Contrast with **SYMBOLIC CODING**.

absolute movement Moving an object on the screen by providing the new location in terms of a specific X-Y coordinate pair.

absolute value The value of the number without reference to positive or negative sign. Denoted in mathematical notation by enclosure in vertical bars: $|+38| = |-38| = 38$.

abstract A summary of a document.

AC An abbreviation for **ALTERNATING CURRENT**, the type of electricity found in homes, schools, and businesses.

acceptance test A test used to demonstrate the capabilities and workability of a new computer system. It is usually conducted by the manufacturer to show the customer that the system is in working order.

access   Generally, the obtaining of data. To locate the desired data.

access arm   A mechanical device in a disk file storage unit that positions the reading and writing mechanism.

access code   A group of characters or number that identifies a user to the computer system.

access mechanism   A mechanical device in the disk storage unit that positions the read/write heads on the proper tracks.

accessory   A peripheral device, such as a floppy disk drive.

access time   The time a computer takes to locate and transfer data to or from storage.

accumulator   A register or storage location that forms the result of an arithmetic or logic operation. Commonly used when a series of calculations are to be totaled.

accuracy   The degree of exactness of an approximation or measurement. ACCURACY normally denotes absolute quality of computed results; PRECISION usually refers to the amount of detail used in representing those results. Thus, four-place results are less precise than six-place results; nevertheless, a four-place table could be more accurate than an erroneously computed six-place table. See PRECISION.

ACM   See ASSOCIATION FOR COMPUTING MACHINERY.

acoustical sound enclosure   A device that fits over a printer or other machine to reduce noise.

acoustic coupler   A modem (**MO**DULATOR/**DEM**ODULATOR) that connects to a telephone handset with rubber cups. The modem converts signals from the computer into audible tones that are detected by the telephone mouthpiece. Incoming signals are converted by the modem into electrical signals that the computer can read. Acoustic couplers, also called acoustic modems, are preferred by many small-computer users because they are compatible with almost any telephone. In contrast, direct-connect modems require a modular telephone jack connected to the phone system. Speed is limited to about 1200 bits per second. See MODEM.

ACP An abbreviation for **A**SSOCIATE **C**OMPUTER **P**ROFES-SIONAL, a program designed to assist two general groups of people. They are: students or recent graduates from computer programs in one-, two- or four-year colleges; and people who have been working in the computer field only a short period of time. Based on curriculum guidelines developed in the field, the ACP selects common areas of competence and their relative importance. The ACP program was designed to measure such basic knowledge. As a computer professional moves to higher positions, senior level programs provide competency measurement. Administered by the INSTITUTE FOR CERTIFICATION OF COMPUTER PROFESSIONALS.

ACPA See **A**SSOCIATION FOR **W**OMEN IN **C**OMPUTING.

acronym A word formed from the first letter (or letters) of each word in a phrase or name (e.g., VDT stands for Visual Display Terminal and IC stands for Integrated Circuit).

action (1) The performance of a particular operation or set of operations in response to a stimulus. (2) The resulting activity from a given condition.

action-oriented management report A report used to alert management to abnormal situations that require special attention.

action statement A statement that tells the computer to perform some action.

active cell In an electronic spreadsheet, the cell on the matrix that is highlighted by the cursor. Information may be entered, altered, or deleted by the user when the cell is active.

active file A file currently being used.

active program Any program currently being executed in the computer.

activity One of the subunits of work that comprise a task.

activity ratio When a file is processed, the ratio of the number of records in the file that have activity to the total number of records in that file.

actuator In a disk drive, a mechanism that moves the read/write head to the desired position over the disk surface.

ACU An abbreviation for **AUTOMATIC CALLING UNIT**. A device that allows a business machine to make dial calls on a telephone network.

Ada A high-level programming language developed in the late 1970s for the U.S. Department of Defense. It is named for Ada Augusta Lovelace, the first female programmer. ADA is intended particularly for embedded systems. It stresses modularity, reliability, and maintainability, and bears a strong resemblance to Pascal. Here is a sample program written in ADA:

```
with SQRT, SIMPLE_IO;
procedure PRINT_ROOT is
    use SIMPLE_IO;
    X: FLOAT;
begin
    GET(X);
    PUT(SQRT(X));
end PRINT_ROOT;
```

adapter A device that allows compatibility between different equipment.

adapter boards The printed circuit boards that connect a system board to peripheral I/O devices or add specialized functions to the system.

adaptive system A system displaying the ability to learn, change its state, or otherwise react to a stimulus. Any system capable of adapting itself to changes in its environment.

adder A device capable of forming the sum of two or more quantities.

add-in Refers to a component that can be placed on a printed circuit board already installed in a computer. For example, the addition of additional memory chips to empty slots in a microcomputer.

addition record A record that results from the creation of a new record during the processing of a file.

add-on Component or device added to a computer system to increase its storage capacity, to modify its architecture, or to upgrade its performance.

address An identification, such as a label, number, or name that designates a particular location in storage or any other data destination or source.

address bus A bus that conveys address data from one system component to another.

address decoder Circuitry that enables data to be obtained from a particular location when its character code is provided.

addressing Techniques for locating a required piece of data.

address modification An operation that causes an address to be altered in a prescribed way by a computer.

address register A register containing the address of the instruction currently being executed.

address space The complete range of addresses available to a computer user.

address translation The process of changing the address of an instruction or item of data to the address in main memory at which it is to be loaded or relocated.

advanced BASIC An advanced implementation of the BASIC programming language.

aesthetic Having to do with beauty as opposed to usefulness or moral or emotional content.

AFCET An acronym for ASSOCIATION FRANCAISE POUR LA CYBERNETIQUE ECONOMIQUE ET TECHNIQUE. A professional organization whose purpose is to bring together French scientists, computer users, computer manufacturers, and engineers interested in computer technology and applied mathematics.

AFIPS See AMERICAN FEDERATION OF INFORMATION PROCESSING SOCIETIES.

AI An abbreviation for artificial intelligence, the branch of computer science that works on getting computers to think like human beings.

AISP See ASSOCIATION OF INFORMATION SYSTEMS PROFESSIONALS.

alarm A warning signal that is displayed or activated whenever a critical deviation from normal conditions occur.

ALGOL An acronym for **ALGORITHMIC LANGUAGE**, an international high-level programming language used to code mathematical and number problems. The language has had a strong impact on programming language design. ALGOL is essentially a "dead" language that managed to spawn others, most notably Pascal and Modula-2.

algorithm A prescribed set of well-defined, unambiguous rules or processes for the solution of a problem in a finite number of steps; for example, a full statement of an arithmetic procedure for evaluating cosine x to a stated precision. A computer can carry out the steps in many different types of algorithms. Thus the study of computers and the study of algorithms are closely related subjects. Contrast with HEURISTIC.

algorithmic language A language designed for expressing algorithms. See ALGOL.

aliasing Undesirable visual effects in computer-generated images caused by improper sampling techniques. The most common effect is a jagged edge along object boundaries. See STAIRCASING.

aligning edge That edge of a form that, in conjunction with the leading edge, serves to position correctly a document to be scanned by an OCR device.

alignment An adjustment of tolerances within the mechanism of a device so it will operate properly.

allocate To assign a resource for use in performing a specific job.

allocation The process of reserving computer storage areas for instructions or data. Allocation is sometimes done by a programmer, or sometimes automatically by a program.

alphabetic Referring to data that consists of letters and special symbols.

alphabetic string A string in which the characters are letters, or pertain to an agreed alphabet set.

alphameric   A contraction of alphanumeric.

alphanumeric   A general term for alphabetic letters (A through Z), numerical digits (0 through 9), and special characters (-, /, *, $, (,), +, etc.) that are machine-processable.

alphanumeric display terminal   A device for entering alphanumeric information into a computer system and displaying it on a screen.

alphanumeric sort   A process in which a computer system puts a list into alphabetical or numerical order, or both.

alpha testing   Trying a new product out on the employees of one's own company before subjecting it to a beta test. See BETA TESTING.

alternate routing   In data communications, the process of switching the path between two locations to an alternate when the normal path is not available.

alternating current   The type of electricity found in schools, homes, and businesses.

ALU   An abbreviation for ARITHMETIC-LOGIC UNIT, the portion of the central processing unit (CPU) where arithmetic and logical operations are performed. A basic element of the CPU.

ambient conditions   The environmental conditions that surround a computer system, such as light, temperature, and humidity.

ambient temperature   The temperature surrounding a piece of equipment.

American Federation of Information Processing Societies (AFIPS)   As the American representative of the International Federation for Information Processing (IFIP), AFIPS represents the majority of the major computer science and data processing organizations in the country. Activities include sponsorship of the annual National Computer Conference, and committee work on education, research, government activities, standards and practices, and the history of computing.

American National Standards Institute (ANSI) An organization that acts as a national clearing-house and coordinator for voluntary standards in the United States.

American Society for Information Science (ASIS) A professional organization that provides a forum for librarians, information specialists, and scientists who seek to improve the communication of information.

American Standard Code for Information Interchange See ASCII.

Amiga™ The brand name of a family of microcomputers manufactured by Commodore International, Ltd. The Amiga is a revolutionary product in many respects. It uses a Motorola 68000 microprocessor, includes color graphics, multi-tasking and an IBM-PC compatible option. There are three members to this family: Amiga 500™, Amiga 1000™, and Amiga 2000™.

analog Referring to the representation of numerical quantities by the measurement of continuous physical variables: for example, the magnitude of an electrical signal might represent a number. Contrast with DIGITAL.

analog computer A computer that measures continuously changing conditions, such as temperature and pressure, and converts them into quantities. See COMPUTER. Contrast with DIGITAL COMPUTER.

analog data A physical representation of information such that the representation bears an exact relationship to the original information. For example, the electrical signals on a telephone channel are analog data representation of the original voice data. Contrast with DIGITAL DATA.

analogical reasoning Drawing conclusions about a system by studying a model of it.

analog-to-digital converter Mechanical or electrical device used to convert continuous analog signals to discrete digital numbers.

analysis The investigation of a problem by some consistent, systematic procedure. See SYSTEMS ANALYSIS.

analysis graphics Types of graphics programs that are designed to allow users to more clearly examine and analyze data, making it easier for them to develop conclusions about what the data itself means. The major component of business graphics, analytical graphics programs, consist basically of bar, area, line, and pie charts.

analyst A person skilled in the definition and development of techniques for solving a problem, especially those techniques for solutions on a computer. See PROGRAMMER/ANALYST and SYSTEMS ANALYST.

ancillary equipment See PERIPHERAL EQUIPMENT.

AND A logical connector, as in the statement A AND B, which means that the statement is true if, and only if, both A and B are true simultaneously.

AND-gate **(1)** A binary circuit with two or more inputs and a single output, in which the output is logic 1 only when all inputs are logic 1, and the output is logic 0 if any one of the inputs is logic 0. **(2)** In a computer, a gate circuit with more than one input terminal. No output signal will be produced unless a pulse is applied to all inputs simultaneously. Contrast with OR-GATE.

android A human-like male robot.

angstrom A unit of measurement, 1/250 millionth of an inch. Angstroms are used to measure the elements in electronic components on a chip.

animation Process of making an object appear to move by rapidly displaying a series of pictures of it, each one in a slightly different position. The technique used for producing computer-generated movies.

annotation A comment, note or descriptive remark added to a program or flowchart.

annotation symbol A symbol used to add messages or notes to a flowchart, attached to other flowcharting symbols by dashed lines.

ANSI An acronym for AMERICAN NATIONAL STANDARDS INSTITUTE. An organization that acts as a national clearinghouse and coordinator for voluntary standards in the United States.

answer mode   The ability of a modem to accept an incoming call from another modem.

answer/originate   In telecommunications, refers to the alternatives of sending (originating) or receiving (answering) a phone call.

anti-aliasing   A filtering technique to give the appearance of smooth lines and edges in a raster display image.

antistatic mat   A floor mat placed in front of a device such as a disk unit that is sensitive to static, to prevent shocks that could cause loss of data during human handling of the unit.

APL   An abbreviation for **A** **P**ROGRAMMING **L**ANGUAGE, a mathematically structured programming language, popular for problem-solving applications. In its simplest mode of operation, APL performs the functions of an intelligent calculator. The power of the language is demonstrated by its extended single operators that allow a user to perform directly such calculations as taking the inverse of a matrix or solving a set of linear equations. Here is a program written in APL.

```
      ∇ INVEST
 [1]  P←1000
 [2]  I←5
 [3]  N←10
 [4]  A←P x (1 + I) ÷ 100) * N
 [5]  A
 [6]  ∇
      INVEST
1628.894627
```

append   To add on, for example, to add new records to a data base or to add to the end of a character string or list.

Apple™   **(1)** The brand name for a family of microcomputers manufactured by Apple Computer, Inc., including the Apple II™, Apple IIPlus™, Apple IIc™, Apple IIe™, and Apple IIGS™. **(2)** One of the largest microcomputer manufacturers. The company, located in Cupertino, California, was founded by Steven P. Jobs and Stephen G. Wozniak.

AppleBus   An external device that allows a Macintosh microcomputer to be connected to other computers to form a network so information may be passed from one computer to another.

Apple Pascal A high-level programming language designed for use on the Apple II™ family of microcomputers. The Apple Pascal system incorporates UCSD Pascal and extensions for graphics, sound, paddles, and other functions. See PASCAL and UCSD PASCAL.

AppleLine A hardware device that enables a Macintosh microcomputer to exchange information with IBM mainframe systems.

Applesoft BASIC An extended version of the BASIC programming language used with Apple II+, IIc, IIe and IIGS™ computers and capable of processing numbers in floating-point form. An interpreter for creating and executing programs in Applesoft BASIC is built into the computer.

Appleworks™ An integrated software package containing word processing, spreadsheet, and data base services that can share data with one another. The package is widely used in educational institutions. Developed by Apple Computer, Inc.

application Task to be performed by a computer program or system. Broad examples of computer applications are computer-aided design, numerical control, airline seat reservations, business forecasting, and hospital administration. Word processing or electronic spreadsheet programs are examples of applications that run on microcomputer systems.

application-oriented language A problem-oriented programming language whose statements contain or resemble the terminology of the computer user.

application programmer A computer programmer who develops application programs.

application programming The preparation of programs for application to specific problems in order to find solutions. Contrast with SYSTEM PROGRAMMING.

application programs The programs normally written by programmers within an organization that enable the computer to produce useful work; for example, inventory control, attendance accounting, linear programming, or medical accounting tasks. Contrast with SYSTEM PROGRAMS.

application software See APPLICATION PROGRAMS.

applied mathematics Mathematics put to practical use, as in mechanics, physics, or computer science.

approximation A number that is not exact, but has been rounded off to a prescribed decimal place: 3.14 and 3.14159 are both approximations for π.

APT An abbreviation for **A**UTOMATIC **P**ROGRAMMED **T**OOL. A programming system that is used in numerical control applications for the programmed control of machine functions. The APT language allows a user to define points, lines, circles, planes, conical surfaces, and geometric surfaces. See NUMERICAL CONTROL and PARTS PROGRAMMER.

arcade game Computer video games popularized by coin-operated machines, characterized by high-resolution color graphics, high-speed animation, and sound. Players often use joysticks to control a screen object, and the computer assigns scores based on the game's rules.

architecture (1) The physical structure of a computer's internal operations, including its registers, memory, instruction set, input/output structure, and so on. (2) The art of building with solid materials, enclosing space in a useful and pleasing way. (3) The composite of specific components and the way in which they interact, that form a computer system.

archival Pertaining to the long-term storage of data.

archive (1) To copy programs and data onto an auxiliary storage medium such as a disk or tape for long-term retention. (2) To store data for anticipated normal long-term use.

area chart Area charts are usually a combination of two line charts with the difference between the two highlighted to accentuate that difference.

area search The examination of a large group of documents to select those that pertain to one group, such as a specific category or class.

argument A variable to which either a logical or a numerical value may be assigned.

arithmetic Pertaining to computing by adding, subtracting, multiplying, or dividing.

arithmetic-logic unit A basic element of the central processing unit (CPU). The portion of the CPU where arithmetic and logical operations are performed. Abbreviated ALU.

arithmetic operation The addition, subtraction, multiplication, or division of numerical quantities.

arithmetic operator A symbol that tells a computer to perform addition, subtraction, multiplication, division or raising to a power.

ARPANET A network established by the **A**DVANCED **RE**SEARCH **P**ROJECTS **A**GENCY (ARPA) of the Department of Defense so that information can be exchanged between the computers of universities and defense contractors all over the country.

arrangement Order of index terms or system.

array (1) A series of related items. (2) An ordered arrangement or pattern of items or numbers, such as a determinant, matrix, vector, or table of numbers. See MATRIX and VECTOR.

array processor A processor that performs matrix arithmetic much faster than standard computers. It is capable of performing operations on all the elements in large matrices at one time. Also known as a vector processor.

arrival rate The number of characters or messages arriving over a data communications medium per unit of time.

artificial intelligence The branch of computer science that studies how smart a machine can be, which involves the capability of a device to perform functions normally associated with human intelligence, such as reasoning, learning, and self-improvement. See EXPERT SYSTEMS, HEURISTIC, KNOWLEDGE-BASED SYSTEMS, and MACHINE LEARNING. Abbreviated AI.

artificial language A language based on a set of prescribed rules that are established prior to its usage: computer programming languages, such as BASIC and Pascal are artificial languages. Contrast with NATURAL LANGUAGE.

ARTSPEAK A programming language designed to help inexperienced users produce computer drawings on digital plotters.

ASAP An acronym for "AS SOON AS POSSIBLE."

ascender The portion of lower-case letters that extends above the main portion of the letter, such as the tops of b, d, and h.

ascending order The order that ranges from smallest to largest or first to last.

ASCII An acronym for **AMERICAN STANDARD CODE FOR IN-FORMATION INTERCHANGE**. Pronounced "asskey." A 7-bit standard code adopted to facilitate the interchange of data among various types of data processing and data communications equipment. Compare EBCDIC.

Ashton-Tate A California software company that produces software for microcomputers. Two of their programs are dBASE™ III and Framework™.

ASIS See **AMERICAN SOCIETY FOR INFORMATION SCIENCE**.

ASM See **ASSOCIATION FOR SYSTEMS MANAGEMENT**.

aspect ratio In computer graphics, the relationship of the height and width of the video display screen frame or image area.

assemble (1) To gather, interpret, and coordinate data required for a computer program, translate the data into computer language, and project it into the final program for the computer to follow. (2) To translate symbolic code into equivalent machine code.

assembler A computer program that takes nonmachine language instructions prepared by a computer user and converts them into a form that may be used by the computer. A computer program that assembles.

assembling The automatic process by which a computer converts a symbolic source language program into a machine language, usually on an instruction-by-instruction basis. See CROSS COMPILING/ASSEMBLING.

assembly The process of translating a program written in symbolic code into its equivalent machine code.

assembly language A programming language that allows a computer user to write a program using mnemonics instead of numeric instructions. It is a low-level symbolic programming language that closely resembles machine code language. Same as low-level language. Contrast with PROBLEM-ORIENTED LANGUAGE and PROCEDURE-ORIENTED LANGUAGE. Here is a sample program written in assembly language.

```
          START   256
BEGIN     BALR    15 0
          USING   *,15
          L       3,OLDOH
          A       3,RECPT
          S       3,ISSUE
          ST      3,NEWOH
          SVC     0
OLDOH     DC      F'9'
RECPT     DC      F'4'
ISSUE     DC      F'6'
NEWOH     DS      F
          END     BEGIN
```

assembly listing A printed output produced by an assembler. It lists the original assembly language program, the machine language version of the program, storage assignments, error messages, and other information useful to the programmer.

assembly program See ASSEMBLER.

assignment operator An operator used in an assignment statement that causes the value on the right to be placed into the variable on the left of the operator. In BASIC, the assignment operator is the = sign. In Pascal, the assignment operator is the := sign.

assignment statement A programming language statement that gives a value to a variable, such as in $x = x + 1$ or $y = 6$.

Associate Computer Professionals See ACP.

Association for Computers and the Humanities (ACH) ACH is an international organization devoted to the encouragement of computer-aided research in language and literary studies, history, anthropology, and related social sciences as well as the use of computers in the creation and study of art, music, and dance.

Association for Computing Machinery (ACM) World's largest educational and scientific society committed to the development of technical skills and professional competence of computer specialists. Founded in 1947, ACM has earned a reputation for technical excellence by publishing prestigious journals and sponsoring numerous conferences that promote an ongoing dialogue among students, educators, and practitioners.

Association for Systems Management (ASM) Founded in 1947, ASM is an international organization engaged in keeping its members abreast of the rapid growth and change occurring in the field of systems management and information processing. It has five technical departments: Data Communications, Data Processing, Management Information Systems, Organization Planning, and Written Communications. An ASM member can belong to one or more of these departments.

Association for Women in Computing (AWC) Nonprofit, professional organization comprised of people who have an interest in the field of computer data processing. Main goals are to promote communication among, further the professional development and advancement of, and promote the education of women in computing.

Association of Computer Programmers and Analysts (ACPA) International organization of professionals that offers members a voice in professional issues plus opportunities to develop professional skills through seminars, workshops, and conferences. Provides informative national and chapter publications and promotes exchange of ideas with other professionals at chapter activities.

Association of Information Systems Professionals (AISP) Founded in 1972 as the International Word Processing Association, AISP has members worldwide with organized chapters in more than 100 metropolitan areas of the United States and Canada. Membership is intended for professional level employees involved in all aspects of information systems.

associative storage   Storage device whose storage locations are identified by their contents (rather than by names or positions, as in most computer storage devices).

asterisk   A symbol (*) used to represent a multiplication operator in many programming languages.

asynchronous   Pertaining to a mode of data communications that provides a variable time interval between characters during transmission.

asynchronous device   A device that transmits signals at irregular intervals to the system with which it is communicating.

asynchronous transmission   A method of transmission that allows data to be sent at irregular intervals by preceding each character with a "start bit" and following it with a "stop bit."

Atari™   (1) The brand name of a popular line of personal computers and peripheral equipment manufactured by Atari Corporation. Examples include the Atari 520ST™ and Atari 1024ST™. (2) A large manufacturer of personal computers. Despite its Japanese name, the company is American and has been so since its inception.

ATM   See AUTOMATED TELLER MACHINE.

atom   (1) Elementary building block of DATA STRUCTURES. Corresponds to a record in a file and may contain one or more fields of data. (2) A basic element in a list. In list processing languages, the term usually refers to one item in a list: for example, in the list "the little red schoolhouse," each word is an atom.

attach   To connect a peripheral to a computer in order to increase its capacity.

attenuation   The decrease in the strength of a signal as it passes through a control system. Opposite of GAIN.

atto   Prefix meaning one quintillionth, or a billionth of a billionth, 10^{-18}. Abbreviated a.

attribute   (1) A word that describes the manner in which a variable is handled by the computer. (2) A characteristic quality of a data type, data structure, element of a data model, or system. (3) A feature of a device.

audible Capable of being heard.

audio Sound that can be heard by a human.

audio device Any computer device that accepts sound and/or produces sound. See VOICE RECOGNITION SYSTEM and VOICE SYNTHESIS.

audio output Computer output generated through voice synthesizers that create audible signals resembling a human voice. See VOICE SYNTHESIS.

audio response device An output device that produces a spoken response. See VOICE OUTPUT.

audio-visual Pertaining to the nonprint materials—such as films, tapes, cassettes—that record information by sound and/or sight.

audit trail A means for identifying the actions taken in processing input data or in preparing output. By use of the audit trail, data on a source document can be traced to a specific output, and an output can be traced to the source items from which it was derived. For example, it could reveal that Tom Wilson changed the inventory figures in the lamp bulb account at 10:34 A.M. on March 12.

authoring system A computer system capable of executing an author language.

authorized program A computer program capable of altering the fundamental operation or status of a computer system.

author language A programming language that is used for designing instructional programs for COMPUTER ASSISTED INSTRUCTION (CAI) systems.

authorization A system control feature that requires specific approval before processing can take place.

authors People who design instructional material for COMPUTER ASSISTED INSTRUCTION (CAI) systems.

auto-answer A modem that can automatically answer incoming telephone calls from computers and pipe the data into another computer.

auto-dial A modem capable of connecting to the telephone system and dialing a number. The modem and communications software perform the proper communications procedures so that computers may exchange data.

auto dialing modem   A modem that can automatically dial a phone number and redial a busy number until a connection is made.

auto-load   A key on some computer keyboards that activates the computer. It essentially boots the operating system into main storage and starts execution of the system. See OPERATING SYSTEM.

automata   The theory related to the study of the principles of operation, and the application, and behavioral characteristics of automatic devices.

automated data processing   A largely self-regulating process in which information is handled with a minimum of human effort and intervention.

automated flowchart   A flowchart drawn by a computer controlled printer or plotter.

automated office   Result of the merger of computers, office electronic devices, and telecommunications technology in an office environment.

automated teller machine   A special-purpose device used by banks for data communications with the bank's computer system.

automatic   Pertaining to a process or device that, under specified conditions, functions without intervention by a human operator.

automatic carriage   A control mechanism for a printer that can automatically control the feeding, spacing, skipping, and ejecting of paper or preprinted forms.

automatic check   An equipment check built in specifically for checking purposes. Also called BUILT-IN CHECK.

automatic coding   The machine-assisted preparation of machine language routines.

automatic computer   A computer that can process a specified volume of work, its assigned function, without requiring human intervention except for program changes. See COMPUTER.

automatic error correction A technique for detecting and correcting errors that occur in data transmission or within the system itself.

automatic loader A hardware loader program, usually implemented in a special ROM, that allows loading of an auxiliary storage unit (disk or magnetic tape). See BOOTSTRAPPING.

automatic message switching See MESSAGE SWITCHING.

automatic programming (1) The process of using a computer to perform some stages of the work involved in preparing a program. (2) The production of a machine language computer program under the guidance of a symbolic representation of the program.

automatic quality control Technique for evaluating the quality of a product being processed by checking it against a predetermined standard, and then automatically taking the proper corrective action if the quality falls below the standard.

automatic scrolling Same as CONTINUOUS SCROLLING.

automatic shutdown Refers to the ability of some systems software to stop a network or a computer system as a whole in an orderly fashion.

automatic teller machine (ATM) A banking terminal that provides customers with 24-hour deposit and withdrawal service. Special-purpose device connected to the bank's computer system. To use the automatic teller, the customer inserts a plastic identification card, enters a special password code, and communicates with the system by using a numeric keypad and a visual display.

automation (1) The implementation of processes by automatic means. (2) Automatically controlled operation of an apparatus, process, or system by mechanical or electronic devices that take the place of human observation, effort, and decision. (3) Refers to the use of machines to do work that was once done by people.

automaton A machine designed to simulate the operations of living things.

automonitor **(1)** A computer's record of its functions. **(2)** A computer program that records the operating functions of a computer.

autopolling A contraction of automatic polling. A process whereby terminals in a computer network are scanned periodically to determine whether they are ready to send information. Autopolling is a combination of hardware and software that polls the terminals in a computer network.

auto-repeat A feature of some keyboards that allows a key to automatically repeat when held down.

auto-restart The capability of a computer to perform automatically the initialization functions necessary to resume operation following an equipment or power failure.

autoscore In word processing, an instruction that causes text to be underlined.

auxiliary equipment Equipment not under direct control of the central processing unit. See OFFLINE.

auxiliary memory See AUXILIARY STORAGE.

auxiliary operation An operation performed by equipment not under control of the central processing unit. See OFFLINE.

auxiliary storage A storage that supplements the main storage of a computer, such as magnetic disks, floppy disks, and magnetic tapes. Same as SECONDARY STORAGE. Contrast with MAIN STORAGE.

availability The ratio of the time that a hardware device is known or believed to be operating correctly to the total hours of scheduled operation. Often called OPERATING RATIO.

available time The time that a computer is available for use.

AWC See ASSOCIATION FOR WOMEN IN COMPUTING.

axis In a two-dimensional coordinate system, lines used as references for vertical (*y*) and horizontal (*x*) measurement.

B

b An abbreviation for byte or baud. Use bytes when referring to storage, or baud rate when referring to communications.

Kb = 1000 bytes or baud (technically 1K = 1024 bytes). See BAUD and BYTE.

babble The cross talk from a large number of channels in a system. See CROSS TALK.

background (1) In multiprogramming, the environment in which low priority programs are executed. (2) That part of a display screen not occupied with displayed characters or graphics (foreground).

background job See BACKGROUND PROGRAM.

background noise In optical scanning, electrical interference caused by such things as ink tracking or carbon offsetting.

background processing The execution of lower-priority computer programs during periods when system resources are not required to process high-priority programs. See BACKGROUND PROGRAM. Contrast with FOREGROUND PROCESSING.

background program A program that can be executed whenever the facilities of a multiprogramming computer system are not required by other programs of higher priority. Contrast with FOREGROUND PROGRAM.

backing store A backup memory to the computer's main memory. More commonly called AUXILIARY STORAGE.

backing-up Making backup copies of files to prevent loss of their contents in the event the originals are damaged or lost.

back panel The back of a computer case, with a number of sockets for connecting peripheral devices to the computer.

backplane The circuitry and mechanical elements used to connect the boards of a system. The main circuit board of a computer into which other circuit boards are plugged. Also called MOTHERBOARD and SYSTEM BOARD.

backspace A keyboard operation that moves the cursor one place to the left. Backspacing allows modification of what has already been typed.

backspace tape The process of returning a magnetic tape to the beginning of the preceding record.

backtracking The operation of scanning a list in reverse.

backup **(1)** Pertaining to procedures or standby equipment that are available for use in the event of failure or overloading of the normally used equipment or procedures. **(2)** To make a copy of a program or data in case the original is lost, damaged, or otherwise inaccessible. **(3)** To so duplicate hardware, software or data.

backup copy A copy of a file or data set that is kept for reference in case the original file or data set is destroyed.

backward chaining A goal-driven method of reasoning that proceeds from the desired goal to the facts already known.

backward read A feature available on some magnetic tape systems whereby the magnetic tape units can transfer data to computer storage while moving in reverse.

badge reader A terminal equipped to read credit cards or specially coded badges.

bad sector A sector on a disk that will not read or write correctly. Usually due to a minor physical flaw in the disk.

balance The visual arrangement of colors, shapes, or masses to create a sense of equilibrium.

ball printer A printer that has the printing elements on the face of a ball-like replacement element. Type fonts can easily be changed by changing the TYPEBALL.

band printer An output printing device that uses a steel band or polyurethane belt to carry the character set.

bandwidth In data communications, the difference between the highest and lowest frequencies of a band. The term is used as a measure of the capacity of a communication channel, expressed in bits per second.

Bank Street Writer™ A word processing program developed by Broaderbund Software. The program is widely used on school and home microcomputer systems.

bank In communications, a range of frequencies, as between two specified limits. **(2)** range, as scope, of operation.

bar chart Widely used chart in business graphics.

bar-code A type of code used on labels to be read by a scanner. Bar codes are used to identify retail sales items, library books, and other items. See UNIVERSAL PRODUCT CODE.

bar graph A method presenting business data as a clear comparison between two or more items. Also called BAR CHART.

bare board A printed circuit board with no electronic components on it.

bar printer An impact printing device that uses several "type bars" positioned side by side across the line.

base (1) The radix of a number system. (2) The region between the emitter and collector of a transistor that receives minority carriers ejected from the emitter. (3) On a printed circuit board, the portion that supports the printed pattern.

base address A specified address that is combined with a RELATIVE ADDRESS to form the ABSOLUTE ADDRESS of a particular storage location.

baseband transmission Method of using low-frequency transmission of signals across coaxial cables for short-distance, local area network transmission.

base 8 See OCTAL.

baseline document A document that is a reference for changes to a computer system.

base 16 See HEXADECIMAL.

base 10 See DECIMAL.

base 2 See BINARY.

BASIC An acronym for BEGINNER'S ALL-PURPOSE SYMBOLIC INSTRUCTION CODE, an easy-to-learn, easy-to-use, algebraic programming language with a small repertory of commands and simple statement formats. For this reason, BASIC is widely used in programming instruction, in personal computing, and in business and industry. The BASIC language has been implemented on most microcomputers, minicomputers, and larger machines. See ADVANCED BASIC, BASIC-PLUS, INTEGER BASIC, FLOATING POINT BASIC, and TRUE BASIC. Here is a sample program written in BASIC.

```
100 REM ***********************
110 REM **** HOUSE MORTGAGE ****
120 REM ***********************
130 REM ** M - MONTHS **
140 REM ** B - BALANCE **
150 REM ** P - MONTHLY PAYMENT **
160 REM ** I - INTEREST FOR PRESENT MONTH **
170 REM ** P1 - PRINCIPLE FOR PRESENT MONTH **
180 PRINT ''MONTH'', ''BALANCE'',
    ''INTEREST'', ''PRINCIPLE''
190 LET B = 45000
200 LET P = 375
210 FOR M = 1 TO 72
220 REM **** CALCULATING INTEREST FOR PRESENT
    MONTH ****
230 LET I = B * (.08 * (1 / 12))
240 REM **** CALCULATING PRINCIPLE FOR PRESENT
    MONTH ****
250 LET P1 = P - 1
260 PRINT M, B, I, P1
270 REM **** CALCULATING NEW BALANCE ****
280 LET B = B - P1
290 NEXT M
300 END
```

Basic FORTRAN An approved American Standard version of the FORTRAN programming language. See FORTRAN.

basic linkage A linkage used repeatedly in one routine, program, or system that follows the same set of rules each time. See CALLING SEQUENCE and LINKAGE.

BASIC-PLUS An extension of the BASIC programming language. The language includes more powerful capabilities, especially for data manipulation.

batch A group of records or programs that is considered a single unit for processing on a computer.

batch processing (1) A technique by which programs to be executed are coded and collected together for processing in groups or batches. The user gives the job to a computer center, where it is put into a batch of programs and processed, and then returned. The user has no direct access to the machine. (2) Processing as a group data that has been accumulated over a period of time or must be done periodically, as in payroll and billing applications. See REMOTE BATCH PROCESSING.

battery backup Auxiliary power provided to a computer so that volatile information is not lost during a power failure.

baud A unit for measuring data transmission speed. One baud is 1 bit per second. Since a single character requires approximately 8 bits to represent it, divide the baud rate by 8 to calculate the characters per second (cps) to be transmitted. For example, 300 baud equal 37.5 cps, 1200 baud equal 150 cps, 2400 baud equal 300 cps. Most commercial information services (CompuServe, The Source, and Dow Jones News/Retrieval) offer both 300 and 1200 baud. Sometimes abbreviated b. See BYTE.

bay A cabinet or rack in which electronic equipment is installed.

BCD An abbreviation for BINARY CODED DECIMAL.

BCS An abbreviation for BRITISH COMPUTER SOCIETY, a professional computer society in the United Kingdom.

BDOS An acronym for BASIC DISK OPERATING SYSTEM. In some operating systems, the part of the system that customizes it to a specific disk drive.

bedlam Wild uproar and confusion.

beep An audible sound produced by a computer's speaker. Also a command in some programming languages that causes the computer's speaker to emit a sound.

bell 103 Standard format for transmitting data by telephone at speeds of 300 baud or less.

bells-and-whistles An informal description of the special or extra features of a computer system, including graphics, color displays, sound, and many peripherals.

bell 212A Standard format for transmitting data by telephone at a speed of 1200 baud.

benchmark A point of reference from which measurements can be made; such as the use of a program to evaluate the performance of a computer. Any standard against which products can be compared.

benchmark problem A problem designed to evaluate and compare the performance of computers.

benchmark tests Tests used in the measurement of computer equipment performance under typical conditions of use, such as a computer program run on several different computers for the purpose of comparing execution speed, throughput, and so forth.

Bernoulli™ box A removable hard disk system for microcomputers, manufactured by Iomega Corp. The main advantage of this cartridge system is that one hard disk system can be used for multiple libraries of hard disk data.

beta testing Pretesting of hardware and software products with selected "typical" users, to discover bugs before the product is released to the general public. See ALPHA TESTING.

bias The amount by which the average of a set of values departs from a reference value.

bibliography (1) An annotated catalog of documents. (2) An enumerative list of books. (3) A list of documents pertaining to a given subject or author. (4) The process of compiling catalogs or lists.

bi-directional Data flow may go in either direction on a wire. At each end of the wire there are transceivers to both receive and transmit. Common bi-directional buses are tristate or open collector transistor-transistor logic.

bi-directional printer A printer that prints from left to right as well as from right to left. A bi-directional printer is faster but slightly more complicated than conventional serial printers. This type of printer avoids a carriage return delay.

bifurcation A condition whereby two, and only two, outcomes can occur, such as on or off, 0 or 1, true or false.

Big Blue Nickname for International Business Machines Corporation (IBM).

billisecond See NANOSECOND.

bill of materials A listing of all the subassemblies, parts, materials, and quantities required to manufacture one assembled product or part, or to build a plant. A bill of materials can be generated automatically on a CAD/CAM system.

binary Pertaining to the number system with a radix of 2, or to a characteristic or property involving a choice or condition in which there are exactly two possibilities.

binary arithmetic A mathematical numeration system equivalent to our decimal arithmetic system but involving only two digits: 1 and 0.

binary code A coding system in which the encoding of any data is done through the use of bits—that is, 0 or 1.

binary coded character One element of a notation system representing alphanumeric characters—such as decimal digits, alphabetic letters, and special symbols—by a predetermined configuration of consecutive binary digits.

binary coded decimal (BCD) A computer coding system in which each decimal digit is represented by a group of four binary 1s and 0s.

binary device (1) A device that can register two conditions, such as an electrical switch that can be ON or OFF. (2) In computer science, equipment that records data in binary form or that reads the data so coded.

binary digit Either of the characters 0 or 1. Abbreviated BIT.

binary file A file containing programs in machine code.

binary notation A numeral system written in base 2 notation.

binary number A numeral, usually of more than one digit, representing a sum in which the quantity represented by each digit is based on a radix of 2. The digits used are 0 and 1.

binary point Radix point in a mixed binary numeral, separating the fractional part from the integer part. In the binary numeral 110.011, the binary point is between the two 0s.

binary search Search method in which a series of items is divided into two parts, one of which is rejected, and the process is repeated on each unrejected part until the item with the desired property is found. Often the best method when the list to be searched is known to be in order and relatively uniform. Many database systems use this method for locating items in their indexes.

binary system Numeral system with a base or radix of 2. The numeral 111 in the binary system represents the quantity 1, plus 1×2^1, plus 1×2^2—that is, 7 in the decimal system.

binary-to-decimal conversion The process of converting a numeral written to the base 2 to the equivalent numeral written to the base 10.

binary-to-hexadecimal conversion The process of converting a numeral written to the base 2 to the equivalent numeral written to the base 16.

binary-to-octal conversion The process of converting a numeral written to the base 2 to the equivalent numeral written to the base 8.

binding time The stage at which a compiler replaces a symbolic name or address with its machine language form.

biochip The computer industry's attempt to turn living organisms into microchips. Some predictions call for a reduction in size by 500 times from current silicon chips, but other scientists say the chips could be 80 years in the making. Biochips are made from existing biosystems, such as large protein molecules, to produce electronic circuits and switches, or by synthesizing an electron-trained molecule from scratch. A futuristic process of creating organic microchips from protein and manufacturing genetically engineered bacteria.

bionics The study of living systems for the purpose of relating their characteristics and functions to the development of mechanical and electronic hardware (hardware systems).

BIOS An acronym for BASIC INPUT/OUTPUT SYSTEM. In some operating systems, the part of the program that customizes it to a specific computer.

bipolar Pertaining to the most popular fundamental kind of integrated circuit, formed from layers of silicon with different electrical characteristics. Bipolar literally means "having two poles," unlike the earlier MOS Field Effect Transistor (MOSFET), which is unipolar ("having one pole"). As in MOSFET, the current flow of majority carriers goes in one direction only, such as, from source to drain. In a bipolar transistor, the current in the EMITTER region splits and flows toward two terminals (poles), the BASE and the COLLECTOR.

bit A binary digit; a digit (1 or 0) in the representation of a number in binary notation. The smallest unit of information recognized by a computer and its associated equipment. Several bits make up a byte, or a computer word.

bit image A collection of bits stored in a computer's memory, arranged into a rectangular matrix. The computer's display screen is a bit image that is visible to the user.

bit manipulation The act of turning bits on and off. Sometimes called bit-flipping.

bit map (1) An area in the computer's storage reserved for graphics. The bit map holds the picture that is continuously transmitted to the display screen. (2) An array of bits whose on-off status corresponds to the status of an array of other things.

bit mapped screen A screen display that associates each pixel on the screen with a memory location in the computer's RAM. Pixels are turned on or off depending upon the state of the memory location associated with each pixel. See PIXEL.

bit rate The rate at which binary digits, or pulse representations, appear on communication lines or channels.

bi-state A situation in which a computer component takes on one of only two possible conditions.

bit-slice processor This approach to microprocessors allows microcomputer organizations of variable word sizes, with processor units separated into 2-, 4- or 8-bit slices on a single chip. These devices can be paralleled to yield an 8-, 12-, 16-, 24- or 32-bit microcomputer when assembled with the other necessary overhead components of the system.

bit stream Referring to a binary signal without regard to groupings by character.

bit test A program check to determine whether a specific bit is on (1) or off (0).

bit transfer rate   The number of bits transferred per unit time, usually expressed in bits per second.

black box   An electronic or mechanical device that alters input signals in a predictable manner but whose inner workings are often a mystery to the user.

blank   **(1)** A part of a medium in which no characters are recorded. **(2)** In electronic spreadsheets, a command that will erase the contents of a cell or range of cells. **(3)** An empty space.

blank character   A character, or bit pattern, used to produce a space in data.

blanking   On a display screen, not displaying a character or leaving a space.

blind search   A time-consuming type of search that uses an orderly scheme but no knowledge to exhaust all possibilities.

blinking   A graphics aid that makes a predefined graphic entity blink on the CRT to attract the attention of the designer.

block   A group of digits, characters, or words that are held in one section of an input/output medium and handled as a unit, such as the data recorded between two interblock gaps on a magnetic tape.

block diagram   A graphic representation of the logical sequence by which data is processed. See FLOWCHART.

block gap   See INTERRECORD GAP.

block header   A brief record of data that describes a block of memory and its contents.

blocking   Combining two or more logical records into one block usually to increase the efficiency of computer input and output operations.

blocking factor   The number of logical records per physical record on a magnetic tape or disk.

block length   A measure of the size of a block, usually specified in units such as records, words, characters, or bytes.

block move   **(1)** Process in which a block of text is moved from one part of a document or file to another, or from one document or file to another. **(2)** In word processing, a feature that allows the user to identify a block of text and move it anywhere in a file. Electronic equivalent of "cut and paste."

block structure A programming technique in which a program is constructed by grouping sequences of instructions into hierarchical blocks: a block structure is used to create programs that are easy to understand. A characteristic of languages like Ada, Pascal or Modula-2.

block transfer Relocation of an entire block of data from one area of storage to another.

blow-up **(1)** The changing of a smaller format picture into a larger format picture. **(2)** Unexpected halt to a program due to a bug or because it encounters data conditions it cannot handle.

Blue Chip™ Personal Computer A low-cost IBM Personal Computer XT compatible that is made in Korea by Hyundai.

blue ribbon program A computer program that executes properly on the first try and does not require any debugging.

board Short for printed circuit board. A flat, thin rectangular component of a computer or peripheral that includes one or more layers of printed circuitry and to which chips and other electronic parts are attached. Sometimes called a card.

board computer A computer in which all electronic components are laid out on a single circuit board.

board exchange warranty A warranty that provides a customer with a new replacement board when the original needs repair.

boilerplate Pieces of text that get used over and over again, word for word, in different documents.

boldface A type font in which the main strokes of the letter are thicker than normal.

boldfacing A feature of some printers and word processing systems that lets them imitate the look of a boldface type font. On many printers, boldfacing is produced by shadow printing.

bold printing The ability to make certain letters darker than the surrounding test. Some printers produce bold characters by overstriking or shadow printing.

bomb A term used to denote a spectacular failure in a program. A computer user "bombs" a system when he/she deliberately writes a program that will disrupt the system. See CRASH.

bookkeeping See HOUSEKEEPING.

Boolean algebra A branch of symbolic logic that is similar in form to algebra, but instead of dealing with numerical relationships, it deals with logical relationships. An algebra named for George Boole.

Boolean operator A logic operator, each of whose operands and whose result has one of two values.

boot Derived from "bootstrap." To start or restart a computer system by reading instructions from a storage device into the computer's memory. It involves loading part of the operating system into the computer's main memory. If the computer is already turned on, it's a "warm boot;" if not, it's a "cold boot."

bootstrapping The process of using a small initialization program bootstrap to load another program and to start up an inactive computer. See BOOT.

bore The diameter of a hole, such as on a floppy disk.

Borland International A manufacturer of microcomputer software, founded by Philippe Kahn. Software products include Turbo Pascal, Sidekick, Turbo PROLOG, Turbo C and Turbo BASIC.

BOT An acronym for BEGINNING-OF-TAPE, a mark that shows where to start recording on a magnetic tape.

bottleneck See LIMITING OPERATION.

bottom up technique An implementation technique wherein the bottom level modules are written and tested, after which the next lowest level of modules are written and tested. This process continues until all of the modules have been completed.

bound Pertaining to whatever limits system performance, such as processor bound or I/O bound, indicating which component of a system is the bottleneck preventing faster performance.

bpi An abbreviation for BITS PER INCH or bytes per inch.

bps An abbreviation for BITS PER SECOND or sometimes bytes per second.

branch The selection of one or more possible paths in the flow of control, based on some criterion. A programming instruction that causes transfer of control to another program sequence. See CONDITIONAL TRANSFER, JUMP, and UNCONDITIONAL TRANSFER.

branch instruction An instruction to a computer that enables it to choose between alternative program paths, depending upon the conditions determined by the computer during the execution of the program.

branchpoint A place in a program where a branch is selected.

breadboard A board on which developing or experimental electronic circuits can be laid out: so called from the times when radios were constructed at home on a breadboard.

break An interruption of a transmission. To interrupt execution of a program.

break key On some computers, a keyboard key that will interrupt what the computer is doing.

breakpoint A specified point in a program at which the program may be interrupted by manual intervention or by a control routine. Breakpoints are generally used as an aid in testing and debugging programs.

bridgeware Computer programs used to translate instructions written for one type of computer into a format that another type of computer understands.

briefcase computer Portable computer that will fit inside a briefcase. See LAP COMPUTER, MICROCOMPUTER, and PORTABLE COMPUTER.

brightness (1) In computer graphics, the relative presence or absence of shading (whiteness to grayness to blackness). (2) On some visual display terminals, the ability to vary the intensity of the screen display. Especially useful in highlighting selected segments.

broadband As applied to data communications, used to denote transmission facilities capable of handling frequencies greater than those required for voice grade communications. Broadband communication channels can transmit data at rates up to five million baud; for example, microwaves, fiber optics, and laser beams.

broadcast In data communications, the dissemination of information to a number of stations simultaneously.

browsing Looking at files or computer listings in search of something interesting, often without authorization to do so.

brush In computer graphics, a blob of color that can be moved anywhere on the display screen by means of a joystick, paddle or similar input device. As the brush moves, it leaves behind a trail of color. See PAINTBRUSH.

brute-force technique Any mathematical technique that depends on the raw power of a computer to arrive at a non-elegant solution to a mathematical problem. Most computer users try to avoid brute-force techniques unless they have no practical alternative.

bubble memory A method by which information is stored as magnetized dots (bubbles), that rest on a thin film of semiconductor material. Offers a compact nonvolatile storage capability.

bubble sort A sort achieved by exchanging successive pairs of elements until the list is in the desired order. Also called ripple sort.

budget forecasting model Model generally used to consolidate budget information provided by separate departments by using standard accounting practices. May include capabilities to generate forecasts of cash flow, earnings per share, and other financial ratios resulting from performance according to budget. Such models are usually incorporated into SPREADSHEET programs.

buffer An area of storage used to temporarily hold data being transferred from one device to another. Used to compensate for the different rates at which hardware devices process data: for example, a buffer would be used to hold data waiting to print, in order to free the CPU for other tasks, since it processes data at a much faster rate.

buffered computer A computer that provides for simultaneous input/output and process operations.

buffering The delaying and temporary storing of data in a data communications path.

bug A term used to denote a mistake in a computer program or system or a malfunction in a computer hardware component. Hence, to debug means to remove mistakes and correct malfunctions. See MALFUNCTION and MISTAKE.

building block principle A system design that permits the addition of other equipment units to form a larger system. See MODULARITY.

built-in check See AUTOMATIC CHECK.

built-in fonts Fonts that come with a particular printer. In some cases, you can then add other fonts.

bulk eraser See DEGAUSSER.

bulk storage Large capacity data storage, generally long term. See AUXILIARY STORAGE.

bulletin board A computer system that allows users to post messages or programs for other users. Also called electronic bulletin board.

bundle To include software, peripherals, and services as part of the purchase price of a computer system.

bundled Pertaining to inclusion by a computer manufacturer of the entire line of computer products and services in a single price. Contrast with UNBUNDLED.

burn To ruin circuitry by subjecting it to excessive current or heat.

burn-in The process of testing electronic circuits and components by running the circuits at elevated temperatures in an oven. For example, a typical test might be to run components continuously for a week at 50 degrees C (122 degrees F). This testing process causes weak links in the circuit to burn out; the failed circuitry is replaced with components that will withstand the test.

burning The process of programming a read-only memory. See PROM PROGRAMMER.

burst (1) In computer operations, to separate continuous-form paper into discrete sheets. (2) In data transmission, a sequence of signals counted as one unit (an unbroken stream of bits).

burster A mechanical device that takes apart a multipage computer printout. It separates copies and removes carbon paper.

burst mode A method of reading or writing data that does not permit an interrupt to occur.

bus A channel or path for transferring data and electrical signals.

business graphics (1) Pie charts, bar charts, scattergrams, graphs, and other visual representations of the operational or strategic aspects of a business, such as sales vs. costs, sales by department, comparative product performance and stock prices. (2) The application programs that allow the user to display data as visual presentations.

business machines Word processors, computers, copy machines, terminals, and other electronic and mechanical equipment involved in business operations.

business software Programs specifically designed for business applications. Examples are electronic spreadsheets, database management systems, business graphics packages, payroll programs, and accounting programs.

bus network A system in which all stations, or computer devices, communicate by using a common distribution channel, or bus.

bus system A network of paths inside the computer that facilitate data flow. Important buses in a computer are identified as data bus, control bus, and address bus.

buzzword A word or phrase that happens to be the popular cliche of a group of people.

bypass A parallel path around one or more elements of a circuit.

byte **(1)** A grouping of adjacent binary digits operated on by the computer as a unit. The most common size byte contains 8 binary digits. **(2)** A group of binary digits used to encode a single character. Sometimes abbreviated b.

bytes per inch (BPI) The number of bytes that can be contained on one inch of magnetic tape.

C

C The full name of a programming language designed for use on microcomputers. The language combines high-level statements with low-level machine control to deliver software that is both easy to use and highly efficient. Here is a sample program written in C.

```
main()
   [
        int length, width area, circum;

        length = 40;
        width = 30;

        area = length * width;
        circum = 2 * (length + width);

        printf(''Length          %5d\n'',
        length);
        printf(''Width           %5d\n'',
        width);

        printf(''\n'');
        printf(''Area            %5d\n'',
        area);
        printf(''Circumference   %5d\n'',
        circum);
   ]
```

cable An electrical wire or bundle of wires used to connect two parts of the system together. It carries electrical power or electrical signals.

cable connector Plugs (male/female) that are used for connecting cables between a computer and peripherals.

cabling diagram A diagram showing connections and physical locations of system or unit cables, and used to facilitate field installation and repair of wiring systems.

cache memory A small high-speed memory for the temporary storage of information, usually used between a slower large memory and a fast central processing unit. Also called SCRATCHPAD.

CAD See COMPUTER-AIDED DESIGN.

CADAM An acronym for COMPUTER-GRAPHICS AUGMENTED DESIGN AND MANUFACTURING, the process of, or methods for, using computer systems as tools in design and manufacturing applications.

CAD/CAM An acronym for COMPUTER-AIDED DESIGN/COMPUTER-AIDED MANUFACTURING. A rapidly growing branch of computer graphics, currently relying primarily on calligraphic graphics but now branching out to incorporate raster graphics. It is used to design auto parts, buildings, bridges, and integrated circuits.

CADD See COMPUTER-AIDED DESIGN AND DRAFTING.

CAE An acronym for COMPUTER-AIDED ENGINEERING. Analysis of a design for basic error-checking, or to optimize manufacturability, performance, and economy. Information drawn from the CAD/CAM design data base is used to analyze the functional characteristics of a part, product, or system under design, and to simulate its performance under various conditions.

cage A chassis in which printed circuit cards are mounted.

CAI See COMPUTER-ASSISTED INSTRUCTION.

CAL See COMPUTER-AUGMENTED LEARNING.

calculating Reconstructing or creating new data by compressing certain numeric facts.

calculations Mathematical processes performed on data.

calculator Any mechanical or electronic machine used for performing calculations. Calculators, as distinguished from computers, usually require frequent human intervention. See HAND CALCULATOR.

calculator mode Operating mode on some interactive computer systems that allows the terminal (or keyboard/display in case of microcomputer systems) to be used as a desk calculator. The user types an expression; the computer then evaluates it and returns the answer immediately.

calibration The process of determining by measurement or by comparison with a standard the correct value of each scale reading on a meter or the correct value of each setting of a control knob.

call (1) To transfer control to a specific closed subroutine. (2) In communications, the action performed by the calling party, or the operations necessary in making a call, or the effective use made of a connection between two stations. Synonymous with cue.

calligraphic graphics Method of forming an image from scanlines oriented in arbitrary directions and drawn in an arbitrary order. Expensive electronics are required, but spatial anti-aliasing is not. Typical of this style of graphics are the "wire-frame" models that were considered synonymous with computer graphics in the early days.

calling sequence A specified set of instructions and data necessary to call a given subroutine.

call instruction An instruction that, after diverting execution to a new sequence of instructions (subroutine), permits a return to the program's original sequence.

CAM Acronyms for COMPUTER-AIDED MANUFACTURING AND COMPOSITION AND MAKE-UP.

Canadian Information Processing Society (CIPS) An organization formed to bring together Canadians with a common interest in the field of information processing. CIPS has a membership of several thousand persons, including scientists, businesspeople, and others who make their careers in computing and information processing.

cancel A keyboard operation that deletes the line currently being typed.

canned software Programs prepared by computer manufacturers or another supplier and provided to a user in ready-to-use form. This packaged software is general enough to be used by many businesses and individuals. Contrast with CUSTOM SOFTWARE.

Canon engine™ The internal mechanism of a Canon office photocopier, used in most laser printers.

capacitance A measure of the ability to store electric charge; the basic unit of measurement being a farad.

capacitor An electronic component that stores a charge of static electricity and when properly stimulated, releases this charge. This is the way bits are written to, and read from, computer storage.

capacitor storage A storage device that utilizes the capacitance properties of materials to store data.

capacity The number of items of data that a storage device is capable of containing. Frequently defined in terms of computer words, bytes, or characters.

caps Capitals, or uppercase letters. ALL CAPS WOULD LOOK LIKE THIS.

capstan The rotating shaft within a magnetic tape drive that pulls the tape across the recording heads at a constant speed.

capture (of data) The recording of data on a form or its entry into a computer.

carbon ribbon Ribbon used with printers to produce extremely sharp characters with excellent definition.

card (1) Another term for printed circuit board. (2) A storage medium in which data is represented by means of holes punched in vertical columns in an 18.7 cm by 8.3 cm (7 3/8 inches by 3 1/4 inches) paper card.

card cage Chassis inside the computer housing on which printed circuit boards are mounted.

card reader A machine that translates symbols coded on punched cards into electrical signals to send to a computer.

caret (1) A symbol used to indicate the location of the radix point of a number. (2) ∧ or > mark, used on a screen as a cursor to show where text should be inserted. (3) Symbol for exponentiation in BASIC.

carriage A control mechanism for a printer that automatically feeds, skips, spaces, and ejects paper forms.

carriage control tape A tape punched with information needed to control line feeding on a line printer.

carriage return In a character printer, the operation that causes the next character to be printed at the left margin. Abbreviated CR.

carrier frequency A constant signal transmitted between communicating devices that is modulated to encode binary information.

carry (1) Process of bringing forward. Special condition that occurs when the sum of two digits in a single column is equal to or greater than the number base. (2) Carry digit, or the digit to be added to the next higher column.

cartesian chart A rectangular planar grid based on two perpendicularly intersecting axes, an X axis (vertical), and a Y axis (horizontal).

cartesian coordinate system System named for French mathematician Rene Descartes whereby, in a flat plane, a point can be located by its distances from two intersecting straight lines, called the axes, the distance from one axis being measured along a parallel to the other axis. The numbers associated with the point are called the coordinates of the point.

cartridge A plug-in module that contains software permanently stored in ROM. A cartridge is convenient, easy to use, durable, soundless, and cannot be erased. A cartridge is inserted into a special slot built into the computer. It cannot be erased or copied to disk or tape. Also called SOLID STATE CARTRIDGE and ROM CARTRIDGE.

cascade connection Two or more similar component devices arranged in tandem, with the output of one connected to the input of the next.

cassette recorder A device designed to use cassettes to record and store digital data and, at a later time, reload this data into the computer's main storage.

cassette tape Magnetic tape, approximately 1/8 inch wide, that is housed in a small plastic container. Cassette tape is read by a cassette recorder.

CAT An acronym for COMPUTERIZED AXIAL TOMOGRAPHY and COMPUTER-ASSISTED TRAINING.

catalog (1) An ordered compilation of item descriptions and sufficient information to afford access to the items, such as a listing of programs or data file names that are stored on a floppy disk. To catalog a disk is to instruct the computer to print out a list of all of the files on the disk. (2) To so enter information into a table.

catena A connected series. See CONCATENATE.

cathode ray tube An electronic tube with a screen upon which information may be displayed. Abbreviated CRT. See DISPLAY, SCREEN, and VIDEO DISPLAY TERMINAL.

CBASIC A popular language compiler that is much faster in execution than the more popular interpreter BASIC. This high-level language is not interactive. A CBASIC program is translated into object code before it is executed. Here is a sample program written in CBASIC.

```
        REM   Accept an input from the operator
   10   INPUT  ''Enter a number between 1 and
        5:'';N%
        IF N%;<1 THEN GOTO 10
        IF N%>5 THEN GOTO 10
        ELSE ON N% GOTO

  100, Print \ ''one''
  200, Print \ ''two''
  300, Print \ ''three''
  400, Print \ ''four''
  500, REM Print ''five''

  100   PRINT   ''one''        :STOP      REM
1 input
```

```
    200    PRINT    ''two''      :STOP     REM
2 input
    300    PRINT    ''three''    :STOP     REM
3 input
    400    PRINT    ''four''     :STOP     REM
4 input
    500    PRINT    ''five''     :STOP     REM
5 input
       END
```

CBL See COMPUTER-BASED LEARNING.

CCD An abbreviation for CHARGE COUPLED DEVICE. A memory device within which stored information circulates rather than remains in fixed locations.

CCITT An abbreviation for CONSULTATIVE COMMITTEE INTERNATIONAL TELEGRAPH AND TELEPHONE, an organization established by the United Nations to develop worldwide standards for data communications.

CCP An abbreviation for CERTIFICATE IN COMPUTER PROGRAMMING. CCP examinations are given annually at test centers in colleges and universities in the United States, Canada, and several international locations. Three separate full-day examinations test a common core of programming knowledge and an area of specialization: business programming, scientific programming, or systems programming. The common core of knowledge emphasizes such areas as data and file organization, techniques of programming, programming languages, interaction with hardware and software, and interaction with people. Administered by the INSTITUTE FOR CERTIFICATION OF COMPUTER PROFESSIONALS.

CDC An abbreviationm for CALL DIRECTING CODE, a two- or three-character code used to route a message or command automatically.

CDP An abbreviation for CERTIFICATE IN DATA PROCESSING. CDP examinations are given annually at test centers in colleges and universities in the United States, Canada, and several international locations. This broad-based examination consists of five sections and requires half a day to complete. In addition to having experience requirements and espousing the Code of Ethics, CDP candidates must successfully complete all five sections of the examination to receive the certificate. Administered by the INSTITUTE FOR CERTIFICATION OF COMPUTER PROFESSIONALS.

CE See CUSTOMER ENGINEER.

cell (1) The storage for one unit of information, usually one character, one byte, or one word. A binary cell is a cell of one binary digit capacity. (2) A single coordinate location within the grid, or matrix, that constitutes the basic form of an electronic spreadsheet.

centi Prefix meaning hundredth.

center A keyboard function that places the information being typed in the center of the line.

centisecond One hundredth of a second.

central information file The main data storage system.

centralized data processing A concept by which a company has all its computing equipment located at the same site, and field-office operations have no effective data processing capability. Contrast with DISTRIBUTED DATA PROCESSING.

centralized design An information structure in which a separate information processing department provides information processing facilities for the organization.

centralized network configuration The structure of a computer network whose dominating feature is a central computer that, in one way or another, is involved in everything that happens in the system. Also called a STAR NETWORK.

central processing unit (CPU) The component of a computer system with the circuitry to control the interpretation and execution of instructions. The CPU includes the arithmetic-logic unit and control unit.

central processor See CENTRAL PROCESSING UNIT.

central site The main installation of a distributed information processing system.

central tendency The probability of data conforming to expected values.

Centronics interface A popular parallel interface used generally to connect printers to microcomputers. Centronics was one of the original printer manufacturers to use the parallel scheme for communications between microcomputers and printers.

Certificate in Computer Programming See CCP.

Certificate in Data Processing See CDP.

certification (1) Acceptance of software by an authorized agent, usually after the software has been validated by the agent, or after its validity has been demonstrated to the agent. (2) A voluntary system of attesting that a person has achieved a certain professional status, usually by passing a rigorous examination. See ACP, CCP, CDP, CSP, and INSTITUTE FOR CERTIFICATION OF COMPUTER PROFESSIONALS.

Certified Systems Professional See CSP.

chain (1) Linking of records by means of pointers in such a way that all like records are connected, the last record pointing to the first. (2) A set of operations that are to be performed sequentially.

chained files Data files where data blocks are chained together using pointers.

chained list A list in which each item points to the next item and the order of retrieval need not have any relation to the storage order.

chain field A field in a record that defines the location and storage device of other data items logically related to the original record but not physically attached.

chaining (1) A process of linking a series of records, programs, or operations together. (2) A method of allowing the execution of programs larger than the main memory of a computer by loading and executing modules of the same program sequentially.

chain printer An impact line printer that has its character set assembled on a chain revolving horizontally past all print positions; it prints when a print hammer (one for each column on the paper) presses the paper against an inked ribbon that in turn presses against the appropriate characters on the aligned print chain.

channel **(1)** A path for electrical or electronic transmission between two or more points. Also called a path, link, line, facility, or circuit. **(2)** A transmission path that connects auxiliary devices to a computer.

channel adapter A device that enables data communications between channels on different hardware devices.

channel capacity In data communications, an expression of the maximum number of bits per second that can be accommodated by a channel. This maximum number is determined by the bandwidth modulation scheme and certain types of noise. The channel capacity is most often measured in bauds, or bits per second.

chaos Utter confusion and disorder.

character Any symbol, digit, letter, or punctuation mark stored or processed by computing equipment.

character checking The checking of each character by examining all characters as a group or field.

character code A code designating a unique numerical representation for a set of characters.

character density A measure of the number of characters recorded per unit of length or area.

character generator A circuit that forms the letters or numbers on a screen or printer.

characteristic That part of a floating-point number that represents the size of the EXPONENT.

character map A grid of blocks on a display screen, where each block corresponds to a letter, number, punctuation mark, or special character.

character pitch In a line of text, the number of characters per inch. See ELITE TYPE and PICA.

character printer A printer in which only a single character is composed and determined within the device prior to printing.

character recognition The technology of using machines to automatically identify human-readable symbols, most often alphanumeric characters, and then to express their identities in machine-readable codes. This operation of transforming numbers and letters into a form directly suitable for electronic data processing is an important method of introducing information into computing systems.

character set Comprises the numbers, letters, and symbols associated with a given device or coding system. All of the characters recognized by a computer system.

characters per inch Method of expressing the output from printers as determined by the size and style.

characters per second Unit for measuring output of low-speed serial printers.

character string A string of alphanumeric characters.

character template A device used to shape an electron beam into an alphanumeric character for a CRT display.

charge A quantity of unbalanced electricity in a body.

charged coupled device (CCD) A semiconductor memory device within which stored information circulates rather than remains in fixed locations.

Charles Babbage Institute An organization for the study of the "information revolution" from a historical perspective. It is intended as a clearinghouse for information about research resources related to this history and a repository for archival materials.

chart A diagram showing the relationships of two or more variable quantities. Also called a graph. See FLOWCHART.

chassis A metal frame upon which the wiring, sockets, and other parts of an electronic assembly are mounted.

check digits One or more digits carried within a unit item of numerical data to provide information about the other digits in the unit in such a manner that, if an error occurs, the check fails, and an indication of error is given.

checkout See DEBUG.

check plot A pen plot generated automatically by a CAD system for visual verification and editing prior to final output generation.

checkpoint   A specified point at which a program can be interrupted, either manually or by a control routine. Used primarily as an aid in debugging programs.

check problem   A testing problem designed to determine whether a computer or a computer program is operating correctly. See BUG, DEBUG, and TEST DATA.

check sum   A summation of digits or bits used primarily for checking purposes and summed according to an arbitrary set of rules. The check sum is used to verify the integrity of data.

chief programmer   An individual designated as the leader of a programming team who has the overall responsibility of seeing that an entire project is successfully completed.

chief programmer team   An organization for computer programming wherein a very superior programmer is the technical leader of a team consisting, as a minimum, of a chief programmer, a backup programmer, and a programming librarian/programming secretary. As needed, the team may be augmented with two to three additional members and may consult specialists. The key concepts are **(1)** Making programming a public "engineering" practice instead of a private art. **(2)** Providing support so that a very superior creator can concentrate on creating.

child   A data record that can be created based upon only the contents of one or more other records (parents) already in existence. See PARENT and PARENT/CHILD RELATIONSHIP.

chip   A small component that contains a large amount of electronic circuitry. A thin silicon wafer on which electronic components are deposited in the form of integrated circuits. Chips are the building blocks of a computer and perform various functions, such as doing arithmetic, serving as the computer's memory, or controlling other chips.

chip family   A group of related chips, each of which (except the first) evolved from an earlier chip in the family.

chop   To discard unneeded data.

chroma   Color attributes, such as shade, saturation, and hue.

chunking along A slang term referring to the operation of a long running, dependable program.

CIM (1) An acronym for COMPUTER INPUT MICROFILM. A technology that involves using an input device to read the contents of microfilm directly into the computer. (2) An acronym for COMPUTER-INTEGRATED MANUFACTURING.

cipher A secret method of representing information to ensure computer security.

CIPS See CANADIAN INFORMATION PROCESSING SOCIETY.

circuit (1) A pathway designed for the controlled flow of electrons. (2) A system of conductors and related electrical elements through which electrical currents flow. (3) A communication link between two or more points.

circuit board A thin insulating board used to mount and connect various electronic components and microchips in a pattern of conductive lines. This circuit pattern is etched into the board's surface. Also called a PRINTED CIRCUIT BOARD.

circuitry A complex of circuits describing interconnection within or between systems.

circuit switching A physical connection between two nodes in a communication network that dedicates bandwidth of that circuit until the connection is dropped.

circular list A linked list, usually of data elements, in which the last element points to the first one. Also called a RING.

circular shift A shifting operation whereby bits or characters shifted off one end of a register enter the register on the opposite end.

cladding In fiber optics, the second layer of the fiber optics unit that bounces the light waves back into the core of the unit.

class A group having the same or similar characteristics.

classify To categorize or place data with similar characteristics into the same category.

clear (1) A keyboard function that removes the contents from the display screen. (2) To change the contents of a storage location.

clearing (1) Replacing the information in a register, storage location, or storage unit with zeros or blanks. (2) Erasing displayed text and/or graphic images from a display screen.

click The process of pressing the mouse button.

click art A disk of drawings and pictures that are ready to clip out and use in computer-produced documents. See CUT-AND-PASTE.

clicking A term used to describe the pressing of a button on the top of a mouse. See MOUSE.

clip art Graphics you can "cut" out and use. Clip art comes in both printed form and images stored on floppy disks.

clipboard A portion of a computer's memory set aside to store data being transferred from one file or application to another.

clipping The process of removing portions of an image that are outside the boundaries of the display screen.

clobber To write new data over the top of good data in a file or otherwise damage a file so that it becomes useless. To wipe out a file.

clock (1) A timing device that generates the basic periodic signal used to control the timing of all operations in a synchronous computer. (2) A device that records the progress of real time, or some approximation of it, and whose contents are available to a computer program.

clocking A technique used to synchronize a sending and a receiving data communications device. Permits synchronous transmission at high speeds.

clockwise Moving from left to right.

clone In non-biological terms, it is a product or idea that is an exact duplicate or copy of another.

closed file A file that cannot be accessed for reading or writing. Contrast with OPEN FILE.

closed loop A loop that is completely circular. See LOOP.

closed routine See CLOSED SUBROUTINE.

closed shop   The operation of the computer center by professional operators. Programs and data are carried by messengers or transmitted over telephone lines, avoiding the necessity of users entering the computer room. This enables a much more efficient use of the computer and is the opposite of the "open shop," in which each user puts her or his own program in the machine and fiddles with the switches on the console. Contrast with OPEN SHOP.

closed subroutine   A subroutine stored at one place and linked to one or more calling routines. Contrast with OPEN SUBROUTINE.

cluster controller   A down-line processor that collects data from a number of low-speed devices then transmits "concentrated" data over a single communications channel. See CONCENTRATOR.

clustered devices   Refers to a group of terminals connected to a common controller.

clustering   Refers to the process of grouping things with similar characteristics.

CMI   An abbreviation for COMPUTER-MANAGED INSTRUCTION.

CMS   An abbreviation for CONVERSATIONAL MONITOR SYSTEM, operating system for IBM mainframe computers.

CMOS   An abbreviation for complementary MOS. A method of making metallic oxide semiconductor chips that uses almost no power and works faster than MOS.

coaxial cable   A special type of communications cable that permits the transmission of data at high speed. Usually employed in local networks.

COBOL   An acronym for COMMON BUSINESS ORIENTED LANGUAGE, a high-level language developed for business data processing applications. Every COBOL source program has four divisions: (1) Identification Division identifies the source program and output of a compilation; (2) Environment Division specifies those aspects of a data processing problem that are dependent upon the physical characteristics of a particular computer; (3) Data Division describes the data that the object program is to accept as input, manipulate, create, or produce as output; and (4) Procedure Division specifies the procedures to be performed by the object program, using English-like statements. Here is part of a sample program written in COBOL.

```
00510    PROCEDURE DIVISION.
00520    START-IT.
00530        OPEN INPUT IN-FILE.
00540        OPEN OUTPUT OUT-FILE.
00550    DO-IT.
00560        MOVE SPACES TO CHECK-REGISTER.
00570        READ IN-FILE AT END GO TO END-
             IT.
00580        MOVE AMOUNT TO AMOUNT-OUT.
00590        MOVE CHK-NUMBER TO CHK-NUMBER-
             OUT.
00600        MOVE ISSUED-TO TO ISSUED-TO-OUT.
00610        MOVE MONTH TO MONTH-OUT.
00620        MOVE DAY-IN TO DAY-OUT.
00630        MOVE YEAR TO YEAR-OUT.
00640        WRITE CHECK-REGISTER.
00650    END-IT.
00660        CLOSE IN-FILE, OUT-FILE.
00670        STOP RUN.
```

code (1) A set of rules outlining the way in which data may be represented. (2) Rules used to convert data from one representation to another. (3) To write a program or routine (i.e., a programmer generated code). Same as ENCODE.

code conversion A process for changing the bit groupings for characters in one code into the corresponding character bit groupings for a second code.

coded decimal number A number consisting of successive characters or a group of characters that usually represents a specific figure in an associated decimal number.

code level The number of bits used to represent a given character.

coder A person who writes programs designed by other, usually more experienced, programmers or systems analysts.

coding (1) The writing of a list of instructions that will cause a computer to perform specified operations. (2) An ordered list or lists of the successive instructions that will cause a computer to perform a particular process.

coding form A form on which the instructions for programming a computer are written.

coercion In programming language expressions, an automatic conversion from one data type to another.

COGO An acronym for **CO**ORDINATE **GE**OMETRY. A problem-oriented programming language used to solve geometric problems. Used primarily by civil engineers.

coherence Assumption used in raster scan display technology that attributes the same value of an individual pixel to its adjacent pixel.

cohesion The degree to which a module performs one general function.

cold boot The act of turning a computer on and loading an operating system into it. Contrast with WARM BOOT.

cold fault A computer fault that is apparent as soon as the machine is switched on.

cold start The restart activity used when a serious failure has occurred in a system making the contents of the direct access storage inaccessible so that no trace of the recent processing can be used. The system must be reloaded and activity restarted as though at the beginning of a day. More simply, restarting the computer by turning it off and then on again—all programs and data in memory are lost. See COLD BOOT.

collate To MERGE two or more sequenced data sets to produce a resulting data set that reflects the sequencing of the original sets.

collating sort Sort that uses a technique of continuous merging of data until one sequence is developed.

collation sequence Order that the computer will use when it arranges items from first to last. Typically, this order is alphabetical for words and numerical for numbers. However, the question becomes complex when one must take into account upper-case and lower-case, mixed numbers and words, punctuation, numbers that are not filled to the same length with leading zeros, and other factors.

collator   Machine used to collate or merge sets of cards or other documents into a sequence.

collection   The process of gathering data from various sources and assembling it at one location.

collision detection   (1) In computer graphics, particularly in arcade-type games, a program often must determine when two objects have collided. There are several programming techniques that may be used to detect a collision. (2) A task performed in a multiple-access network to prevent two computers from transmitting at the same time. (3) A method of defining which operation will be performed whenever two keyboard operations are activated simultaneously.

color camera   An output device that is used to record data on film from raster scan display devices. See FILM RECORDER.

color graphics   Refers to a system that is used to create graphs, draw pictures, and so forth, using colors.

color monitor   An RGB (red-green-blue) or composite monitor. An RGB monitor uses separate video signals for red, green, and blue, the three primary video colors. It uses these signals to display almost any number of hues, depending on the software and display circuitry (on an adapter card or in the computer) that is used. This type of monitor usually produces clearer, sharper colors and images. Composite monitors use one signal that combines the three primary colors.

color printer   An output device that can produce text, charts, graphics and artwork in several colors.

color saturation   A measure of the amount of white light in a hue. High saturation means that there is no white-light component and that the color is of good quality.

column   (1) The vertical members of one line of an array. (2) A position of information in a computer word. (3) A vertical division of an electronic spreadsheet. Together with rows, columns serve to form the spreadsheet matrix. Contrast with ROW.

COM An acronym for COMPUTER OUTPUT MICROFILM. A technology that permits the output information produced by computers to be stored on microfilm. See COMPUTER OUTPUT MICROFILM (COM) RECORDER.

combinatorial explosion A condition that occurs in problem solving when the possibilities to be examined become too numerous even for a very large computer.

combinatorics The study of methods of counting how many objects there are of some type, or how many ways there are to do something.

COMDEX An acronym for COMMUNICATIONS and DATA PROCESSING EXPOSITION, a large computer trade show held in the United States and other locations.

command (1) A control signal. (2) Loosely, a mathematical or logic operator. (3) Loosely, a computer instruction. See OPERATION CODE.

command-driven software Programs that make little or no effort to guide the terminal user with menus. Instead, command-driven software expects the operator to know what commands are available and when each is appropriate.

command key Any keyboard key used to perform specific functions.

command language A language used to give instructions to an operating system. See JOB CONTROL LANGUAGE.

command processing The reading, analyzing, and performing of computer instructions.

comments English prose that may be interspersed among the computer language statements of a computer program to explain their action to readers of the program. Special markers on the comments cause the computer to ignore them. Properly done comments are a valuable form of internal documentation because they are embedded in the program itself; therefore they stay with the program. Comments provide helpful notes for future users who may later attempt to understand or alter the program.

Commodore International, Ltd. A manufacturing company that has developed a number of popular microcomputers including the C-64™, C-128™, Amiga 500™, Amiga 1000™, and Amiga 2000™.

common carrier A government-regulated private company that provides telephone, telegraph, and other telecommunications facilities for public use.

common language A computer programming language that is sensible to two or more computers with different machine languages. BASIC, Pascal, FORTRAN, COBOL and Modula-2 are common languages.

common storage A section of memory for each user that holds data or parameters that are accessible to all programs.

communicating The process of transmitting information to a point of use.

communications (1) The flow of information from one point (the source) to another (the receiver). (2) The act of transmitting or making known. (3) A process by which information is exchanged between individuals through the use of a commonly accepted set of symbols. See DATA COMMUNICATIONS.

communications channel The physical means of connecting one location or device to another for the purpose of transmitting and receiving data.

communications control unit Usually, a small computer whose only job is to handle the flow of data communications traffic to and from a mainframe computer.

communications link The method by which information is transmitted between computer devices.

communications processor A computer that provides a path for data transfer between the computer system and the data communications network.

communications protocol A set of communication rules that provide for error checking between devices and ensure that transmitted data are not lost.

communications satellites Earth satellites placed in different spots in the geostationary orbit 22,250 miles above the equator that serve as relay stations for communications signals transmitted from Earth stations. These satellites orbit

Earth once every 24 hours, giving the impression that they are "parked" in one spot over the equator. Once in this orbit, a satellite is capable of reaching 43 percent of Earth's surface with a single radio signal. Most communications satellites are launched by NASA, weigh several thousand pounds, and are powered by solar panels.

communications server A device that connects local area networks to wide area or telecommunications networks.

communications software Programs that allow computers to communicate through a MODEM. Some communications programs are capable of automatic telecommunications, such as auto-answering, auto-dialing, and even dialing another computer at a preset time to establish communication and send and receive information. Some programs allow operation of an unattended remote computer—accessing disk files, operating peripherals, and so forth.

communications system A system that consists of senders, physical channels, and receivers of data communications.

Compaq Computer Corporation A manufacturer of several microcomputers compatible with IBM microcomputer systems.

compare To examine the representation of a quantity to determine its relationship to zero, or to examine two quantities, usually for the purposes of determining identity or relative magnitude.

comparison The act of comparing. The common forms are comparison of two numbers for identity, comparison of two numbers for relative magnitude, comparison of two characters for similarity, and comparison of the signs of two numbers.

compart A term that means COMPUTER ART.

compatibility (1) A property of some computers that allows programs written for one computer to run on another (compatible) computer, even though it is a different model. (2) The ability of different devices, such as a computer and a printer, to work together. (3) The ability of one program to use data from another program, such as a word processor using data from a spreadsheet in a report.

compatible A quality possessed by a computer system that enables it to handle both data and programs devised for some other type of computer system.

compatible software Programs that can be run on different computers without modification.

compilation One of the two principal means of translating programs written in high-level languages into machine language instructions that can be directly executed by the processor. Compilation entails translating a complete program before any execution. This contrasts with interpretation, in which each instruction is translated when it is to be executed.

compilation time The time during which a source language program is translated (compiled) into an object program (machine language). Contrast with RUN TIME.

compile To prepare a machine language program (or a program expressed in symbolic coding) from a program written in a high-level programming language such as FORTRAN, COBOL, or Pascal.

compile-and-go An operating technique by which the loading and execution phases of a program compilation are performed in one continuous run. This technique is especially useful when a program must be compiled for a one-time application.

compiler A computer program whose purpose is that of translating high-level language statements into a form that can directly activate the computer hardware. Translates a complete program before any execution. See INTERPRETER.

compiler language A source language that uses a compiler to translate the language statements into an object language.

compile time The time required to compile a program. The point in the processing of a program when it is being translated from source code to object code by a translator (compiler). Also called compilation time.

complement A number used to represent the negative of a given number. Obtained by subtracting each digit of the number from the number representing its base and, in the case of two's complement and ten's complement, adding unity to the last significant digit.

completeness check Establishes that none of the fields is missing and that the entire record has been checked.

complex number Any number of the form a + bi, where a and b are real numbers and i is the square root of -1; i is called the imaginary unit, a is called the real part, and the real coefficient b is called the imaginary part.

component A basic part; an ELEMENT; a part of a computer system; a portion of an application.

composite A type of video signal in which all three primary video color signals (red, green, blue) are combined, which limits the sharpness of the monitor image. This type of video signal is used in some monitors and TV sets that use only one electron gun to generate the three primary colors. See RGB.

composite symbol A symbol consisting of more than one character, for example, the composite symbol < > stands for "not equal to" in some software systems.

composite video Color output from a computer color display described in terms of its hue and its brightness and encoded in a single video signal. The color control signal is a single data stream that must be decoded into three colors (red, green and blue). Inexpensive color monitors called composite monitors use composite video and produce a slightly better picture than a TV set. Such monitors, however do not produce the high quality of RGB monitors. See RGB.

Composition And Make-up (CAM) terminal A CRT display device capable of showing and changing exact point sizes and character widths. Used for computer phototypesetting.

compound statement A single instruction that contains two or more instructions that could be used separately.

CompuServe A major information service network used by individuals as well as businesses. It features timely news features, stock market reports, electronic mail, educational programs, programming aids, and more. Personal computer owners can reference the CompuServe network via the common telephone system. Compare SOURCE (THE).

computability   Property by which computational problems are classified.

computation   Result of computing.

compute-bound   A program or computer system that is restricted or limited by the speed of the central processing unit.

computer   A device capable of solving problems or manipulating data by accepting data, performing prescribed operations (mathematical or logical) on the data, and supplying the results of these operations. See ANALOG COMPUTER, BRIEFCASE COMPUTER, DESKTOP COMPUTER, DIGITAL COMPUTER, HOME COMPUTER, HAND-HELD COMPUTER, LAP COMPUTER, MAINFRAME, MICROCOMPUTER, MICROPROCESSOR, MINICOMPUTER, PERSONAL COMPUTER, PORTABLE COMPUTER, SMALL BUSINESS COMPUTER, and SUPERCOMPUTER.

computer-aided design (CAD)   A process involving direct, real-time communication between a designer and a computer, generally by the use of a video display terminal and a light pen.

Computer-Aided Design and Drafting (CADD)   Drafting is the producing of drawings; design is the ordering of intentions. Drafting is the most common way of giving form to designs, much as typing is the most common way of giving form to writing. CADD systems are graphics systems that permit automatic drafting and design functions. These systems are used widely in numerical control, robotics, manufacturing resources planning and computer-aided process planning.

computer-aided design/computer-aided manufacturing   Efforts to automate design and manufacturing operations. Abbreviated CAD/CAM.

computer-aided factory management   A system for managing a production facility in which computers schedule operations, keep accurate accounts on parts inventories, and order new supplies as required from supply houses.

computer-aided instruction   See COMPUTER-AUGMENTED LEARNING.

computer-aided manufacturing (CAM) The use of computer technology in the management, control, and operation of manufacturing.

computer architecture The area of computer study that deals with the physical structure (hardware) of computer systems and the relationships among these various hardware components.

computer art An art form produced by artists using computer equipment. For the artist, the computer can be considered a tool, as a paint brush, a charcoal pencil, or an extension of the mind. The artist can dream lovely images and use the computer to bring them to vivid reality. Computer art is usually produced on visual displays, graphics printers, digital plotters or film copying devices.

computer artist A person who uses computers as tools in producing art. See COMPUTER ART.

computer-assisted diagnosis Using a computer as a diagnostic tool to save doctors time and assist in a speedy, accurate diagnosis.

computer-assisted instruction (CAI) The use of computers to augment individual instruction by providing students with programmed sequences of instruction under computer control. The manner of sequencing and progressing through the materials permits students to progress at their own rate. CAI is responsive to students' individual needs.

computer-augmented learning (CAL) A method of using a computer system to augment, or supplement, a more conventional instructional system, such as by using simulation programs to aid in problem solving in a course of instruction.

computer awareness Generally, an understanding of what a computer is, how it works, and the role and impact of computers in society.

computer-based learning (CBL) A term used to embrace all the present forms of educational computing.

computer binder A binder designed to hold and protect printouts produced by printers.

computer camp A camp, usually held during the summer weeks, where campers not only swim and eat, but also learn to use microcomputers.

computer center A facility that provides computer services to a variety of users through the operation of computer and auxiliary hardware, and through ancillary services provided by its staff.

computer center director An individual who directs the activities, operations, and personnel in a computer center.

computer circuits Circuits used in digital computers, such as gating circuits, storage circuits, triggering circuits, inverting circuits, and power amplifying circuits.

computer classifications Computers fall into two major classifications: digital and analog. A third classification, called hybrid, combines both digital and analog computers. Digital computers vary in size from huge supercomputers to minute microprocessors.

computer code A machine code for a specific computer.

computer conferencing A system that enables humans to conduct a conference even though widely scattered geographically, by communicating through a computer network.

computer control console See CONTROL PANEL.

computer crime Intentional act to misuse a computer system. Computer crimes can range from simple fraud schemes to crimes of violence. Use of computers to commit unauthorized acts. Legally, not yet well-defined.

computer design The conception, planning, and making of specifications for a computer.

computer drawing A specific image prepared by a computer output device usually drawn by a graphics printer or plotter, or a visual display representation reproduced as a 35mm slide or an instant photograph.

computer enclosure The cabinet or housing for a computer's circuit boards and power supply.

computer engineering The field of knowledge that includes the design of computer hardware systems. Computer engineering is offered as a degree program in several colleges and universities. See SOFTWARE ENGINEERING.

computerese The jargon and other specialized vocabulary of people working with computers and information processing systems.

computer family All the models, collectively, of a single type of computer, sharing the same logical design.

computer flicks Movies made by a computer.

computer game Interactive software or firmware in which the input data consists of the human player's physical actions and the output is an interactive graphics display. See COMPUTERIZED GAME PLAYING.

computer graphicist A specialist who uses computer graphics systems to produce graphs, charts, animated diagrams, art forms, and graphics designs.

computer graphics A general term meaning the appearance of pictures or diagrams, as distinct from letters and numbers, on the display screen or hard-copy output device.

computer-independent language A high-level language designed for use in any computer equipped with an appropriate compiler (i.e., BASIC, COBOL, FORTRAN, Pascal, and so forth).

computer industry An industry composed of businesses and organizations that supply computer hardware, software, and computer-related services.

computer information system A coordinated collection of hardware, software, data, people, and support resources to perform an integrated series of functions that can include processing, storage, input, and output. Abbreviated CIS.

computer input microfilm (CIM) A technology that involves using an input device to read the contents of microfilm or microfiche directly into the computer.

computer instruction See INSTRUCTION.

computer integrated manufacturing (CIM) The concept of a totally automated factory in which all manufacturing processes are integrated and controlled by a CAD/CAM system. CIM enables production planners and schedulers, shop-floor foremen, and accountants to use the same data base as product designers and engineers.

computer interface unit A device used to connect peripheral devices to a computer. Abbreviated CIU.

computerization The application of a computer to an activity formerly done by other means. The actual reshaping of society by the widespread adoption and use of computers.

computerize (1) To equip a business or organization with computers so as to facilitate or automate procedures. (2) To convert a manual operation into one that is performed by a computer.

computerized tomography (CT) A computer controlled X-ray technique that shows a picture of a site through the body at a given depth. The computer is used to bring out the details of this picture. The computer records X-rays passing through the body in changing directions and generates an image of the body's structure.

computerized data base A set of computerized files on which an organization's activities are based and upon which high reliance is placed for availability and accuracy.

computerized game playing Recreational use of (microcomputers, minicomputers, and mainframes) that have been programmed to play a wide variety of games such as tic-tac-toe, Pacman, Breakout, Star raiders, Space war, blackjack, hangman, backgammon, chess, and checkers, among others. See COMPUTER GAME.

computerized mail A technique of delivering mail in electronic form directly to homes and businesses through computer equipment.

computer jargon The technical vocabulary associated with the computer field.

computer language See PROGRAMMING LANGUAGE.

computer leasing company A company that specializes in leasing computer equipment that it purchases from a computer manufacturer.

computer letter A personalized form letter produced by a word processing system.

computer literacy A broad knowledge of how to use computers to solve problems, general awareness of the functioning of the software and hardware, and an understanding of the societal implications of computers. It is the nontechnical study of the computer and its effect upon society that provides one with some of the knowledge, tools, and understanding to live in a computer-oriented society. It is a state of being able to function comfortably as a user in a computerized environment but not necessarily possessing technical comprehension.

computer-managed instruction (CMI) An application of computers to instruction in which the computer is used as a record keeper, manager, and/or prescriber of instruction.

Computer Museum An archive for computer history, located in Boston, Massachusetts, whose collection contains many early computer systems and taped presentations of computer pioneers.

computer music Music employing computer equipment at any stage of its composition or realization as sound.

computer network A complex consisting of two or more interconnected computer systems, terminals, and communication facilities.

computernik An avid computer user who chooses to spend a large amount of time using computers.

computer numerical control A technique in which a machine-tool control uses a computer to store numerical control instructions generated earlier by CAD/CAM for controlling the machine.

computer-on-a-chip A complete microcomputer on an integrated circuit chip. See MICROCOMPUTER CHIP and MICROPROCESSOR.

computer operations That part of a computer installation responsible for the day-to-day collection, production, distribution, and maintenance of data.

computer operations manager The person who oversees the computer operations area in an organization. The computer operations manager is responsible for hiring personnel and scheduling work that the system is to perform.

computer operator   A person skilled in the operation of the computer and associated peripheral devices. Performs other operational functions that are required in a computer center, such as loading a disk drive, removing printouts from the line printer rack, and so forth.

computer output microfilm (COM)   A technology that involves recording computer output on microfilm or microfiche.

computer output microfilm (COM) recorder   A device that records computer output on photosensitive film in microscopic form.

computerphobia   The fear of computers, especially an inordinate amount of fear.

computer processing cycle   The steps involved in using a computer to solve a problem: write the program in a programming language such as BASIC or Pascal; input the program into the computer; compile and execute the program.

computer professional   A person whose regular job is directly related to the computer.

computer program   A formal expression of the sequence of actions required for a data processing task. The program is the programmer's specification of the task(s) to the computer in a formal notation that can be processed by the computer. A program consists of a series of statements and instructions that cause a computer to perform a particular operation or task.

computer programmer   A person whose job is to design, write, and test programs and the instructions that cause a computer to do a specific job.

computer revolution   The name given to the present era because of the impact of computer technology on society. Most often referred to as the Information Revolution.

computer science   The field of knowledge embracing all aspects of the design and use of computers. Offered as a degree program in many colleges and universities.

computer security   The preservation of computing resources against abuse or unauthorized use, especially the protection of data from accidental or deliberate damage, disclosure, or modification. See DATA SECURITY.

computer services company A company that provides computer services to other individuals and organizations. Sometimes called SERVICE BUREAU. See COMPUTER UTILITY.

computer simulation A representation of a real or hypothetical system, constructed from a computer program.

computer specialist An individual who provides computer services to computer-using organizations; for example, a systems analyst, a programmer, and so forth.

computer store A retail store where customers can select, from the floor or shelf, a full computer system or just a few accessories. These stores typically sell software, books, supplies, and periodicals. In a broad-based computer store, one can examine and operate several types of microcomputer systems.

computer system A system that includes computer hardware, software, and people. Used to process data into useful information.

computer typesetting The use of a special-purpose computer to process an input medium resulting in a justified, hyphenated, and formatted output medium.

computer user A person who uses a computer system or its output.

computer users group A group whose members share the knowledge they have gained and the programs they have developed on a computer or class of computers of a certain manufacturer. Most groups hold meetings and distribute newsletters to exchange information, trade equipment, and share computer programs.

computer utility A service that provides computational ability, usually a time-shared computer system. Programs, as well as data, may be made available to the user. The user also may have her or his own programs immediately available in the central processing unit, or have them on call at the computer utility, or load them by transmitting them to the computer prior to using them. Certain data and programs are shared by all users of the service; other data and programs, because of their proprietary nature, have restricted access. Computer utilities are generally accessed by means

of data communications subsystems. See COMPUTER SER-
VICES COMPANY and SERVICE BUREAU.

computer vendor A person or organization that manufactures,
sells, or services computer equipment.

computer word A fixed sequence of bits, bytes, or characters
treated as a unit and capable of being stored in one storage
location. See WORD.

computing The act of using computing equipment for processing data; in other words, the art or science of getting
the computer to do what the user wants.

computing system See COMPUTER SYSTEM.

COM recorder A device that records computer output on photosensitive film in microscopic form. See COMPUTER OUT-
PUT MICROFILM.

concatenate To link together or join two or more character
strings into a single character string, or to join one line of
a display with the succeeding line. For example, "MICRO"
concatenated with "COMPUTER" equals "MICROCOMPU-
TER." To compress. Contrast with DECATENATE.

concatenated data set A collection of logically connected data
sets.

concatenated key More than one data item used in conjunction to identify a record.

concentrator A device that allows a number of slow-speed devices to utilize a single high-speed communications line.
Also called MULTIPLEXER.

conceptual tool A tool for working with ideas instead of
things.

concordance An alphabetical list of words and phrases appearing in a document, with an indication of where those
words and phrases appear.

concurrent Pertaining to the occurrence of two or more
events or activities within the same specified interval of
time.

concurrent processing The performance of two or more data processing tasks within a specified interval. Contrast with SIMULTANEOUS PROCESSING.

concurrent program execution Two or more programs being executed at the same time.

concurrent programming The development of programs that specify the parallel execution of several tasks.

condition (1) A given set of circumstances. (2) A definite state of being.

condition code Refers to a limited group of program conditions such as carry, borrow, and overflow, pertinent to the execution of instructions.

conditional branching See CONDITIONAL TRANSFER.

conditional jump instruction An instruction that causes a jump to occur if the criteria specified are met.

conditional paging A word processing feature that causes printing to begin on the next page if a specified block of text will not fit completely within the remaining space on a page.

conditional statement A statement that is executed only when a certain condition within the routine has been met.

conditional transfer An instruction that may cause a departure from the sequence of instructions being followed, depending upon the result of an operation, the contents of a register, or the settings of an indicator. Contrast with UNCONDITIONAL TRANSFER.

conditioning The improvement of the data transmission properties of a voiceband transmission line by correction of the amplitude phase characteristics of the line amplifiers.

CONDUIT A nonprofit publisher of educational software. CONDUIT reviews, tests, packages, and distributes instructional computer programs and related printed materials.

conferencing See COMPUTER CONFERENCE.

confidentiality Quality of protection against unauthorized access to private or secret information.

configure To assemble a selection of hardware or software into a system and to adjust each of the parts so that they all work together.

configuration An assembly of machines that are interconnected and are programmed to operate as a system. The layout or design of elements in a hardware or information processing system.

configuration management The task of accounting for, controlling, and reporting the planned and actual design of a product throughout its production and operational life.

connecting cable A cable used to transfer electrical impulses between two pieces of equipment.

connect node In computer-aided design, an attachment point for lines or text.

connector (1) A coupling device that provides an electrical and/or mechanical junction between two cables, or between a cable and a chassis or enclosure. (2) A device that provides rapid connection and disconnection of electrical cable and wire terminations. See FEMALE CONNECTOR, JACK, MALE CONNECTOR, and PLUG.

connector symbol A flowcharting symbol used to represent a junction in a line of flow. It connects broken paths in the line of flow and connects several pages of the same flowchart. A small circle containing some identifier is used to represent this symbol.

connect time In time-sharing, the length of time you are "on" the computer; that is, the duration of the telephone connection. Connect time is usually measured by the duration between "sign-on" and "sign-off." See CPU TIME.

consecutive Pertaining to the occurrence of two sequential events without the intervention of any other such event.

consistency check A check to ensure that specific input data falls within a predetermined set of criteria. A control method wherein like data items are checked for consistency of value and form.

console The part of a computer system that enables human operators to communicate with the system. See FRONT PANEL.

console operator Same as COMPUTER OPERATOR.

console printer See CONSOLE TYPEWRITER.

console typewriter A typewriter on-line to the computer that allows communication between the machine and the COMPUTER OPERATOR.

constant A value that does not change during the execution of the program. Contrast with VARIABLE.

constraint A condition that limits the solutions to a problem.

consultant An expert in the use of computers in specific applications environments, such as business data processing, education, military systems, or health-care systems. Often helps to analyze and solve a specific problem.

contention A condition on a multipoint communications channel when two or more locations try to transmit at the same time. Also occurs when two CPUs attempt to control the same device at once.

contents directory A series of queues that indicate the routines in a given region of main storage.

context sensitive help key A key available on many video display terminals. When this key is pressed on a keyboard, help that is specific to the problem at hand is automatically displayed on the screen.

contiguous Adjacent or adjoining.

contiguous data structure See SEQUENTIAL DATA STRUCTURE.

contingency plan A plan for recovery of a computer information system following emergencies or disasters.

continuous forms Fanfold or roll paper that is used on printers, which has small holes on the outer edges for automatic feeding of the paper. It can be blank sheets or preprinted forms such as checks, invoices, stationary, or tax forms.

continuous tone Dots produced by a printer that vary incrementally in color saturation.

continuous processing The input of transactions into a system in the order they occur and as soon after they occur as possible.

continuous scrolling Moving text, line by line, forward or backward, through a window.

continuous tone image A color or black and white image formed of combinations of separate areas made up of different color tones or gray tones.

contour analysis A technique in optical character recognition that uses a spot of light to search for the outline of the character by moving around its exterior edges.

contouring In computer graphics, it refers to the creation of the outline of a body, mass, or figure.

contrast In optical character recognition, the differences between color or shading of the printed material on a document and the background on which it is printed.

contrast enhancement Improvement of light-to-dark distinction. A real digitizing process typically involves some kind of nonlinear detector that destroys the light-to-dark relationships of the object scanned. The correct contrast can be reintroduced if the characteristics of the detector are known. In fact, the contrast can even be heightened if desired.

control The function of performing required operations when certain specific conditions occur or when interpreting and acting upon instructions. See CONTROL SECTION and CONTROL UNIT.

control block A storage area through which a particular type of information required for control of the operating system is communicated among its parts.

control break A point during program processing at which some special processing event takes place.

control character A character whose occurrence in a particular context initiates, modifies, or stops a control operation.

control circuits The electrical circuits within a computer that interpret the program instructions and cause the appropriate operations to be performed.

control console That part of a computer system used for communication between the console operator or customer service technician and the computer.

control data One or more items of data used as a control to identify, select, execute, or modify another routine, record, file, operation, or data value.

Control Data Corporation A large manufacturer of computer equipment including supercomputers. CDC is also the developer of the computer-based education system PLATO. See CYBER.

control field A field in a data record used to identify and classify the record. Same as KEY.

control key A special function key on a computer keyboard. Used simultaneously with another key to enter a command instructing the system to perform a task.

controlled variable A variable that takes on a specific set of values in an iterative structure in a programming language.

controller A device required by the computer to operate a peripheral device.

control logic The order in which processing functions will be carried out by a computer.

control panel The part of a computer control console that contains manual controls. Same as FRONT PANEL.

control program An operating system program responsible for the overall management of the computer and its resources. See OPERATING SYSTEM.

controls Methods and procedures for ensuring the accuracy, integrity, security, reliability, and completeness of data or processing techniques.

control section That part of the central processing unit responsible for directing the operation of the computer in accordance with the instructions in the program. Same as CONTROL UNIT.

control sequence The normal order of selection of instructions by a digital computer wherein it follows one instruction order at a time.

control signal A computer-generated signal for automatic control of machines and processes.

control statement   An operation that terminates the sequential execution of instructions by transferring control to a statement elsewhere in the program.

control structures   The facilities of a programming language that specify a departure from the normal sequential execution of statements.

control total   An accumulation of numeric data fields that are used to check on the accuracy of the input, processed data or output data.

control unit   The portion of the central processing unit that directs the step-by-step operation of the entire computing system.

control words   A series of special reserved character sequences that have a special meaning to the program that reads them. See RESERVED WORDS.

convention   Standard and accepted procedures in computer program development and the abbreviations, symbols, and their meanings as developed for particular programs and systems. A programming style rule, providing consistency among different programs.

convergence   The putting together of previously separate technologies: such as telephone and computer technology.

conversational   Pertaining to a program or a system that carries on a dialog with a terminal user, alternately accepting input and then responding to the input quickly enough for the user to maintain his or her train of thought. See INTERACTIVE PROCESSING.

conversational interaction   Interaction with a computer that takes the form of a dialogue between the user and the machine.

conversational language   A programming language that uses a near-English character set that facilitates communication between the user and the computer. BASIC is a conversational language.

conversational mode   A mode of operation that implies a dialog between a computer and its user in which the computer program examines the input supplied by the user and formulates questions or comments, that are directed back to the user. See INTERACTIVE PROCESSING and LOGGING-IN.

conversational operation   The transmission of data between a video display terminal (VDT) and a computer in which data travels one character at a time.

conversational system   See INTERACTIVE SYSTEM.

conversion   (1) The process of changing information from one form of representation to another, such as from the language of one type of computer to that of another or from punch cards to magnetic disk. (2) The process of changing from one data processing method to another or from one type of equipment to another. (3) The process of changing a number written in one base to the base of another numeral system.

conversion table   A table comparing numerals in two different numeral systems.

convert   (1) To change data from radix to radix. (2) To move data from one type of storage to another, such as floppy disk to magnetic tape.

converter   (1) A device that converts data recorded on one medium to another medium, such as a unit that accepts data from printed pages and records it on floppy disks. (2) A device that converts data in one form into data in another form, such as analog to digital. See MODEM.

cookbook   A step-by-step document describing how to install and use a program.

coordinate   (1) An ordered set of absolute or relative data values that specify a location in a Cartesian coordinate system. (2) In an electronic spreadsheet, the intersection of two numbers and/or letters that uniquely identify the column and row of a cell. (3) Two numbers used to position the cursor, or pointer, on the screen.

coordinate dimensioning   A system of dimensioning where points are defined as a specified dimension and direction from a reference point measured with respect to defined axes.

coordinate paper A continuous-feed graph paper that is used for graphs or diagrams produced on a digital plotter.

coprocessor (1) An auxiliary processor that performs time consuming tasks to free the central processing unit, thus resulting in faster execution time for the overall system. (2) A CPU that works in tandem with another to increase the computing power of a system. (3) An auxiliary microprocessor that lets one computer imitate a different computer.

copy To reproduce data in a new location or other destination, leaving the source data unchanged, although the physical form of the result may differ from that of the source; for example, to make a duplicate of all the programs or data on a disk. Contrast with DUPLICATE.

copy holder A device used to hold papers so they can be easily read by the user when typing on a keyboard. Its purpose is to reduce back, shoulder, neck, and eye strain.

copy protection Methods used by software developers to prevent any copying of their programs. To protect against illegal copying of software, many manufacturers build copy protection routines into their programs. Copy protection techniques are sometimes sophisticated, although several commercial programs exist that allow users to override many standard copy protection techniques. It is illegal to make a copy of copyrighted software and pass it along to another person.

coroutine Instructions used to transfer a set of inputs to a set of outputs.

corporate model Mathematical representation or simulation of a company's accounting practices and financial policy guidelines. Used to project financial results under a given set of assumptions and to evaluate the financial impact of alternative plans. Long-range forecasts are also calculated by using such models. Such a model would ideally be put into an "equation processor," but spreadsheets are often used.

corrective maintenance The activity of detecting, isolating, and correcting failures after they occur. Contrast with PREVENTIVE MAINTENANCE.

correspondence quality High-quality printing obtained by laser, daisy-wheel and certain dot-matrix printers. The high-resolution mode of a dot-matrix printer is used to improve print quality by increasing the number of dots used to form the characters.

cost analysis A technique used to determine the overall cost of a given system and to compare it to cost factors estimated for a new design.

cost/benefit analysis A quantitative form of evaluation in which benefits are assessed and the costs associated with achieving the benefits are determined.

cost effectiveness Effectiveness of a system or an operation in terms of the relationships of the benefits received to the resources expended to attain them. A system, where the received benefits exceed the associated costs, is considered cost-effective.

costing A method of assigning costs to a project, job or function.

cottage key people People who work at home and transmit work to the company by telecommunications, floppy disks, or other means.

coulomb Basic SI unit of electric charge. A group of 6.25 x 10^{18} electrons has a charge of 1 coulomb.

count The successive increase or decrease of a cumulative total of the number of times an event occurs.

counter A device, such as a register or computer storage location, used to represent the number of occurrences of an event.

counterclockwise Moving from right to left.

counting loop A program loop used to perform some action a fixed number of times.

coupling An interaction between systems or between properties of a system.

courseware The name given to computer programs written especially for educational applications, such as teaching reading, physics, art appreciation, arithmetic, German, or English skills. See COMPUTER-ASSISTED INSTRUCTION.

cpi An abbreviation for CHARACTERS PER INCH.

CP/M An abbreviation for CONTROL PROGRAM FOR MICRO-COMPUTERS, an operating system for microcomputers. A collection of programs on a floppy disk, CP/M provides specific commands for transferring information among the devices connected to the computer system, for executing programs, and for manipulating files conveniently. It is produced by Digital Research of Pacific Grove, California.

cps An abbreviation for CHARACTERS PER SECOND.

CPU An abbreviation for CENTRAL PROCESSING UNIT.

CPU time The amount of time devoted by the central processing unit to the execution of program instructions. See CONNECT TIME.

CR An abbreviation for CARRIAGE RETURN.

crash (1) The cessation of the operation of a computer. (2) A system shutdown caused by a hardware malfunction or a software mistake. See HEAD CRASH.

crash conversion A method of converting from one system to another by ceasing to operate the old system when the new one is implemented.

Cray (1) A line of supercomputers manufactured by Cray Research, Inc, including the Cray 2™, which can process a billion operations a second. (2) Cray Research, Inc., founded by Seymour Cray, is a manufacturer of supercomputers.

create (1) Refers to making a new file on a disk as opposed to modifying an existing file. (2) To define the fields for a data base record, specifying field name, length, field type, and so on.

creeping A type of scrolling in which text moves horizontally across the screen like a news wire moving along the bottom of a television program.

critical path That path through a network that defines the shortest possible time in which the entire project can be completed.

critical path method A management technique for control of large-scale, long-term projects involving the analysis and determination of each critical step necessary for project completion. Abbreviated CPM.

CROM An acronym for **CONTROL ROM**, an integral part of most central processing unit (CPU) chips. The CROM is the storage for the microinstructions that the CPU assembles into a sequence to form complex macroinstructions, such as Division or Logical compare, that the computer user normally uses.

crop In computer graphics, to cut off some part of an image.

cross-assembler Refers to an assembler run on one computer for the purpose of translating instructions for a different computer.

cross-check To check the computing by two different methods.

cross-compiler A compiler that runs on a machine other than the one for which it is designed to compile code.

cross-compiling/assembling A technique whereby one uses a minicomputer, large-scale computer, or time-sharing service to write and debug programs for subsequent use on microcomputers.

cross hairs On an input device, two intersecting lines—one horizontal and one vertical—whose intersection marks the active cursor position of a graphics system.

crosshatching In computer graphics, it refers to the shading of some portion of a drawing with a pattern of intersecting lines or figures repeated across the area being shaded.

cross-reference dictionary A printed listing that identifies all references of an assembled program to a specific label. In many systems, this listing is provided immediately after a source program has been assembled.

cross talk The unwanted energy transferred from one circuit, called the "disturbing circuit," to another circuit, called the "disturbed circuit." Generally, occurs when signals from one circuit emerge onto another circuit as interference.

crowbar A circuit that protects a computer system from dangerously high voltage surges.

CRT An abbreviation for CATHODE RAY TUBE, the picture tube of a video display terminal.

CRT plot A computer-generated drawing or graph projected onto the screen of a cathode ray tube.

crunch A nontechnical term used by computer people to refer to the computer's capacity to process numbers and perform routine arithmetic functions. Computers can process, or crunch, a lot of numbers quickly. Also referred to as number crunch.

cryoelectronic storage A storage device consisting of materials that become superconductors at extremely low temperatures.

cryogenics The study and use of devices that utilize the properties assumed by materials at temperatures near absolute zero.

cryptanalysis Operation of converting encrypted messages to the corresponding PLAINTEXT without initial knowledge of the key employed in the encryption.

cryptography Any of various methods for writing in secret code or cipher. As society becomes increasingly dependent upon computers, the vast amounts of data communicated, processed, and stored within computer systems and networks often have to be protected, and cryptography is a means of achieving this protection. It is the only practical method for protecting information transmitted through accessible communications networks, such as telephone lines, satellites, or microwave systems.

crystal A quartz crystal that vibrates at a specific frequency when energy is supplied to it. These vibrations provide an accurate frequency by which to time the clock within a computer system.

CSP An abbreviation for CERTIFIED SYSTEMS PROFESSIONAL. The CSP designation has the following four objectives: To identify systems practitioners who have attained a specified level of knowledge and experience in the principles and practices of systems, information resource management and related disciplines; to provide tools, guidelines and assessment methods necessary to achieve professional status; to foster continuing professional development; and to encourage adherence to professional standards. Administered by the INSTITUTE FOR CERTIFICATION OF COMPUTER PROFESSIONALS.

CT An abbreviation for **C**OMPUTERIZED **T**OMOGRAPHIC.

CTRL An abbreviation for CONTROL.

current A flow of electrons through a conductor. Current is measured in amperes, where 1 ampere equals 6.25×10^{18} electrons per second.

current location counter A counter kept by an assembler to determine the address that has been assigned to either an instruction or constant being assembled.

current mode logic (CML) A logic circuit that employs the characteristics of a differential amplifier circuit in its design.

cursive scanning A scanning technique used with a video display terminal in which the electrons being sent toward the screen are deflected to form the outlines of the picture one line at a time in the same way an artist might draw the same image.

cursor (1) A moving, sliding, or blinking symbol on a CRT screen that indicates where the next character will appear. (2) A position indicator used on a video display terminal to indicate a character to be corrected or a position in which data is to be entered.

cursor control The ability to move a video display prompt character to any position on the screen.

cursor control keys The keyboard keys used to position the cursor on the display screen. They are easiest to use when arranged in a compass pattern.

cursor tracking Positioning a cursor on a display screen by moving a stylus on a digitizer connected to the computer.

curve fitting A mathematical technique for finding a formula that best represents a collection of data points. Usually the formula is used to plot the best-fit line through the points.

custodian The person or organization responsible for physical maintenance and safeguarding of data stored on floppy disks, tape reels, disk packs, and so forth. See LIBRARIAN.

customer service technician   An individual responsible for field maintenance of computer hardware and software. Also called CUSTOMER ENGINEER, and FIELD ENGINEER.

custom IC   An integrated circuit (IC) manufactured to a specific customer's design and specification.

customize   The process of altering a piece of general purpose software or hardware to enhance its performance, usually to fit a specific user's need.

custom software   Programs that are prepared specifically for a business or organization and tailored to the business's needs. Contrast with CANNED SOFTWARE.

cut   The act of removing text or graphics from a document. Compare *paste*.

cut-and-paste   A method employed by some word processing and graphic systems to move text and illustrations from one location to another. Such systems usually permit the performance of other operations between the cut and the paste steps. Abbreviated cut' n' paste.

cyber   A line of mainframe computers (including supercomputers) manufactured by Control Data Corporation.

cybernetics   The branch of learning that seeks to integrate the theories and studies of communication and control in machines and living organisms. See ARTIFICIAL INTELLIGENCE.

cycle   As related to computer storage, a periodic sequence of events occurring when information is transferred to or from the storage device or a computer. It is the time it takes to reference an address, remove the data, and be ready to select it again.

cycle stealing   A technique that allows a peripheral device to temporarily disable computer control of the I/O bus, thus allowing the device to access the computer's internal memory.

cycle time   **(1)** The minimum time interval between the starts of successive accesses to a storage location. **(2)** The time required to change the information in a set of registers.

cylinder As related to magnetic disks, a vertical column of tracks on a magnetic disk pack. The corresponding tracks on each surface of a disk pack.

D

DA See DIRECT ACCESS.

D-A converter See DIGITAL-TO-ANALOG CONVERTER.

daisy chain Refers to a specific method of propagating signals along a bus. This method permits the assignment of device priorities based on the electrical position of the device along the bus.

daisy wheel The printing element in a daisy-wheel printer. Characters are embossed on spokes radiating from a central hub. A character is printed by simply rotating the wheel.

daisy-wheel printer An impact printer that uses a plastic or metal disk with printed characters along its edge. The disk rotates until the required character is brought before a hammer that strikes it against a ribbon. A popular letter-quality printer used with microcomputers and word processing systems.

dark bulb A type of cathode ray tube, almost black in appearance when turned off, that gives good contrast to video displays.

darkness Intensity, especially low intensity or limited brightness.

DASD An acronym for DIRECT ACCESS STORAGE DEVICE. A device such as a magnetic disk storage unit.

DAT An acronym for DYNAMIC ADDRESS TRANSLATION.

data A formalized representation of facts or concepts suitable for communication, interpretation, or processing by people or by automatic means. The raw material of information. Individual pieces of quantitative information, such as dollar sales of carpets, numbers of building permits issued, units of raw material on hand. Historically, data is a plural noun, datum is singular—a distinction now generally ignored in data processing terminology.

data acquisition The retrieval of data from remote sites initiated by a central computer system. The collection of data from external sensors.

data administrator See DATA BASE ADMINISTRATOR.

data aggregate A collection of data items within a record, that is given a name and referred to as a whole.

data bank See DATA BASE.

data base A collection of logically related records or files. A data base consolidates many records previously stored in separate files so that a common pool of data records serves as a single central file for many data processing applications.

data base administrator The individual who has the responsibility of maintaining the data base management system, and in general maintaining the accuracy and the integrity of the data that is stored in the computer system.

data base analyst A key person in the analysis, design, and implementation of data structures in a data base environment.

data base environment That environment resulting from the integration of users, data, and systems by implementing the data base.

data base management A systematic approach to storing, updating, and retrieving information stored as data items, usually in the form of records in a file, by which many users, or even many remote installations, will use common data bases.

data base management system (DBMS) The collection of hardware and software that organizes and provides access to a data base. The computer program provides you with the mechanisms needed to create a computerized data base file, to add data to the file, to alter data in the file, to organize data within the file, to search for data in the file, and so forth. In other words, it manages data.

data base manager A program that allows the user to enter, organize, sort, and retrieve information.

data base, on line   See ON-LINE DATA BASE.

data base packages   See DATA BASE MANAGEMENT SYSTEM.

data base specialist   A person who works with data bases.

data bus   A bus system that interconnects the CPU, storage, and all the input/output devices of a computer system for the purpose of exchanging data.

data byte   The 8-bit binary number representing one character of data the computer will use in an arithmetic or logical operation, or store in memory.

data capturing   Gathering or collecting information for computer handling, the first step in job processing. Also called DATA COLLECTION.

data catalog   An organized listing by full name of all data elements used by an organization.

data cell   A direct-access magnetic storage device, developed by the IBM Corporation, that handles data recorded on magnetic strips arranged in cells.

data center   A computer equipped location that processes data and converts it into a desired form, such as reports.

data chaining   A process of linking data items together. Each data item contains the location of the next data item.

data channel   A communications link between two devices or points.

data clerk   A person who does clerical jobs in a computer installation.

data collection   **(1)** The gathering of source data to be entered into a data processing system. **(2)** The act of bringing data from one or more points to a central point. Also called DATA CAPTURING.

data communications   **(1)** The movement of encoded information by means of electrical transmission systems. **(2)** The entire process and science of enabling digital devices, such as computers, to communicate with each other.

data communications equipment   The equipment associated with the transmission of data from one device to another.

Examples are modems, remote terminals and communications processors. See INPUT/OUTPUT CHANNEL and MODEM.

data communications system   A system consisting of computers, terminals and communications links.

data compression   A technique that saves computer storage space by eliminating empty fields, gap redundancies, or unnecessary data to reduce the size or the length of records.

data concentration   **(1)** Collection of data at an intermediate point from several low- and medium-speed lines for retransmission across high-speed lines. **(2)** Addition of one item at the end of others to produce one longer data item.

data control section   The organization or group responsible for meeting quality control standards for processing and for collecting input from, and delivering output to, computer users.

data conversion   The process of changing the form of data representation.

data definition   In programming, a statement that gives the size, type, and often the content of a field or record. That portion of a program that identifies the data to be used in analysis.

data definition language (DDL)   A language used by a data base administrator to create, store, and manage data in a data base environment. Also called DATA DESCRIPTION LANGUAGE.

data description language (DDL)   A language that specifies the manner in which data are to be stored and managed in a data base environment by a data base management system. Also called DATA DEFINITION LANGUAGE.

data dictionary   A list of all the files, fields, and variables used in a data base management system. A data dictionary helps users remember what items they have to work with and how they have been defined. Particularly helpful when writing a large number of linked procedures or programs that share a data base.

data diddling A technique whereby data is modified before it goes into a computer file where it is less accessible.

data directory An ordered collection of data element names and/or identifiers and their attributes that provides the location of the elements. It describes where the data are located.

data directory/dictionary An ordered collection of data elements that combines the features of a data catalog, data dictionary, and data directory. It describes and locates each data element.

data division One of the four main components of a COBOL program.

data editing A procedure to check for irregularities in input data. See EDIT.

data element One or more data items that forms a unit or piece of information, such as the social security number in an employee-payroll data base.

data encryption A coding technique used to secure sensitive data by mixing or jumbling the data according to a predetermined format.

data encryption standard A method of data protection, developed by IBM and accepted by the National Bureau of Standards, that uses a single "private key" to encrypt data.

data entry The process of converting data into a form suitable for entry into a computer system, such as by keying from a keyboard onto magnetic disks.

data entry device The equipment used to prepare data so that the computer can accept it.

data entry operator A person who uses a keyboard device to transcribe data into a form suitable for processing by a computer. Often a member of a computer operations staff who is responsible for keying data into a computer system.

data entry specialist A person responsible for inputting information into the computer for processing.

data export The capacity to transport (write) information from one data base in a form that can be used (read) by another program, such as a word processor for form letters and reports, a spreadsheet, or a different data base. Opposite of DATA IMPORT.

data field   One column or consecutive columns used to store a particular piece of information.

data field masking   Using special characters to offset or divide data fields. For date fields, the slash or hyphen characters are often used to divide the month, day, and year (e.g., 03/10/88). For telephone numbers, the parentheses and hyphen characters may be desired: (904) 672-2187. Similar types of characters may be used for part numbers or in other fields where such offsets improve the readability of character strings. These masks can be inserted by the computer, so that an operator does not have to enter the hyphen or other character manually (e.g., only the numbers 031088 are entered in the above date field, with the slashes inserted automatically by the computer program). This feature greatly simplifies data entry and ensures standardization. Some programs routinely mask fields, such as date and telephone number.

data file   A collection of related data records that have been organized in a specific manner.

data file processing   The updating of data files to reflect the effects of current data.

dataflow   A generic term that pertains to algorithms or machines whose actions are determined by the availability of the data needed for these actions.

dataflow analysis   The study of the movement of data among processing activities.

dataflow diagram   A graphic systems analysis and design tool that enables a systems analyst to represent the flow of data through a system. See SYSTEM FLOWCHART.

data gathering   The task of collecting data from internal and/or external sources. See DATA COLLECTION.

Data General Corporation   A manufacturer of minicomputer systems.

data import   The ability to use (read) information developed with another program. This is particularly important in the use of integrated software where several programs will use the information gathered or produced by one program. Opposite of DATA EXPORT.

data independence Status of a data base system with storage structure and accessing strategy that can be changed without significantly affecting the application.

data integrity The accuracy, consistency, and completeness of data that are maintained by the computer system.

data interchange format (DIF) A standard among software developers that allows data from one program to be accessible to another program.

data item An item of data used to represent a single value. A data item is the smallest unit of named data.

data leakage Illegal removal of data from a computer facility.

data librarian A person who maintains custody and control of disks, tapes, and procedures manuals by cataloging and monitoring the use of these data resources.

data link Equipment that permits the transmission of information in data format. See CHANNEL.

data logging Recording of data about events that occur in time sequence.

data management (1) A general term that collectively describes those functions of a system that provide access to hardware, enforce data storage conventions, and regulate the use of input/output devices. (2) A major function of operating systems that involves organizing, cataloging, locating, retrieving, storing, and maintaining data.

data management system (1) A system that provides the necessary procedures and programs to collect, organize, and maintain the data required by information systems. (2) A system that assigns the responsibility for data input and integrity in order to establish and maintain the data bases within an organization.

data manipulation The process of using language commands to add, delete, modify or retrieve data in a file or data base.

data manipulating language (DML) A language that allows a user to interrogate and access the data base of a computer system by using English-like statements.

data medium The material in or on which a specific physical variable may represent data, such as magnetic disk or magnetic tape.

data model A formal language for describing data structures and operations on those structures. It is usually divided into a DATA DESCRIPTION LANGUAGE and a DATA MANIPULATION LANGUAGE.

data modem See MODEM.

data movement time The time taken to transfer data to or from a disk once the read/write head is properly positioned on a disk track.

data name The name of the variable used to indicate a data value, such as PI for 3.14159. . . .

data origination The translation of information from its original form into machine-sensible form.

data packet A means of transmitting serial data in an efficient package that includes an error-checking sequence.

dataphone™ A trademark of the AT&T Company used to identify data sets manufactured and supplied by AT&T for use in the transmission of data over the telephone network.

data point A numeric value for charting purposes. In a simple line chart, the time may be plotted across the x-axis and another value against the y-axis, the intersection being a data point.

data preparation The process of organizing information and storing it in a form that can be input to the computer.

data preparation device A device that permits data capture in which the source data is collected and transformed into a medium or form capable of being read into a computer.

Datapro A research/publishing company that provides in-depth information about computer hardware and software products.

data processing **(1)** One or more operations performed on data to achieve a desired objective. **(2)** The functions of a computer center. **(3)** A term used in reference to operations performed by data processing equipment. **(4)** Operations performed on data to provide useful information to users.

data processing center A computer center equipped with devices capable of receiving information, processing it according to human-made instructions, and producing the computed results. Also called an information processing center.

data processing curriculum A course of study, normally offered by a school, that prepares students for entry-level jobs as application programmers, system programmers, or systems analysts.

data processing cycle The combined functions of input, processing and output.

data processing management Managing the data processing function, its people, and its equipment. Since this activity follows the well-recognized principles of planning, control, and operation, its basic prerequisites are the same skills that are needed to manage any other enterprise.

Data Processing Management Association (DPMA) The largest professional association in the field of computer management. Its purpose is to engage in education and research activities focused on the development of effective programs for the self-improvement of its membership. It seeks to encourage high standards of competence and promotes a professional attitude among its members. DPMA sponsors high school clubs and college chapters.

data processing manager A person who runs the data processing center, usually including the operation of the computer. The biggest part of the manager's job is concerned with developing new systems and keeping them running.

data processing system A network of data processing hardware, software, people, and procedures capable of accepting information, processing it according to a plan, and producing the desired results.

data processing technology The science of information handling.

data processor Any device capable of performing operations on data, such as a desk calculator or a microcomputer.

data protection Measures to safeguard data from undesired occurrences that intentionally or unintentionally lead to de-

struction, modification, or disclosure of data. See DATA SE-
CURITY.

data rate   The rate at which a channel carries data, measured
in bauds (bits per second).

data record   A collection of data fields pertaining to a particular subject. Part of a data file.

data reduction   The process of transforming raw data into useful, condensed, or simplified intelligence. Often adjusting,
scaling, smoothing, compacting, editing, and ordering
operations are used in the process.

data scope   A special display device that monitors a data communications channel and displays the content of the information being transmitted over it.

data security   The protection of data from accidental or ma-
licious destruction, disclosure, or modification. See COM-
PUTER SECURITY, DISK LIBRARY, and TAPE LIBRARY.

data set   **(1)** A device that permits the transmission of data
over communications lines by changing the form of the data
at one end so that it can be carried over the lines; another
data set at the other end changes the data back to its original form so that it is acceptable to the machine (computer,
and so forth) at that end. The dataphone is an example. **(2)**
A collection of related data items.

data sharing   The ability of computer processes or of computer users at several nodes to access data at a single node.

data sheet   A special form used to record input values in a
format convenient for keypunching. See CODING FORM.

data storage device   A unit for storing large quantities (millions) of characters, typically, a magnetic disk unit or tape
unit.

data storage techniques   Methods used by a program to store
data files.

data stream   The serial data that is transmitted through a
channel from a single input/output operation.

data structure   The structure of relationships among files in a
data base and among data items within each file.

data structures The relationships between the data elements in a computer file.

data tablet A manual input device for graphic display consoles. Same as DIGITIZER.

data terminal A point in a computer system or data communications network at which data can be entered or retrieved. See TERMINAL and VIDEO DISPLAY TERMINAL.

data transfer operations Operations that move data, whether externally through data communication channels or within the main computer storage by copying from one location to another.

data transfer rate The rate of transfer of data from one place to another, such as from computer main memory to disk or from one computer's memory to another computer's memory.

data transmission The sending of data from one part of a system to another part. See DATA COMMUNICATIONS.

data type An interpretation applied to a string of bits, such as integer, real, or character.

data validation Measures taken to ensure that data fields conform to desired specifications. Fields may be checked for inappropriate characters or for deviation from specified lengths or values.

data value Any string of symbols that serves as the representative of some item of information.

data word An ordered set of characters, usually of a preset number, that is stored and transferred by the computer's circuits as a fundamental unit of information.

data word size Refers to the specific length of data word that a particular computer is designed to handle. See WORD and WORD LENGTH.

datum A unit of data.

daughter board A circuit board that plugs into a motherboard.

dBASE III™ A relational data base management package that can open (access) more than one file at a time as opposed to a file manager that can open only one file at a time. With

its built-in command-processing language, the relational capabilities let the user create complex data bases and reports, along with screens that ask questions when input is
needed. This enables experienced programmers to set up
systems for use by less-experienced users. Developed by
Ashton-Tate.

DBMS An abbreviation for **DATA BASE MANAGEMENT SYS-
TEM**. A complete collection of hardware and computer programs that organizes and provides access to a data base.

DB-25 connector A plug with either 25 pins (male) or 25 slots
(female). Most commonly used with an RS-232C interface
connection.

DC An abbreviation for **(1) DATA CONVERSION, (2) DESIGN
CHANGE, (3) DIGITAL COMPUTER, (4) DIRECT CURRENT, (5)
DIRECT CYCLE, (6) DISPLAY CONSOLE**.

DCTL An abbreviation for **DIRECT COUPLED TRANSISTOR
LOGIC**.

DDD An abbreviation for **DIRECT DISTANCE DIALING**, the facility used for making long-distance telephone calls without
the assistance of a telephone operator. Also used for **DATA
COMMUNICATIONS**.

DDL A language for declaring data structures in a data base.
See **DATA DEFINITION LANGUAGE** and **DATA DESCRIPTION
LANGUAGE**.

dead halt A halt situation in which the system cannot return
to the point before it halted.

dead letter box In message switching systems, a file for capturing undeliverable messages.

deadlock Unresolved contention for the use of a resource.

deallocation The release of a resource by a program when the
program no longer needs it. The opposite of allocation.

debit card A card issued by a specific bank that allows the
user to deduct money directly from his/her bank account
when making purchases in stores that have accounts with
the same bank.

deblocking Extracting a logical record from a block or group
of logical records.

debounce To prevent spurious closures of a key or switch from being recognized. One method is to introduce time delays that give the switch contacts time to settle down.

debug To detect, locate, and remove all mistakes in a computer program and any malfunctions in the computing system itself. Synonymous with troubleshoot. See BUG, DEBUGGING AIDS, and TEST DATA.

debugging aids Computer routines that are helpful in debugging programs (e.g., tracing routine, snapshot dump, or post mortem dump).

debugging-a-program The process of locating, removing, and correcting all mistakes in a computer program.

DEC An acronym for DIGITAL EQUIPMENT CORPORATION, a large manufacturer of minicomputer systems.

decatenate To separate into two or more parts. Contrast with CONCATENATE.

deceleration time The time required to stop a magnetic tape after reading or recording the last piece of data from a record on that tape.

decimal A characteristic or property involving a selection, condition, or choice in which there are ten possibilities; for example, the numeration system with a radix of 10.

decimal code Describing a form of notation by which each decimal digit is expressed separately in some other number system.

decimal digit A numeral in the decimal numeral system. The radix of the decimal system is 10, and the following symbols are used: 0, 1, 2, 3, 4, 5, 6, 7, 8, and 9.

decimal number A numeral, usually of more than one digit, representing a sum, in which the quantity represented by each digit is based on the radix of 10.

decimal point Radix point in a mixed decimal numeral, separating the fractional part from the integer part. In the decimal numeral 68.82, the decimal point is between the two 8s.

decimal system Base-10 positional numeration system.

decimal-to-binary conversion   The process of converting a numeral written in base 10 to the equivalent numeral written in base 2.

decimal-to-hexadecimal conversion   The process of converting a numeral written in base 10 to the equivalent numeral written in base 16.

decimal-to-octal conversion   The process of converting a numeral written in base 10 to the equivalent numeral written in base 8.

decision   The computer operation of determining if a certain relationship exists between data in storage and of taking alternative courses of action. A determination of future action.

decision instruction   An instruction that affects the selection of a branch of a program, such as a conditional jump instruction.

decision structure   Same as SELECTION STRUCTURE.

decision symbol   A diamond-shaped flowcharting symbol that is used to indicate a choice or a branching in the information processing path.

decision table   A table listing all the contingencies to be considered in the description of a problem, together with the corresponding actions to be taken. Decision tables are sometimes used instead of flowcharts to describe the operations of a program.

decision theory   A broad spectrum of concepts and techniques that have been developed both to describe and rationalize the process of decision making; that is, making a choice among several possible alternatives.

decision tree   A pictorial representation of the alternatives in any situation.

declaration statement   A part of a computer program that defines the nature of other elements of the program or reserves parts of the hardware for special use.

decode   To translate or determine the meaning of coded information. The reverse of ENCODE.

decoder **(1)** A device that decodes. **(2)** A matrix of switching elements that selects one or more output channels according to the combination of input signals present.

decollate To arrange copies of continuous forms in sets and remove the carbon paper from them.

decrement The amount by which a value or variable is decreased. Contrast with INCREMENT.

decryption The process of taking an encrypted message and reconstructing from it the original meaningful message. The opposite of ENCRYPTION.

DECUS An acronym for the DIGITAL EQUIPMENT COMPUTER (DEC) USERS SOCIETY. A user group whose objective is the exchange and dissemination of ideas and information pertinent to computers manufactured by Digital Equipment Corporation.

dedicated Pertaining to programs, machines, or procedures that are designed or reserved for special use.

dedicated computer A computer whose use is reserved for a particular task.

dedicated device A device that is designed to perform only certain functions and that cannot be programmed to perform other functions.

dedicated lines Telephone lines leased for exclusive use by a group or individual for telecommunications. The user pays a set fee rather than per-call or per-minute charges for leased lines.

dedicated system A computer-based device with one primary function, such as word processing. A dedicated word processor would typically have special function keys labeled with commands such as delete word, delete sentence, or insert. A dedicated system is usually easier to use for its intended task than for any other. General-purpose systems, on the other hand, are usually more flexible.

dedicated word processor A system whose hardware and software is expressly designed for, and generally limited to, word processing.

default An assumption made by a system or language translator when no specific choice is given by the program or the user.

default drive The disk drive assigned by a system when no drive number is specified by the user.

default value An assigned quantity for a device or program that is set by the manufacturer. A default value in a program is usually the most common or safest answer.

deferred address An indirect address. See DEFERRED ENTRY, DEFERRED EXIT, and INDIRECT ADDRESSING.

deferred entry An entry into a subroutine that occurs as a result of a deferred exit from the program that passed control to it.

deferred exit The passing of control to a subroutine at a time determined by an asynchronous event rather than at a predictable time.

definition of a problem The art of compiling logic in the form of algorithms, and program descriptions that clearly explain and define the problem.

degausser A device that is used to erase information from magnetically recorded media (disks or tapes). Also called bulk eraser.

degradation A condition in which a system continues to operate but at a reduced level of service. Unavailability of proper equipment maintenance and computer programs not maintained to accommodate current needs are the two most common causes.

deinstall To remove a program or hardware device from active service.

dejagging A computer graphics technique for drawing smooth lines, characters, and polygons.

delay circuit An electronic circuit that deliberately delays the delivery of a signal for a present interval.

delay line storage A storage device that consists of a delay line and a means for regenerating and reinserting information into the delay line. This device was used in early computers.

delete To remove or eliminate. To erase data from a field or to eliminate a record from a file. A method of erasing data.

deletion record A new record that will replace or remove an existing record of a master file.

delimit To fix the limits of something, such as to establish maximum and minimum limits of a specific variable.

delimiter A special character, often a comma or space, used to separate variable names or items in a list or to separate one string of characters from another, as in the separation of data items.

delivery A final step in the program development cycle where the program or system is given to the users for execution against actual data.

demagnetization The process of erasing information stored on magnetic disks or tapes. See DEGAUSSER.

demand paging In virtual storage systems, the transfer of a page from external page storage to real storage at the time it is needed for execution.

demand report A report produced only upon request and used in strategic decision making to provide responses to unanticipated queries.

demodulation In data communications, the process of retrieving an original signal from a modulated carrier wave. This technique is used in data sets to make communications signals compatible with computer terminal signals.

demodulator A device that receives signals transmitted over a communications link and converts them into electrical pulses, or bits, that can serve as inputs to a data processing machine. Contrast with MODULATOR.

demount To remove a magnetic storage medium from a device that reads or writes on it, such as to remove the disk pack from the disk drive.

demultiplexer A circuit that applies the logic state of a single input to one of several outputs. Contrast with MULTIPLEXER.

denominator In the expression a/b, b is the denominator and a is the numerator.

dense binary code A code in which all possible states of the binary pattern are used.

dense list See SEQUENTIAL LIST.

density The number of characters that can be stored in a given physical space. It measures how close together data is recorded on a magnetic medium. As the recording density increases, the capacity of a storage device increases. See DOUBLE DENSITY.

dependency A relationship where the execution of one job has to have been completed before another can begin.

depersonalization The tendency to remove or deemphasize personal identification. The state of being without privacy or individuality.

depth queuing A technique, such as shading, used to enhance the three-dimensional appearance of a two-dimensional object.

deque A double-ended queue that allows insertions and deletions at both ends of a list.

descender The portion of lower-case letters (g, j, p, q, and y) that extends below the baseline of other characters. Also called kern.

descending order Order that ranges from highest to lowest in numeric value or alphabetically. Contrast with ASCENDING ORDER.

descriptive statistics The numerical values representing important features of a set of quantitative information, such as the arithmetic mean, range, standard deviation, ratios, percentages, and rates of change.

descriptor A significant word that helps to categorize or index information. Sometimes called a KEYWORD.

design aids Computer programs or hardware elements that are intended to assist in implementing a computer system. See DEBUGGING AIDS and PROGRAMMING AIDS.

design automation The use of computers in the design and production of circuit packages, new computers, and other electronic equipment.

design costs The costs associated with systems design, programming, training, conversion, testing, and documentation.

design cycle **(1)** In a hardware system, the complete cycle of development of equipment, which includes breadboarding, prototyping, testing, and production. **(2)** In a software system, the complete plan for producing an operational system, which includes problem description, algorithm development, coding, program debugging, and documentation.

design engineer A person involved in the design of a hardware product, such as a visual display device or a microcomputer.

design heuristics Guidelines that can be followed when dividing a larger problem or program into smaller, more manageable modules.

design language A programming language whose statements and syntax facilitate its use in performing design work.

design phase The process of developing an information system based upon previously established system requirements.

design specifications The result of an analysis of information needs of a specific system within the organization. Included are specifications for input, output, and processing.

desk accessories In a graphics-based system, working tools available during use with other documents.

desk checking A manual checking process in which representative sample data items, used for detecting errors in program logic, are traced through the program before it is executed on the computer. Same as DRY RUN.

desktop accessory A program that keeps often-needed business tools and services, such as a calculator, handy while using a computer. These on-screen functions can be accessed while an application, such as a spreadsheet program, is in use. See SIDEKICK™.

desktop computer A microcomputer. A small computer containing a microprocessor, input and output devices, and storage, usually in one box or package. A complete computer system designed to fit on the top of a desk. See HOME

COMPUTER, MICROCOMPUTER, and PERSONAL COMPUTER.

desktop organizer See DESKTOP ACCESSORY.

desktop publishing program An application program that permits the use of a microcomputer and a high-quality printer to produce reports, newsletters, brochures, magazines, books, and other publications.

destination The device or address that receives the data during a data transfer operation.

destructive operation A process of reading or writing data which erases the data that is read or that was stored previously in the receiving storage location.

destructive read The process of destroying the information in a location by reading the contents.

detachable keyboard A keyboard that is not built into the same case as the video display. It connects to the video display with a cable and allows greater flexibility in positioning of the keyboard display—one result of ergonomics.

detail A small section of a larger file or graphics picture.

detail diagram A diagram used in HIPO to describe the specific function performed or data items used in a module.

detail file A file containing relatively transient information, such as records of individual transactions that occurred during a particular period of time. Synonymous with TRANSACTION FILE. Contrast with MASTER FILE.

detail flowchart A diagram that depicts the processing steps required within a particular program. See PROGRAM FLOWCHART.

detail printing An operation in which a line of printing occurs for each record read into the computer.

detection Passive monitoring of an event for the purpose of discovering a problem.

deterministic model A mathematical model for the study of data of known fixed values and direct cause-and-effect relationships.

development support library An automated facility with which a programming librarian maintains program development files, including source code versions, test data sets, and narrative documentation. The library contains up-to-date representations of programs and test data in both computer- and human-readable forms. The librarian maintains the library according to a set of office and computer procedures that separate clerical and bookkeeping operations from programming tasks.

development system A computer system with the capabilities required for efficient hardware and software application development for a given microprocessor. Such a system typically includes a microcomputer, monitor, printer, disk storage, PROM programmer, and an in-circuit emulator.

development time The time used for debugging new programs or hardware.

development tools Hardware and software aids intended for use in developing programs and/or hardware systems.

device (1) A mechanical or electrical device with a specific purpose. (2) A computer peripheral. (3) Any piece of physical equipment within or attached to a computer.

device cluster A group of terminals or other devices that share a communications controller.

device code The 8-bit code for a specific input or output device.

device dependent Pertaining to a program or language that must be used with a particular computer or a particular peripheral, such as a printer or modem, or it will not function.

device flag A 1-bit register that records the current status of a device.

device independence The ability to command input/output operations without regard to the characteristics of the input/output devices. See SYMBOLIC I/O ASSIGNMENT. Contrast with DEVICE DEPENDENT.

device media control language A language used by the data base administrator to create the physical description of a data base on a disk storage device.

device name The general name for a kind of device, such as model IBM Personal System/2™ or HP RuggedWriter 480 printer.

device number A number assigned to a particular peripheral device, used to identify it in the computer.

diagnosis The process of isolating malfunctions in computing equipment and of detecting mistakes in programs and systems.

diagnostic routine (1) A routine designed to locate a malfunction in the central processing unit or a peripheral device. (2) A routine designed to locate an error in a program.

diagnostics Messages to the user automatically printed by a computer which pinpoint improper commands and errors in logic. Sometimes called ERROR MESSAGES.

diagram A schematic representation of a sequence of operations or routines. See FLOWCHART.

dial A way to represent, or for the user to control, a setting that is continuous, such as speaker volume or visual display intensity.

dialect A particular version of a computer language. Usually a minor modification of some base language like BASIC or Pascal, but because of vast differences in modifications it may be significantly different from other dialects of the same language.

dialog A question-and-answer session between a computer system and a human.

dial-up In data communications, the use of a dial or push-button telephone to initiate a station-to-station telephone call.

dial-up line The normal switched telephone line that can be used as a transmission medium for data communications. Synonymous with SWITCHED LINE.

dibit One of the following binary number arrangements: 00, 01, 10, or 11.

dichotomizing search See BINARY SEARCH.

dictionary **(1)** Words that are arranged alphabetically and usually defined. **(2)** A lexicon in alphabetic order. **(3)** A list of files stored on a magnetic disk.

dictionary program A spelling check program, often used with word processing systems. Also called a spelling checker program.

diddle To tamper with data.

die The tiny rectangular piece of a circular wafer of semiconductor silicon, sawed or sliced during the fabrication of integrated circuits.

difference The amount by which one quantity or number is greater or less than another.

DIF An acronym for DATA INTERCHANGE FORMAT, a particular standard for data files. It is used by many programs involving forecasting and it allows files created on one software package to be read by another software package—perhaps one produced by an entirely different company. DIF files are not interchangeable between different machines; an Apple DIF file disk cannot be read directly into an IBM machine. While the files are compatible, the disks are formatted differently for different machines.

diffusion A high temperature process by which impurity atoms that have been deposited on the surface of a material, such as a silicon wafer, have sufficient thermal energy to penetrate the material, seeking to equalize their densities by displacing the host atoms and altering the electrical properties of the material in desired ways. Normal diffusion temperatures are between 900 and 1200 degrees C for the most frequently used impurities in silicon.

digit One of the symbols of a numbering system that is used to designate a quantity.

digital Of or relating to the technology of computers and data communications wherein all information is encoded as bits of 1s or 0s that represent on or off states. Contrast with ANALOG.

digital communications The transmissions of information by coding it into discrete on/off electronic signals.

digital computer A device that manipulates digital data and performs arithmetic and logic operations on such data. See COMPUTER. Contrast with ANALOG COMPUTER.

digital control The use of digital technology to maintain conditions in operating systems as close as possible to desired values despite changes in the operating environment.

digital data Data represented in discrete, discontinuous form, as contrasted with ANALOG DATA, which is represented in continuous form.

digital data transmission The transmission of the original electronic signal produced by a computer device. Not all channels have digital capabilities.

Digital Equipment Corporation (DEC) A manufacturer of several popular minicomputer systems, including the PDP-8™, PDP-11™, and VAX™.

digital plotter An output device that uses an ink pen (or pens) to draw graphs, line drawings, and other illustrations.

digital recording A technique for recording information as discrete points onto magnetic recording media.

digital repeater A unit placed in a data communications path to reconstruct digital pulses, which tend to deteriorate as they travel through long conductors.

Digital Research, Inc. A software company that has produced several products, including the CP/M operating system.

digital signal Two electrical states that communicate a code. The two states represent binary data (1s and 0s) that the computer can understand. Each 1 and 0 is a bit, while eight to 10 bits equal a byte, or one character. The digital signal is converted by a modem into an analog, or continuous wave form, signal (modulated), that may be transmitted over phone lines. Incoming analog signals detected by the modem are converted into digital signals (demodulated) the computer can understand.

digital signal processing The art of using computer technologies to enhance, analyze, or otherwise manipulate images, sounds, radar pulses, and other real-world signals.

digital sorting   A sorting technique similar to sorting on tabulation machines. The elapsed time is directly proportional to the number of characters in the sequencing key and the value of data. Also called RADIX SORTING.

digital speech   Recorded speech broken into tiny units of sound. Each tiny unit has characteristics such as pitch, loudness, and so on that can be represented by numbers, which become the digital code for speech. See SPEECH SYNTHESIZER.

digital-to-analog converter   Mechanical or electronic devices used to convert discrete digital numbers to continuous analog signals. Abbreviated D-A CONVERTER. Opposite of ANALOG-TO-DIGITAL CONVERTER.

digital transmission   The transmission of data as discrete impulses.

digitize   **(1)** To transform a graphical representation (picture drawing) into a digital representation of the graphical picture. **(2)** To assign a digital number to a character or symbol. **(3)** To translate analog data into digital data.

digitizer   An input device that normally consists of a flat tablet that the operator traces over with a pen-like stylus or another cursor device. The patterns traced by the operator are automatically entered into the computer system's memory for subsequent processing.

digitizing   The process of converting graphic representations (pictures, drawings, etc.) into digital data that can be processed by a computer system.

digitizing tablet   A type of digitizer. An input device generally consisting of a surface underlaid by a fine grid of wires that converts graphic and pictorial data into binary inputs for use in a computer. Same as GRAPHICS TABLET.

digit place   In positional notation, the site where a digit is located in a word representing a numeral.

dimension   The defined size of an array: for example, the dimension of an array with three rows and four columns is (3,4) or 3 by 4.

diode An electronic device used to permit current flow in one direction and to inhibit current flow in the opposite direction.

diode transistor logic See DTL.

DIP An acronym for DUAL IN-LINE PACKAGE. A device on which an integrated circuit is mounted. It provides a protective casing for the integrated circuit and pin connections for plugging the chip into a circuit board.

DIP switches DUAL IN-LINE PACKAGE switches, small switches found on many computers and peripherals that are used to set up or adjust the equipment.

direct access Pertaining to the process of storing data in, or getting data from, a storage device in such a manner that surrounding data need not be scanned to locate the desired data. Also, the time required to get desired data from the storage device is independent of the location of the data. This method is quicker than sequential access, where each record in the file is read and written in turn. Contrast with SEQUENTIAL ACCESS. Also called RANDOM ACCESS.

direct access processing Processing of data randomly. Same as RANDOM PROCESSING. Contrast with SEQUENTIAL PROCESSING.

direct access storage device A basic type of storage medium that allows information to be accessed by positioning the medium or accessing mechanism directly to the information required, thus permitting direct addressing of data locations. Abbreviated DASD. See MAGNETIC DISK.

direct address An address that specifies the storage location of an operand. Contrast with INDIRECT ADDRESS.

direct-connect modem A modulator/demodulator that plugs directly into a modular telephone jack for use in data transmission. Contrast with ACOUSTIC COUPLER.

direct conversion See CRASH CONVERSION.

direct coupled transistor logic A logic system that uses only transistors as active elements. Abbreviated DCTL.

direct current The flow of electrons in one direction. Contrast with ALTERNATING CURRENT.

direct data entry Entry of data directly into the computer through machine-readable source documents or through the use of on-line terminals.

direct distance dialing See DDD.

direct memory access A method by which data can be transferred between peripheral devices and internal memory without intervention by the central processing unit. Abbreviated DMA.

directory A partition by software into several distinct files; a directory of these files is maintained on a device to locate the files. A file containing the names and locations of all the files contained on a storage medium. Using directories makes it easier to find programs and data files on a disk.

direct processing A technique of handling data in random order, without preliminary sorting, and utilizing files on direct access storage devices. Contrast with SEQUENTIAL PROCESSING.

disable To remove or inhibit a normal capability, i.e., a command that prevents further operation of a peripheral device. Opposite of ENABLE.

disassembler A program that takes machine language code and generates the assembler language code from which the machine language was produced. See ASSEMBLY LANGUAGE.

disaster dump A computer storage dump that occurs as a result of a nonrecoverable mistake in a program.

disaster recovery plan A plan of action in case a tragedy affects either hardware or software.

disc Alternate spelling for disk. See MAGNETIC DISK.

disclaimer A clause associated with many software products that states the vendor is not responsible for any business losses incurred due to the use of the product.

discrete Pertaining to distinct elements or to representation by means of distinct elements, such as bits or characters.

discrete component An electrical component that contains only one function, as opposed to an integrated circuit.

disk A magnetic device for storing information and programs accessible by a computer. A disk can be either a rigid platter (hard disk) or a sheet of flexible plastic (floppy disk). Disks have tracks where data is stored.

disk access time The time required to locate a specific track on a disk. Also called SEEK TIME.

disk buffer An area of a computer's memory set aside to hold information not yet written to disk.

disk controller card A peripheral circuit card that connects disk drives to a computer and controls their operation.

disk copying The process of transferring the entire contents of one disk to another disk. Same as DISK DUPLICATION.

disk crash A condition of a disk unit that makes it unusable. It is usually caused by contact between the read/write head of the disk drive and the surface of the disk. Sometimes called HEAD CRASH.

disk drive A device that reads data from a magnetic disk and copies it into the computer's memory so that it can be used by the computer, and that writes data from the computer's memory onto a disk so that it can be stored.

disk duplication The process of copying information recorded on one magnetic disk onto another disk. Same as DISK COPYING.

disk envelope A removable protective paper sleeve used when handling or storing a diskette. It must be removed before inserting the diskette in a disk drive. Compare with DISK JACKET.

diskette A floppy disk. A low-cost bulk-storage medium for microcomputers and minicomputers. See FLOPPY DISK.

diskette tray A container that is used to store floppy disks.

disk file A file that resides on a magnetic disk. An organized collection of data stored on a disk.

disk jacket A permanent protective covering for a disk, usually made of paper or plastic. The disk is never removed from the jacket, even when inserted in a disk drive. Compare with DISK ENVELOPE.

disk library A special room that houses a file of disk packs under secure, environmentally controlled conditions.

disk memory Storage using rotating disks as its storage element.

disk operating system (DOS) An operating system in which the operating system programs are stored on magnetic disks. Typically, it keeps track of files, saves and retrieves files, allocates storage space, and manages other control functions associated with disk storage.

disk pack A group of removable tiered hard disks that are mounted on a shaft and treated as a unit. A disk pack must be placed on a disk storage unit to be accessed.

disk partition A logical portion of a disk that provides an organization allowing smaller blocks of data to be handled more conveniently.

disk sector Corresponds to a block of data storage area between two successive radials on the disk. The cutting of a disk into sectors is analogous to the way a pie would be sliced.

disk unit See MAGNETIC DISK UNIT.

disk unit enclosure A cabinet designed to hold one or more disk drives and a power supply.

dispatch To select the next task and get it ready for processing.

dispatching priority A number assigned to tasks and used to determine precedence for use by the central processing unit in a multitask situation.

dispersed data processing Same as DISTRIBUTED DATA PROCESSING.

dispersed intelligence A network system in which the computing power is scattered or dispersed throughout the computer network.

dispersion The extent to which data varies from its expected value.

displacement The difference between the base address and the actual machine language address.

display (1) The physical representation of data, as on a screen or display. (2) Lights or indicators on computer consoles. (3) The process of creating a visual representation of graphic data on an output device.

display adapter An adapter board that electronically links the computer to a display screen and determines its capabilities, such as degree of resolution, color vs. monochrome, and graphics vs. no graphics.

display background Refers to the part of displayed graphic data that is not part of the image being processed. The background display is used to highlight the image part of the display (called foreground display). See DISPLAY FORE-GROUND.

display console An input/output device consisting of a display screen and an input keyboard. Sometimes called a WORK-STATION.

display cycle The time it takes a visual display screen to be completely refreshed.

display device A device capable of producing a visual representation of data, such as a graphics printer, plotter, visual display terminal, and film recorder.

display foreground Refers to the graphic data being displayed on a visual display device that is subject to alteration by the user. Contrast with DISPLAY BACKGROUND.

display highlighting A way of emphasizing information on a display screen by using such enhancers as blinking, bold-face, high contrast, reverse video, underlining, or different colors. See highlighting.

display image That portion of a displayed graphics file that is currently visible on the display device.

display menu An on-screen series of program options that allows the user to choose the next function or course of action to be executed, such as to print the contents of the visual display or to save a graphic display on a disk.

display surface The medium upon which a visual representation of graphic data is made, such as visual display screen, printer paper, plotter paper or film.

display terminal Any output device capable of producing a visual representation of graphic data. Examples are visual display devices, plotters, graphics printers and film recorders.

display tolerance The measure of accuracy with which graphic data can be output.

display type The technology of the display; for example, cathode-ray tube (CRT), light emitting diode (LED), liquid crystal display (LCD), and so forth.

display unit A device that provides a visual representation of data. See CATHODE-RAY TUBE, LINE PRINTER, PLASMA DISPLAY, and PLOTTER.

distortion Any undesired change in the waveform of an electric signal passing through a circuit, including the transmission medium. In the design of any electronic circuit, one important problem is to modify the input signal in the required way without producing distortion beyond an acceptable degree.

distributed data base A data base that is spread throughout the computer system of a network.

distributed data processing The concept of performing operations in a computer system whose terminals and central processing unit are separated geographically but are linked together functionally in a communications network. Contrast with CENTRALIZED DATA PROCESSING.

distributed design An information structure that identifies the existence of independent operating units but recognizes the benefits of central coordination and control.

distributed network A network configuration in which all node pairs are connected either directly or by redundant paths through intermediate nodes.

distributed processing system A set of interacting computer systems or data bases situated in different locations.

distributive sort A sort formed by separating the list into parts and then rearranging the parts in order.

distributor A company that buys computer hardware and software supplies and resells them to end-users or retail stores.

disturbance An irregular phenomenon that interferes with the interchange of intelligence during transmission of a signal. See NOISE.

dithering (1) The intermingling of dots of various colors to produce what appears to be a new color. The dots must be so small and closely spaced that the eye fuses them together. (2) A computer graphics technique for increasing the intensity of the display when the image and device resolutions coincide.

dividend In the division operation a/b, *a* is the dividend and b is the divisor. The result is the quotient and remainder.

division check A multiplication check in which a zero-balancing result is compared against the original dividend.

division of labor The assignment of work to teams of workers, each with a limited number of specialized tasks.

divisor The quantity that is used to divide another quantity.

DMA An abbreviation for DIRECT MEMORY ACCESS. A method by which data can be transferred between peripheral devices and internal memory without intervention by the central processing unit.

DML An abbreviation for DATA MANIPULATION LANGUAGE.

DNC An abbreviation for DIRECT NUMERICAL CONTROL. A method of computer control of automatic machine tools whereby control is applied at discrete points in the process rather than applied continuously. See APT and NUMERICAL CONTROL.

DOA An abbreviation for DEAD ON ARRIVAL. Used to describe a product that does not work when it is received from the supplier or manufacturer.

document (1) A handwritten, typewritten, or printed sheet or sheets of paper containing data. (2) Any representation or collection of information or text. (3) To prepare documentation.

documentation During systems analysis and subsequent programming, the preparation of documents that describe such things as the system, the programs prepared, and the changes made at later dates.

documentation aids Aids that help automate the documentation process, such as program description write-ups, algorithms, pseudocode, programs, program runs, and so forth.

documentor A program designed to use data processing methods in the production and maintenance of program flowcharts, text material, and other types of tabular or graphic information.

document reader A general term referring to OCR or OMR equipment that reads a limited amount of information.

document retrieval The process of acquiring data from storage devices and, possibly, manipulating the data and subsequently preparing a report.

domain (1) A set of data values from which a relational attributes may draw its values. (2) The problem area of interest.

domain knowledge Knowledge of the application environment.

domain tip A type of storage device that uses thin films to create magnetic domains for storing digital data. See THIN FILM.

dopant The substance added in the doping process such as phosphorus or arsenic. See DOPING.

dope vector A vector wherein an atom of a linked list describes the contents of the other atoms in the list.

doping The process of introducing impurity elements into the crystalline structure of pure silicon during semiconductor fabrication.

DOS An acronym for **D**ISK **O**PERATING **S**YSTEM. A specialized, disk-oriented program that provides an easy-to-use link between the user and a computer's disk drive.

dot commands An approach to formatting in which a word processor records formatting instructions in the text but does not apply them to the text until it is printed.

dot matrix A technique for representing characters by composing them out of selected dots from within a rectangular matrix of dots.

dot-matrix printer A printer that creates text characters and graphs with a series of closely spaced dots. The printer uses tiny hammers to strike a needle mechanism against the paper at precise moments as the print head moves across the page. Some produce dot patterns fine enough to approach the print quality of daisy wheel printers.

dot pitch The distance in millimeters between individual dots on a monitor screen. The smaller the dot pitch the better, since it allows for more potential dots to be displayed, giving better resolution.

double buffering A software or hardware technique to transfer information between the computer and peripheral devices. Information in one buffer is acted on by the computer while information in the other is transferred in or out.

double-click A method to invoke a command by using the mouse button. The pointer or cursor is placed in the correct position on a display screen and the mouse button is pressed twice in rapid succession. See MOUSE.

double density Having twice the storage capacity of a normal disk or tape. The ability to store twice as much data in a given area on a disk or tape as single density.

double precision Pertaining to the use of two computer words to represent a number in order to gain increased precision. Contrast with SINGLE PRECISION and TRIPLE PRECISION.

double-sided disk A magnetic disk capable of storing information on both of its surfaces. Contrast with SINGLE-SIDED DISK.

doublestriking See OVERSTRIKING.

double word An entity of storage that is two words in length.

doubly linked list List in which each atom contains one pointer that relates to the successor atom.

down A condition that exists when the hardware circuits of a computer are inoperable or there is a failure in the software system. When a computer is "down," it is simply not functioning. Contrast with UP.

Dow Jones Information Service A computer data base containing current information on stock prices and other financial news. The data base can be accessed by subscribers with microcomputers and modems.

down line processor A processor at or near the terminal point in a data communications network that facilitates the transmission of data.

download The process of transferring data from a large central computer system to a smaller, remote computer system. Opposite of UPLOAD.

downtime The length of time a computer system is inoperative due to a malfunction. Contrast with UPTIME and AVAILABLE TIME.

downward compatible Refers to a computer that is compatible with a smaller or previous generation computer.

DPMA See DATA PROCESSING MANAGEMENT ASSOCIATION.

draft mode A low quality printing mode available on some printers. See DRAFT QUALITY.

draft quality A measure of quality for printed output. Usually refers to the result of top-speed printing and therefore not the most precisely defined or fully filled-in characters. Considered acceptable for working copies but not final work. Contrast with LETTER QUALITY.

drag The action of moving the mouse while holding the button down; used to move or manipulate objects on a computer's display screen.

dragging A technique of making a displayed graphics object follow the cursor. This is accomplished in some systems by moving the mouse while holding down the mouse button.

drain One of three connecting terminals of a field effect transistor, the other two being the SOURCE and the GATE. If the charge carriers are positive, conventional current flows from source to drain.

DRAM See DYNAMIC RAM.

drawing The process of creating graphical illustrations with a computer's graphic capabilities. Examples are creating lines with a computer graphics system or producing a detailed graphics image with a drawing/painting program on a microcomputer.

drift A change in the output of an electric circuit. This change slowly occurs over a period of time.

drive The physical components necessary for reading and writing data to and reading data from a floppy disk. A short name for a disk drive.

drive number A numeric value specifying one of the disk drives available in a system.

driver A series of instructions the computer follows to reformat data for transfer to and from a particular peripheral device. The electrical and mechanical requirements are different from one kind of device to another, and software drivers are used to standardize the format of data between them and the central processor.

DRO An abbreviation for DESTRUCTIVE READ OUT. See DESTRUCTIVE READ.

droid A humanlike robot, taken from android (male) or gynoid (female).

drop (1) In a network, a remote terminal location. (2) The distance between the top and bottom of a sheet of computer stationery, measured in millimeters or inches.

drop dead halt A halt from which there is no recovery. Same as DEAD HALT.

drop-in A character that appears erroneously (on a display screen, on a printout or in a file) because the disk drive or tape drive misstored or misread one or more bits. Opposite of DROP OUT.

drop out (1) In data transmission, a momentary loss in signal, usually due to the effect of noise or system malfunction. (2) A character that vanishes (from a display, printout or file) because the disk drive or tape drive misstored or misread one or more bits. Opposite of DROP IN.

drum plotter An output device that draws schematics, graphs, pictures, and so forth on paper with an automatically controlled pen. The paper is wrapped around a cylindrical drum that turns forward and backward at various speeds under one or more pens that slide to and fro, marking the paper.

drum printer A printing device that uses a drum embossed with alphanumeric characters. A type of LINE PRINTER that can print several thousand lines per minute.

drum sorting A sort program that uses magnetic drums for auxiliary storage during sorting.

drum storage See MAGNETIC DRUM.

dry plasma etching A method for developing a mask on a wafer.

dry run A program-checking technique. The process of examining the logic and coding of a program from an algorithm and written instructions and recording the results of each step of the operation before running the program on the computer. Same as DESK CHECKING.

DSL An abbreviation for DYNAMIC SIMULATION LANGUAGE.

DTL An abbreviation for DIODE TRANSISTOR LOGIC. Microelectronic logic based on connections between semiconductor diodes and the transistor.

dual channel controller A controller that enables reading from and writing to a device to occur simultaneously.

dual density (1) Refers to tapes or disks on which data are densely recorded. (2) A floppy disk with double-sided recording capability.

dual disk drive A floppy disk system that contains two disk drives, thus providing an increased storage capacity.

dual in-line package A popular type of integrated circuit package on which a chip is mounted. Abbreviated DIP.

dual intensity Indicates the ability of a terminal or printer to produce characters in regular as well as highlighted or bold formats. See OVERSTRIKING.

dual processors Two central processing units within a computer system that can function simultaneously. For example, two microprocessors in a single microcomputer that allow the use of software designed for either chip.

dual-sided disk drives Disk drives that use two read/write heads to store and retrieve data on both the top and bottom sides of a disk.

dumb terminal A visual display terminal with minimal input/output capabilities and no processing capability. Contrast with INTELLIGENT TERMINAL and SMART TERMINAL.

dummy Pertaining to an artificial argument, instruction, address, or record of data inserted solely to fulfill prescribed conditions.

dummy argument Variables, used as function arguments, that do not have any values.

dummy instruction (1) An artificial instruction or address inserted in a list to serve a purpose other than its execution as an instruction. (2) An instruction in a routine that, in itself, does not perform any functions. Often used to provide a point at which to terminate a program loop.

dummy module Skeleton of module with entry and exit, but no actual processing. Particularly useful in top-down testing when subordinate subfunctions are not ready for integration.

dump The data that results from a "dumping" process. The duplication of the contents of a storage device to another storage device or to a printer.

dumping Copying all or part of the contents of a storage unit, usually from the computer's internal storage, into an auxiliary storage unit or onto a line printer. See STORAGE, DUMP, POST MORTEM DUMP, and SNAPSHOT DUMP.

duplex Pertaining to a communications system or equipment capable of transmission in both directions. See FULL DUPLEX and HALF DUPLEX.

duplex channel A data communications channel that allows simultaneous transmission in both directions. See FULL DUPLEX, HALF DUPLEX, and SIMPLEX.

duplexing   The use of duplicate computers, peripheral equipment, or circuitry so that, in the event of a component failure, an alternate component can enable the system to continue.

duplicate   To copy so that the result remains in the same physical form as the source; for example, to make a new diskette with the same information and in the same format as an original diskette.

duplicate disk   See DISK COPYING.

duplication check   A check requiring that the results of two independent performances of the same operation be identical. The check may be made concurrently on duplicate equipment or at a later time on the same equipment.

dust cover   Dust is one of computer equipment's worst enemies. Plastic dust covers are used to protect microcomputers, disk units, terminals, printers, etc.

Dvorak keyboard   A keyboard arrangement designed by August Dvorak. It provides increased speed and comfort and reduces the rate of errors by placing the most frequently used letters in the center for use by the strongest fingers. In this fashion, finger motions and awkward strokes are reduced by over 90 percent in comparison with the familiar QWERTY keyboard. The Dvorak system, although patented in 1936, did not really become popular until its approval by ANSI in 1982. Today, some businesses are requiring their keyboarding personnel to use this system. Also, several computer companies are now manufacturing keyboards with a switch that will change from one keyboard to the other. The Dvorak keyboard puts the five vowel keys, AOEUI, together under the left hand in the center row, and the five most frequently used consonants, DHTNS, under the fingers of the right hand. See QWERTY KEYBOARD.

dyadic   Pertaining to an operation that uses two operands.

dyadic operation   An operation on two operands.

dynamic   Pertaining to circuitry that stores information as charges on MOS capacitors. Usually volatile, it requires periodic refreshing.

dynamic address translation In virtual storage systems, the change of a virtual storage address to a real storage address during execution of an instruction. Abbreviated DAT.

dynamic dump A dump taken during the execution of a program.

dynamic RAM Storage that the computer must refresh at frequent intervals. Contrast with STATIC RAM.

dynamic relocation The movement of part or all of an active (i.e., currently operating) program from one region of storage to another. All necessary address references are adjusted to enable proper execution of the program to continue in its new location.

dynamic scheduling Job scheduling that is determined by the computer on a moment-to-moment basis, depending upon the circumstances.

Dynamic Simulation Language (DSL) A high-level programming language, suited primarily for simulation of engineering and scientific problems of a continuous nature. Because DSL facilitates the solution of ordinary differential equations that frequently are functions of time, it is particularly useful for transient analysis of dynamic systems.

dynamic storage A memory device that must constantly be recharged or refreshed at frequent intervals to avoid loss of data. A very volatile storage.

dynamic storage allocation Automatic storage allocation. See STORAGE ALLOCATION.

E

e The letter e is used in mathematics to represent the number 2.718. . . . Since it is an irrational number, its decimal expansion never repeats. It is called a universal constant—if there are intelligent beings on other planets, they too will have to use e to do higher mathematics. The letter e is used to honor Leonhard Euler, who published extensive results on the number in 1748. Logarithms are occasionally taken to the base 10, but much more often e is the base. The properties of e are used in calculus and higher mathematics extensively. BASIC, Pascal and other programming languages include built-in functions to compute e^x. If $y = e^x$, then x is the natural logarithm of y.

E A symbol that stands for exponent. Used in floating point numbers to mean "to the power." For example, 23E2 means 23.0×10^2.

EAROM An acronym for ELECTRICALLY ALTERABLE ROM. ROM memory that can be selectively altered without erasing all stored data, as is done with EPROM devices.

eavesdropping Passive wiretapping, interception of messages, usually without detection.

EBAM An acronym for ELECTRON BEAM ADDRESSED MEMORY. An electronic storage device that uses electrical circuits to control a beam that reads from or writes on a metal oxide semi-conductor surface.

EBCDIC An acronym for EXTENDED BINARY CODED DECIMAL INTERCHANGE CODE (pronounced IB-sa-dik). An 8-bit code used to represent data in modern computers. EBCDIC can represent up to 256 distinct characters and is the principal code used in many current computers. Compare ASCII.

echo (1) In data communications, the return of a transmitted signal to its source, with a delay that indicates the signal is a reflection rather than the original. (2) In computer graphics, to provide visual feedback to the designer during graphic input to the system.

echo check A check on the accuracy of a data transfer operation in which the data received is transmitted back to the source and compared with the original data.

ECL An abbreviation for EMITTER COUPLED LOGIC, also called CURRENT MODE LOGIC (CML). ECL is faster than TTL, but much less popular.

ECOM An acronym for ELECTRONIC COMPUTER ORIENTED MAIL, a process of sending and receiving messages in digital form over telecommunications facilities.

edge (1) In computer graphics, the straight line segment that is the intersection of two planes' faces of a solid, such as the edges of a cube. (2) A connection between two nodes in a graph.

edge card A circuit board (or card) with contact strips along one edge, designed to mate with an edge connector.

edge connector A slot-shaped electrical socket that connects a circuit card to a motherboard or chassis.

edge cutter/trimmer A device for removing the sprocketed margin from continuous-form line printer paper.

edge sharpening A process of sharpening the edges of a digitized picture.

edit **(1)** To check the correctness of data. **(2)** To change as necessary the form of data by adding or deleting certain characters. For example, part of the program can edit data for printing, adding special symbols, spacing, deleting, non-significant zeros, and so on.

editing Making the corrections or changes in a program or data. See *data editing*.

editing run In batch processing, the editing program will check the data for ostensible validity (e.g., test to assure that dates and numbers fall within the expected ranges, compare totals with separately entered batch or hash totals, and prove check digits) and identify any errors for correction and resubmission.

edit line A "status report" line displayed on the screen when certain spreadsheet or word processing programs are in use. It tells the user the present location of the cursor, the amount of memory left, and—in some word processing programs—it tells the name of the file in use; in spreadsheets, it will also show the contents or formula of the cell at the cursor location, and one or two more items of information (depending on which spreadsheet is being used).

edit mode Available in many programs, this mode permits easy modification of cell contents, such as changing program lines or word processing text, without rekeying the entire entry.

editor Computer program designed to make it easy to review and alter a file or program interactively. For example, one editing command might locate and display the first occurrence of a given string of characters; a second command might delete or change those characters wherever they occur.

EDP An abbreviation for ELECTRONIC DATA PROCESSING, data processing performed largely by electronic digital computers.

EDS An abbreviation for EXCHANGEABLE DISK STORE.

EEROM A device that can be erased electrically and reprogrammed.

effective address The address that is derived by performing any specified address modification operations upon a specified address.

effectiveness The degree to which the output produced achieves the desired purpose.

efficiency The ratio of resources consumed to produce a given amount of output. For example, the time and other resources used to produce computer output.

EFT An abbreviation for ELECTRONIC FUNDS TRANSFER. An EFT network transfers funds from one account to another with electronic equipment rather than with paper media, such as checks.

ego-less programming The concept of arranging the programming tasks so that credit for success or blame for failure must be shared by several programmers rather than just one person.

EIA An abbreviation for ELECTRONIC INDUSTRIES ASSOCIATION.

EIA interface A standard interface between peripherals and microcomputers and modems and terminals. Another name for RS-232C interface.

electrical communications The science and technology by which information is collected from an originating source, transformed into electric currents or fields, transmitted over electrical networks or through space to another point, and reconverted into a form suitable for interpretation by a receiving entity.

electrical schematic A diagram of the logical arrangement of hardware in an electrical circuit or system using conventional symbols. Can be constructed interactively by computer-aided design.

electrolysis The process of changing the chemical composition of a material by sending an electric current through it.

electromagnetic delay line A delay line whose operation is based on the time of propagation of electromagnetic waves through distributed or lumped capacitance and inductance. Used in early computers.

electromechanical Referring to a system or device for processing data that uses both electrical and mechanical principles.

electron beam deflection system A narrow stream of electrons moving in the same direction under the influence of an electric or magnetic field.

electronic Pertaining to the flow of electricity through semiconductors, valves, and filters, in contrast with the free flow of current through simple conductors. The essence of computer technology is the selective use and combination of electronic apparatus whereby current can be allowed to flow or can be halted by electronic switches working at a very high speed.

electronically programmable Pertaining to a programmable ROM (READ ONLY MEMORY) or any other digital device in which the data 1s and 0s in binary code can be entered electronically, usually by the user with a piece of equipment called a PROM PROGRAMMER.

electronic bulletin board A computer system that maintains a list of messages that people can call up (with their computer systems) and either read those already there or post a message.

electronic cottage The concept of permitting workers to remain at home to perform work using computer terminals connected to a central office.

electronic data processing Data processing performed largely by electronic equipment, especially digital computers.

electronic data processing system A system for data processing by means of machines using electronic circuitry at electronic speed, as opposed to electromechanical equipment.

electronic filing   The way computer systems store information electronically on disks or tapes.

electronic fund transfer (EFT)   A cashless method of paying for goods or services. Electronic signals between computers are used to adjust the accounts of the parties involved in a transaction.

electronic journal   A log file summarizing, in chronological sequence, the processing activities performed by a system.

electronic magazine   A magazine published in a videotape or videodisk format. A type of ELECTRONIC PUBLISHING.

electronic mail   The process of sending, receiving, storing, and forwarding messages in digital form over telecommunication facilities. Also called E-mail.

electronic music   Music in which the sounds are produced by electronic means. See COMPUTER MUSIC and SYNTHESIZER.

electronic office   An office that relies on word processing and computer and data communications technologies.

electronic pen   A penlike stylus commonly used in conjunction with visual display devices for inputting or changing information under program control. Often called a LIGHT PEN.

electronic power supply   A source of electrical energy employed to furnish the tubes and semiconductor devices of an electronic circuit with the proper electric voltages and currents for their operation.

electronic publishing   A technology encompassing a variety of activities that contain or convey information with a high editorial and value added content in a form other than print. Included in the list of presently practiced electronic publishing activities are: educational software disks, on-line data bases, electronic mail videotext, teletext, videotape cassettes, and videodisks. See ELECTRONIC MAGAZINE.

electronics   The branch of science and technology relating to the conduction and control of electricity flowing through semiconducting materials or through vacuum or gases.

electronic spreadsheet A computer program that turns a computer terminal into a huge ledger sheet. The program allows large columns and rows of numbers to change according to parameters determined by the user. A whole range of numbers can be changed when a single entry is varied, allowing complex projections and numerical forecasts to be performed without tedious manual calculations.

electron tube The dominant electronic element found in computers prior to the advent of the transistor.

electroplate To deposit a metal on a surface of certain materials by electrolysis.

electrosensitive paper Printer paper with a thin coating of conductive material, such as aluminum. Print becomes visible because it darkens where a matrix-type print head allows electric current to flow onto the conductive surface.

electrosensitive printer A nonimpact printer that uses electricity to form characters on specially treated paper.

electrostatic plotter An output device that draws graphic data on paper by using static electrical energy.

electrostatic printer A high-speed nonimpact printer that forms characters on chemically treated paper.

electrothermal printer A high-speed printer that uses heated elements to create characters as matrices of small dots on heat sensitive paper.

elegant Designing a program, efficiently written, to use the smallest possible amount of main storage by decreasing the number of instructions used to accomplish various tasks.

element (1) An item of data within an array. (2) Any of the units comprising the larger item.

elementary diagram A wiring diagram of an electrical system in which all devices are drawn between vertical lines that represent power sources. Contains logic elements, components, wire nets, and text. Can be constructed interactively on a CAD system.

elite type A size of type that fits twelve characters into each inch of type.

ELIZA A classic example of the use of LISP in a sample artificial intelligence (AI) application. ELIZA is a program that
"simulates" a patient's discussion with a psychiatrist. While
appearing on the surface to possess "intelligence," the program is actually little more than a simple pattern matcher.
A sample dialogue with ELIZA follows (user input is in lower
case, with ELIZA's responses in upper case):

```
    MAY I HELP YOU?
 :i want you to help me
    WHAT WOULD IT MEAN TO YOU IF YOU GOT ME
    TO HELP YOU?
 :im afraid to tell you
    YOURE NOT REALLY TALKING ABOUT ME, ARE
    YOU?
 :what does that mean
    WHY DO YOU ASK?
 :are you asking me
    WHY ARE YOU INTERESTED IN WHETHER OR NOT
    I AM ASKING YOU?
    :why do you keep answering with
    questions
    DOES THAT QUESTION INTEREST YOU?
 :i dont know
    DONT YOU REALLY KNOW?
 :no
    ARE YOU SAYING NO JUST TO BE NEGATIVE?
 :i think so
    DO YOU REALLY THINK SO?
 :not always
    CAN YOU THINK OF A SPECIFIC EXAMPLE?
  :oh shut up
    IM NOT SURE I UNDERSTAND YOU FULLY?
 :goodbye
    GOODBYE
```

ellipse A geometrical figure like a flattened circle. Ellipse creation is an automatic function of virtually all computer
graphics systems.

E-mail An abbreviation for electronic mail, a communications
service for computer users wherein textual messages are

sent to a central computer system, or electronic "mailbox," and later retrieved by the addressee.

embedded command In word processing, one or more characters inserted into the text that do not print but direct the word processing program or printer to perform some task, such as end a page or skip a line.

embedded systems Computer systems that cannot be programmed by the user because they are preprogrammed for a specific task and are buried within the equipment they serve.

embedding Placing special printer commands within the text as instructions.

emitter An electrode within a transistor.

empty string A string containing no characters. Also called a NULL STRING.

emulate (1) To pattern one hardware system after another, by means of an electronic attachment. The imitating system accepts the same data, executes the same programs, and achieves the same results as the imitated system. (2) To have a program simulate the function of another software or hardware product.

emulator A type of program or device that allows user programs written for one kind of computer system to be run on another system.

emulsion laser storage See LASER STORAGE.

enable To switch a computer device or facility so it can operate. The opposite of DISABLE.

encipher To alter data (scramble) so it is not readily usable unless the changes are first undone. See ENCRYPTION.

enclosure A housing for any electrical or electronic device.

encode To convert data into a code form that is acceptable to some piece of computer equipment. Opposite of DECODE.

encoder A device that produces machine-readable output, such as a floppy disk, either from manual keyboard depressions or from data already recorded in some other code.

encryption The coding of data in such a way as to make it unintelligible without the key to decryption.

end-around carry A carry from the most significant digit place to the least significant digit place.

end-around shift See CIRCULAR SHIFT.

endless loop The endless repetition of a series of instructions with no exit from the loop possible. Occurs when the "defined exit" for a loop has either not been defined or is unattainable by the sequence of instructions as they stand.

end mark A code or signal that indicates termination of a unit of data.

end-of-block Termination of a block. Abbreviated EOB.

end-of-file Termination or point of completion of a quantity of data. End-of-file marks are used to indicate this point on magnetic files. Abbreviated EOF. See END-OF-TAPE MARKER.

end-of-message Termination of a message. Abbreviated EOM.

end-of-page halt A feature that stops the printer at the end of each completed page of output.

end-of-tape marker A marker on a magnetic tape used to indicate the end of the permissible recording area.

end-user Anyone who uses a computer system or its output.

engine Another name for a processor.

engineering units Units of measure as applied to a process variable.

enhancements Hardware or software improvements, additions, or updates to a computer or software system.

E notation A system of notation used to express very large and very small numbers. The notation consists of two parts: a mantissa and an exponent. Also called SCIENTIFIC NOTATION.

ENTER key A special key on some keyboards that means "execute a statement or command." Same as RETURN key on some keyboards. Often used interchangeably with carriage return.

enterprise An organization that performs some task or group of tasks in relation to the rest of the world.

entity An object that has meaning for a particular application. A computer system may be an entity; a job position, a company, or even a technique or concept could be an entity as well.

entrepreneur Someone who starts and manages a business enterprise; lately, this word has taken on a broader meaning—it can refer to someone who is in charge of a specific part of the business within a large organization.

entry In an electronic spreadsheet, the value or information contained within a specific cell.

entry point Any location in a routine to which control can be passed by another routine. Entry is also referred to as the TRANSFER ADDRESS. It is often the first instruction to be executed in a program.

environment In a computing context, this is more likely to refer to the mode of operation (e.g., "in a time-sharing environment") than to physical conditions of temperature, humidity, and so forth. But either kind of environment may affect operational efficiency.

environment division One of the four main component parts of a COBOL program.

EOB An abbreviation for END-OF-BLOCK. Termination of a block.

EOF An abbreviation for END-OF-FILE. When all the records in a file have been processed, the computer is said to have encountered an end-of-file condition.

EOJ An abbreviation for END-OF-JOB.

EOLN An abbreviation for END-OF-LINE. A flag indicating the end of a line of data. Sometimes abbreviated EOL.

EOM See END-OF-MESSAGE.

EOT An abbreviation for END-OF-TRANSMISSION.

EPO An abbreviation for EMERGENCY POWER OFF, meaning the circuit and the buttons activating it that can turn an entire computer off in an emergency. There may be as many as twenty EPO buttons in a large installation.

EPROM An acronym for ERASABLE PROGRAMMABLE READ ONLY MEMORY, a special PROM that can be erased under high-intensity ultraviolet light, then reprogrammed. EPROMs can be reprogrammed repeatedly.

EPROM programmer A special machine that is used to program EPROM chips.

epsilon A small quantity of something.

equality The idea expressed by the equal sign, written =. In many programming languages the = sign is also used as a "replacement symbol."

equation A mathematical sentence with an = sign between two expressions that name the same number; for example, y = x + 3 is an equation.

equipment Part of a computer system. See COMPUTER, HARDWARE, and PERIPHERAL EQUIPMENT.

equipment bay A cabinet or case in which electronic equipment is installed.

erasable programmable read only memory See EPROM.

erasable storage A storage medium that can be erased and reused. Magnetic disks or tapes are mediums that can be erased and reused; punched cards or film cannot.

erase To remove data from storage without replacing it.

erase head In a domestic tape recorder, the erase head is the device that cleans the tape of earlier signals immediately before new matter is recorded. In a computer storage device based on magnetization of ferric-oxide surfaces—such as floppy disks or cassette tapes—the erase head operates immediately before the write head to perform a precisely similar function.

ergonomics The science and technology that emphasize the safety, comfort, and ease of use of human-operated machines, such as computer video display terminals. The goal of ergonomics is to produce systems that are user-friendly, i.e., safe, comfortable, and easy to use. Ergonomics is frequently called human engineering. Tangible results of er-

gonomics are numeric keypads on standard keyboards, tilting display screens, detachable keyboards and nonglare
display screens.

EROM An acronym for ERASABLE ROM. Same as EPROM.

error The general term referring to any deviation of a computed or a measured quantity from the theoretically correct
or true value. Contrast with FAULT, MALFUNCTION, and
MISTAKE. See INTERMITTENT ERROR and ROUND-OFF ER-
ROR.

error analysis The branch of numerical analysis concerned
with studying the error aspects of numerical analysis procedures. It includes the study of errors that arise in a computation because of the peculiarities of computer arithmetic.

error checking (1) Refers to various techniques that test for
the valid condition of data. (2) The process by which two
telecommunicating computers can verify that the data received was error-free.

error control A plan, implemented by software, hardware, or
procedures, to detect and/or correct errors introduced into
a data communications system.

error-correcting code (1) A code in which each acceptable
expression conforms to specific rules of construction. Non-
acceptable expressions are also defined. If certain types of
errors occur in an acceptable expression, an equivalent will
result and the error can be corrected. (2) A code in which
the forbidden pulse combination produced by the gain or
loss of a bit will indicate which bit is wrong. Same as SELF-
CORRECTING CODE.

error correction A system that detects and inherently provides
correction for errors caused by transmission equipment or
facilities.

error-detection code (1) A code in which each expression conforms to specific rules of construction. When expressions
occur that do not conform to the rules of these construc-
tions, an error is indicated. (2) A code in which errors
produce forbidden combinations. A single error-detecting
code produces a forbidden combination if a digit gains or
loses a single bit. A double error-detecting code produces

a forbidden combination if a digit gains or loses either one or two bits, and so on. Also called a SELF-CHECKING CODE.

error file A file generated during data processing to retain erroneous information sensed by the computer, often printed as an error report.

error guessing A test data selection technique. The selection criterion is to pick values that seem likely to cause errors.

error handling A program feature that minimizes the possibility of an error occurring if a keyboard operator pushes the wrong key.

error message A printed or displayed statement indicating the computer has detected a mistake or malfunction.

error rate In data communications, a measure of quality of circuit or equipment; the number of erroneous bits or characters in a sample.

error ratio The ratio of the number of erroneous data units to the total number of data units.

error transmission A change in data resulting from the transmission process.

escape key A standard control key available on most computer keyboards. Abbreviated ESC. It is usually used to take control of the computer away from a program, to escape from a specific program, or to stop a program.

Ethernet A type of network system that allows audio and video information to be carried as well as computer data.

ETX An acronym for END-OF-TEXT.

evaluate To find the value of.

evaluation The process of determining if a newly created computer system is actually doing what it was designed to do.

event An occurrence or happening. An event has no time frame associated with it, but typically serves to mark the start or end of activities and to relate activities to each other.

exception reporting A technique for screening large amounts of computerized data in order to display or print reports containing only specific information.

exchangeable disk See DISK PACK.

exchange buffering A technique using data chaining for eliminating the need to move data in the computer's main storage.

exchange sorting algorithm Another name for a bubble sorting algorithm.

exclusive OR The Boolean operator that gives a truth table value of true if only one of the two variables it connects is true. If both variables it connects are true, this value is false. Abbreviated XOR.

executable statement A program statement that gives an instruction of some computational operation to be performed, such as an assignment statement. Contrast with NONEXECUTABLE STATEMENT.

execute To run a program on a computer or to carry out an instruction. Same as RUN.

execute cycle The period of time during which a machine instruction is interpreted and the indicated operation is performed on the specified operand.

execution The process of carrying out the operations specified in the instructions of a program.

execution time (1) The time it takes for a program to run from start to finish. (2) The phase during which a program is being executed. (3) The time required to fetch, decode, and execute an instruction.

executive A master program that controls the execution of other programs. Often used synonymously with MONITOR, SUPERVISORY SYSTEM, and OPERATING SYSTEM.

exerciser A device that enables users to create and debug programs and hardware interfaces by manual means.

exit That point in an algorithm or program from which control is transferred elsewhere.

expandability The ability to increase the capability of a computer system by adding modules or devices.

expansion card A card added to a system for the purpose of mounting additional chips or circuits to expand the system capability.

expansion interface A circuit board that allows one to add disk drives, additional memory, and other peripherals to a basic computer.

expansion slots Slots, or spaces, inside the main computer housing that are used to connect small circuit boards (cards) to the main circuit board (motherboard). For example, the main memory of a computer can be increased with extra memory boards. Most computers contain expansion slots for these boards, to simplify modification.

expansion unit A device, connected to a computer, which contains extra sockets into which additional printed circuit boards can be plugged.

expert-support system Similar to an expert system, but often used in conjunction with decision-support systems to solve problems by examining subjective, intuitive factors, as opposed to formal rules.

expert system Methods and techniques for constructing human-machine systems with specialized problem-solving expertise. The pursuit of this area of artificial intelligence research has emphasized the knowledge that underlies human expertise and has simultaneously decreased the apparent significance of domain-independent problem solving theory. An expert system assists or replaces an expert to solve problems.

explicit address A storage address explicitly stated (rather than an address symbolically represented) in a source language program. Contrast with SYMBOLIC ADDRESS.

exploded view An illustration of a solid construction showing its parts separately, but in positions that indicate their relationships to the whole.

exponent A symbol or number written above and to the right of another symbol or number that denotes the number of times the latter is used as a factor. A short way of writing $10 \times 10 \times 10$ is 10^3. The 3 is called the exponent; 10 is the base. The exponent 3 tells us how many times 10 is used as a factor. For instance, y^4 means y x y x y x y; 10^7 means 10 x 10 x 10 x 10 x 10 x 10 x 10.

exponential function A function of the form $y = a^x$, where *a* can be any positive number except 1 and is called the base of the function. The most common exponential function is e^x.

exponential smoothing A weighted, moving average method of forecasting in which past observations are geometrically discounted according to their age. The heaviest weight is assigned to the most recent data. The smoothing is called exponential because data points are weighted in accordance with an exponential function of their age.

exponentiation A process or function that enables the user to calculate the power of a number. For example, the result of seven to the fourth power may be calculated in a single step without multiplying 7 x 7 x 7 x 7.

export For a data base system, to write the data out (usually to a disk file) in a form that other programs can use. Many data base programs store their data in some coded form, but will produce for export ASCII files that can be read and edited with a normal text editor. Contrast with IMPORT.

expression **(1)** A general term for numerals, numerals with signs of operation, variables and combinations of these: 6, 3+6, n+10 are all expressions. **(2)** An arithmetic formula coded in a programming language.

extended addressing Pertains to an addressing mode that can reach any place in memory and requires more than one byte to locate the data in memory.

Extended Binary Coded Decimal Interchange Code See EBCDIC.

extender board A debugging aid that allows one to monitor circuit boards more conveniently.

extensible language A concept whereby the user adds new features to a programming language by modifying existing ones.

extension Additional feature added to a programming language or computer system. Feature beyond what is regularly available in the standard.

extent   A collection of physical records that are contiguous in auxiliary storage.

external data file   Data that is stored separately from the program that processes it.

external label   An identification label attached to the outside of a file medium holder identifying the file, such as a paper label or a sticker attached to the cover containing a floppy disk.

external reference   A reference to a symbol defined in another routine.

external sort   The second phase of a multipass sort program, wherein strings of data are continually merged until one string of sequenced data is formed.

external storage   Same as AUXILIARY STORAGE.

external symbol   (1) A control section name, entry point name, or external reference. (2) A symbol contained in the external symbol dictionary.

external symbol dictionary   Control information associated with an object program that identifies the external symbols in the program.

extract   To remove specific information from a computer word as determined by a mask or filter.

F

f   An abbreviation for FREQUENCY.

fabricated language   Same as SYMBOLIC LANGUAGE.

fabrication   Refers to the processing of manufacturing materials to desired specifications. See COMPUTER-AIDED MANUFACTURING.

face   In computer graphics a polyhedron, such as a cube or a prism, is a solid formed by parts of planes, which are called faces of the solid. A cube has six faces.

facilities   A general term that applies to physical equipment, electrical power, communication lines, and other items used in computer and data communications centers.

facilities management   The use of an independent service organization to operate and manage a data processing installation.

facsimile (FAX)   **(1)** Transmission of pictures, maps, diagrams,
and so on. The image is scanned at the transmitter, reconstructed at the receiving station, and duplicated on some
form of paper. **(2)** A precise reproduction of an original document; an exact copy. **(3)** A hard copy reproduction.

facsimile transceiver   A unit used to transmit and receive electronic transmissions of images.

factor analysis   A mathematical technique for studying the
interaction of many factors in order to determine the most
significant factors and the degree of significance.

factorial   A product of factors, computed by multiplying together all the integers from 1 to a specified number. The
exclamation point (!) is used to represent factorial. For example:

```
5! = 1 x 2 x 3 x 4 x 5
7! = 1 x 2 x 3 x 4 x 5 x 6 x 7
n! = 1 x 2 x 3 x 4 . . . (n - 1) x n
```

fail-safe system   A system designed to avoid catastrophe, but
possibly at the expense of convenience. For example, when
a fault is detected in a computer-controlled traffic light system, a fail-safe arrangement might be to set all the traffic
lights to red rather than turn them off. Similarly, in a power
plant operation, overheating might simply disconnect the
power supply. See FAIL-SOFT SYSTEM.

fail-soft system   A system that continues to process data despite the failure of parts of the system. Usually accompanied
by a deterioration in performance. Using the two examples
described under fail-safe system, the traffic lights might turn
to flashing amber rather than red, and the overheat system
might maintain battery power for emergency equipment
while the main source of power was turned off. See FAIL-
SAFE SYSTEM.

failure prediction   A technique that attempts to determine the
failure schedule of specific parts or equipment so that they
may be discarded and replaced before failure occurs.

fairness Condition that holds when every action requested in a system is guaranteed to execute after a finite amount of time.

fall-back A backup system brought into use in an emergency situation, especially the reserve data base and programs that would be switched in quickly, or even automatically, in the event of a detected fault in a real-time system.

fallout The failure of electronic components that is sometimes experienced during the burn-in of a new piece of equipment.

family of computers A series of central processing units allegedly of the same logical design but of different speeds. This philosophy enables the user to start with a slower, less expensive CPU and grow to a faster, more expensive one as the workload builds up, without having to change the rest of the computer system.

FAMOS An acronym for **FLOATING GATE AVALANCHE INJECTION MOS**, a fabrication technology for charge storage devices such as PROMs.

fanfold paper One long continuous sheet of paper perforated at regular intervals to mark page boundaries and folded fan-style into a stack.

fan-in The number of signal inputs to a digital component.

fan-out The number of programming modules below any given module in a structured program.

farad A unit of measure of capacitance. A capacitor has a capacitance of 1 farad if it will store a charge of 1 coulomb when a 1-volt potential is applied across it.

fatal error An unexpected failure or other problem that occurs while the program is executing. A fatal error prevents the computer from continuing to execute the program. If the error is nonfatal, the program will proceed, but not correctly. An example is where an operator makes a mistake that causes the program to crash, destroying the data stored in RAM.

fat bits A software function that enlarges a portion of the display screen to allow precise manipulation of individual screen elements. Useful for precision work or font designing.

father file   A system of updating records that retains a copy of the original record as well as provides an amended version. When a file update program is run, the old master file is termed the father file. The updated file is termed the son file. The file that was used to create the father file is termed the grandfather file. The technique is particularly applicable to files held on magnetic media, such as disk or tape. Sometimes called the grandfather-father-son concept.

fault   A condition that causes a component, a computer, or a peripheral device to not perform to its design specifications (e.g., a broken wire or a short circuit). Contrast with ERROR, MALFUNCTION, and MISTAKE.

fault tolerance   The capability of a system to perform its function in accordance with design specifications, even in the presence of hardware or software failures. If, in the event of faults, the system functions can be performed but do not meet the design specifications with respect to the time required to complete the job or the storage capacity required for the job, the system is said to be partially or quasi fault-tolerant. Fault tolerance is provided by the application of protective reliability. These resources may consist of more hardware, software, or time, or a combination of all three.

FAX   An acronym for FACSIMILE. An equipment configuration that facilitates the transmission of images over a common carrier network.

FCC   An abbreviation for Federal Communications Commission, an organization of the U. S. Government responsible for regulating interstate communcations, communications common carriers, and the broadcast media.

FE   An abbreviation for FIELD ENGINEER, an individual responsible for field maintenance of computer hardware and software. Also called CUSTOMER SERVICE TECHNICIAN.

feasibility study   Study concerned with a definition of a data processing problem, together with alternative solutions, a recommended course of action, and a working plan for designing and installing the system.

feature   Something special that is accomplished in a program or hardware device. For example, the ability of a word processing program to merge graphic images with text.

feature extraction The selection of dominant characteristics for pattern recognition. This enables a computer-controlled video camera to recognize objects by such features as shapes and edges.

Federal Privacy Act Federal legislation prohibiting secret personnel files from being kept on individuals by government agencies or contractors. It allows individuals to know what information about them is on file and how it is used within all government agencies and their contractors. Also known as the PRIVACY ACT OF 1974.

feed The mechanical process whereby lengthy materials are moved along the required operating positions.

feedback (1) Any process whereby output from a sequential task serves to modify subsequent tasks. (2) A means of automatic control in which the actual state of a process is measured and used to obtain a quantity that modifies the input in order to initiate the activity of the control system. (3) In data processing, information arising from a particular stage of processing could provide a feedback to affect the processing of subsequent data; for example, the fact that an area of storage was nearly full might either delay the acceptance of more data or divert it to some other storage area.

feedback circuit A circuit that returns a portion of the output signal of an electronic circuit or control system to the input of the circuit or the system.

feep Another name for the beep that terminals make to get the user's attention.

female connector Pertaining to the recessed portion of a connecting device into which another part fits. See CONNECTOR and MALE CONNECTOR.

femto Prefix indicating one quadrillionth, or a millionth of a billionth, 10^{-15}.

femtosecond One quadrillionth of a second. There are as many of them (the number one followed by 15 zeros) in one second as there are seconds in 30 million years. In two seconds, light travels from Earth past the moon. In 12 femtoseconds, it moves only five microns, roughly one-tenth the width of a human hair. Abbreviated fs.

ferrous oxide The substance that coats recording disks and tapes. It can be magnetized, thereby permitting information to be recorded on it magnetically.

FET An acronym for FIELD EFFECT TRANSISTOR. A semiconductor device used as a storage element.

fetch To locate and load a quantity of instructions or data from storage.

FF An abbreviation for FORM FEED.

fiber optics A data transmission medium made of tiny threads of glass or plastic that transmit huge amounts of data at the speed of light.

fiche Microfiche. A sheet of photographic film containing multiple microimages. See COM.

field A single piece of information, the smallest unit normally manipulated by a data base management system. In a personnel file, the person's age might be a field. A record is made up of one or more fields.

field alterable control element A chip used in some systems to allow the user to write microprograms. Abbreviated FACE.

field effect transistor A three-terminal semiconductor device that acts as a variable charge storage element. The most commonly used type in microcomputers is the Metallic Oxide Semiconductor (MOS) transistor. Abbreviated FET.

field emission The emission of electrons from a metal or semiconductor into a vacuum under the influence of a strong electric field.

field engineer An individual responsible for field maintenance of computer hardware and software. Abbreviated FE. Also called CUSTOMER ENGINEER and CUSTOMER SERVICE TECHNICIAN.

field of view In computer graphics, the limits of what a simulated camera can see, usually expressed as a horizontal angle centered at the camera. For simplicity of computation, computer graphicists assume that what a camera sees lies within a pyramid—rather than a cone—with the apex at the camera.

field upgradable Hardware capable of being enhanced in the field (in one's office or at a local repair center or computer store).

FIFO An acronym for FIRST IN-FIRST OUT. A method of storing and retrieving items from a list, table, or stack, such that the first element stored is the first one retrieved. Contrast with LIFO.

FIFO-LIFO Refers to two techniques for the collection of items to which additions and deletions are to be made. See FIFO and LIFO.

fifth-generation computers The next generation of computers, predicted to be available in the 1990s. They are expected to be true knowledge systems, able to combine one set of facts with other sets to produce sophisticated new solutions. No other computer has been able to do that. To play a central role in society that scientists envision, these machines will be easier to use than the current ones and will understand spoken, written, and graphical input.

figure shift A keyboard key, or the code generated by the key, signifying that the following characters are to be read as figures until a letter shift appears in the message.

file A collection of related records treated as a basic unit of storage.

file backup Copies of data files that can be used to reactivate (restore) a data base that has been damaged or destroyed.

file conversion The process of changing the file medium or structure.

file gap A space at the end of the file that signifies to the system where the file terminates.

file handling routine That part of a computer program that reads data from, and writes data to, a file.

file label An external label identifying a file.

file layout The arrangement and structure of data in a file, including the sequence and size of its components.

file level model   A model concerned with defining data structures for optimum performance of data base application programs or queries.

file librarian   A person who has the responsibility for the safekeeping of all computer files, such as programs and data files on floppy disks, magnetic tapes, microfilm, and so forth.

file maintenance   The updating of a file to reflect the effects of nonperiodic changes by adding, altering, or deleting data; for example, the addition of new programs to a program library on magnetic disks.

file manager   A simple data base management program that uses only simple files and indexes. A little brother to a data base management system.

filename   Alphanumeric characters used to identify a particular file.

filename extension   A code that forms the second part of a filename and that is separated from the filename by a period. It identifies the kind of data in the file.

file organization   The manner in which the applications programmer views the data.

file processing   The periodic updating of master files to reflect the effects of current data, often transaction data contained in detail files; for example, a monthly inventory run updating the master inventory file.

file protection   A technique or device used to prevent accidental erasure of data from a file; for example, a magnetic tape file-protect ring or gummed tab over the write-protect notch of a floppy disk. See FILE-PROTECT RING and WRITE-PROTECT NOTCH.

file-protect ring   A device used to protect data on magnetic tape. Accidental writing on the tape is prevented by removing the ring from the tape reel.

file size   The number of records in a file.

file storage   Devices that can hold a reservoir of mass data within the computer system. Magnetic disk units and magnetic tape units are examples of file storage devices.

file structure The format of fields within a data record. For example, PART NAME in the first field of a record, PART NUMBER in the second field, PRICE in the third field, and so on, specify the structure of a file.

file transfer The movement of a file from one place to another, or from one storage medium to another.

filling In computer graphics, a software function that allows the interior of a defined area to be filled with a color, shading, or crosshatching of the operator's choosing.

film developer The equipment used to develop microfilm for COM devices.

film recorder An output device that records data on photographic film or paper.

FILO An acronym for FIRST IN-LAST OUT. A method of storing and retrieving items from a list, table, or stack, such that the first element stored is the last one retrieved. Same as LIFO. Contrast with FIFO.

filter See MASK.

financial planning system A system that allows the financial planner/manager to examine and evaluate many alternatives before making a final decision.

find The ability of the computer to search within a document for a specific series of characters. See SEARCH.

find and replace A software feature that finds a designated character sequence and if found, replaces it with a new one. Same as SEARCH AND REPLACE.

finder The central element of an operating environment, a program that, among other things, displays and organizes files stored on disks.

finite To have limits, an end, or a last number.

finite element method An approximation technique used to solve field problems in various engineering fields.

firmware A program that has been implanted in a read-only memory (ROM) device. A combination of software and hardware designed for a specific task.

first-generation computers Computers that were built in the late 1940s and 1950s, using vacuum tubes. Now museum pieces.

first in-first out See FIFO.

first in-last out (FILO) A method of storing and retrieving items from a list, table, or stack, such that the first element stored is the last one retrieved.

first-order predicate logic A form of logic, used in PROLOG, that allows assertions to be made about the variables in a proposition.

fitting In computer graphics, it refers to the calculation of a curve, surface, or line that fits most accurately to a set of data points and design criteria.

fixed Refers to a field that always exists within a data record.

fixed area The portion of internal storage that has been assigned to specific programs or data areas.

fixed-head disk unit A storage device consisting of one or more magnetically coded disks on the surface of which data are stored in the form of magnetic spots arranged in a manner to represent binary data. These data are arranged in circular tracks around the disks and are accessible for reading and writing by read-write heads assigned one per track. Data from a given track are read or written sequentially as the disk rotates under or over the read-write head.

fixed-length record A record that always contains the same number of characters. Contrast with VARIABLE-LENGTH RECORD.

fixed point Pertaining to a number system in which each number is represented by a single set of digits and the position of the radix point is implied by the manner in which the numbers are used. Contrast with FLOATING POINT.

fixed-point arithmetic (1) A method of calculation in which the operations take place in an invariant manner without considering the location of the radix point. This is illustrated by desk calculators that require the operator to keep track of the decimal point. This occurs similarly with many automatic computers, in which the location of the radix point is the computer user's responsibility. (2) A type of arithmetic in which the operands and results of all arithmetic operations must be properly scaled to have a magnitude between certain fixed values. Contrast with FLOATING-POINT ARITHMETIC.

fixed-program computer   See WIRED PROGRAM COMPUTER.

fixed-size records   File elements, each of which has the same number of words, characters, bytes, bits, fields, and so on.

fixed spacing   The printing of characters at fixed horizontal intervals on a page.

fixed storage   Storage whose contents are not alterable by computer instructions, such as read-only memory.

fixed word length   Pertaining to a machine word or operand that always has the same number of bits, bytes, or characters. Contrast with VARIABLE WORD LENGTH.

flag   (1) An indicator used frequently to tell some later part of a program that some condition occurred earlier, such as an overflow or carry. (2) A symbol used to mark a record for special attention. For example, on a listing of a program, all statements that contain errors may be flagged for the attention of the program writer. (3) An indicator of special conditions, such as interrupts.

flatbed plotter   A digital plotter using plotting heads that move over a flat surface in both vertical and horizontal directions.

flat pack   A small, low-profile (flat), integrated circuit package that can be spot-welded or soldered to a terminal or a printed circuit board. The pins extend outward rather than pointing down, as on a DIP.

flat-panel display   A compact, thin panel display that uses gas plasma electroluminescent and liquid-crystal technologies. These displays are very portable and are only a few inches deep. See GAS PLASMA DISPLAY.

flat screen   A thin panel screen such as those found on flat panel displays.

flexible disk   A disk made of oxide-coated mylar that is stored in plastic jackets. See FLOPPY DISK.

flicker   An undesirable, unsteady lighting of a display due to inadequate refresh rate and/or fast persistence. Occurs whenever the refresh speed is not fast enough to compensate for natural luminance delay on the screen.

flight computer   A computer resident in a spacecraft, an airplane, or a missile.

flight simulator   A computer-controlled simulator that is used by airline companies to train pilots on new aircraft.

flip-flop   A device or circuit containing active elements, capable of assuming either one of two stable states at a given time. Synonymous with TOGGLE.

flippy diskette   A diskette that has two recording sides.

float   The amount of time following the completion of a task or activity and the start of the next task or activity.

floating point   A form of number representation in which quantities are represented by a number called the mantissa multiplied by a power of the number base. Contrast with FIXED POINT.

floating-point arithmetic   A method of calculation that automatically accounts for the location of the radix point. Contrast with FIXED-POINT ARITHMETIC.

floating-point BASIC   A type of BASIC language that allows the use of decimal numbers.

floating-point constant   A number, usually consisting of two parts. One part contains the fractional component of the number; the other part is expressed as a power of the radix (base) of the number.

floating-point operation   A method of calculation that automatically accounts for the location of the radix point.

floating-point routine   A set of subroutines that cause a computer to execute floating point operations on a computer with no built-in floating point hardware.

FLOP   An acronym for FLOATING POINT OPERATION.

floppy disk   A flexible disk (DISKETTE) of oxide-coated mylar that is stored in paper or plastic jackets. The entire envelope is inserted in the disk unit. Used widely with microcomputers and minicomputers, floppy disks provides storage at relatively low cost. Floppy disks come in three popular sizes:

diameters of 8 inches (20.32 cm), 5¼ inches (13.3 cm), and 3½ inches (9 cm).

floppy-disk case A container, usually made of plastic, for storing and protecting floppy disks.

floppy-disk controller The circuit board or chip that controls a floppy disk unit.

floppy-disk unit A peripheral storage device in which data are recorded on magnetizable floppy disks.

flow A general term to indicate a sequence of events.

flowchart A diagram that uses symbols and interconnecting lines to show (1) the logic and sequence of specific program operations (program flowchart) or (2) a system of processing to achieve objectives (system flowchart). See PROGRAM FLOWCHART and SYSTEM FLOWCHART.

flowcharter A computer program that automatically generates flowcharts with a visual display screen, digital plotter or printer.

flowcharting symbol A symbol used to represent operations, data, flow, or equipment on a flowchart. See ANNOTATION SYMBOL, CONNECTOR SYMBOL, DECISION SYMBOL, INPUT/OUTPUT SYMBOL, PROCESSING SYMBOL, and TERMINAL SYMBOL.

flowchart template A plastic guide that contains cutouts of the flowchart symbols and is used in the preparation of a flowchart.

flowchart text The descriptive information that is associated with flowchart symbols.

flow diagram See FLOWCHART.

flowline On a flowchart, a line representing a connecting path between flowchart symbols. Normal directions are downward and to the right; flowlines going upward or to the left must indicate their directions by arrowheads.

flush (1) To empty a portion of storage of its contents. (2) Pertaining to type set in alignment with the left (flush left) or right (flush right) edge of the line measure. See JUSTIFICATION.

FM An abbreviation for **FREQUENCY MODULATION**. The process of changing the value represented by a signal by varying the frequency of the signal.

focusing Sharpening a blurred image on a display screen.

font (1) A complete set of characters in a consistent and unique typeface. (2) A family or collection of printing characters of a particular size and style.

footer Information printed at the bottom of a page; for example, page numbers. Most word processors can automatically print footers on each page of a document.

footprint The shape and area of floor space required for a piece of equipment.

force To intervene manually in a program and cause the computer to execute a jump instruction.

forecast The extrapolation of the past into the future. It is usually an objective computation involving data, as opposed to a prediction, which is a subjective estimate incorporating the manager's anticipation of changes and new influencing factors.

foreground job See FOREGROUND PROGRAM.

foreground processing The automatic execution of computer programs that have been designed to preempt the use of computing facilities.

foreground program A program that has a high priority and therefore takes precedence over concurrently operating programs in a computer system using multiprogramming techniques. Contrast with BACKGROUND PROGRAM.

foreground task See FOREGROUND PROGRAM.

forest A collection of trees. See TREE.

form (1) A preprinted document requiring additional information to make it meaningful. (2) The format of program output.

formal language Abstract mathematical objects used to model the syntax of programming languages, such as COBOL or BASIC, or of natural languages, such as English or German.

formal logic The study of the structure and form of valid argument without regard to the meaning of the terms of the argument.

format (1) The specific arrangement of data. (2) The programming associated with setting up text arrangements for output. (3) Any method of arranging information that is to be stored or displayed.

formatted display A screen display in which the attributes or contents of one or more display fields have been defined by the user.

formatter The section of a word processing program that formats the text.

form feed The physical transport of continuous paper to the beginning of a new line or page. Abbreviated FF. See LINE FEED.

form letter A document consisting mainly of standard text into which selected pieces of personal information, such as a business name and address, have been inserted.

form-letter program A program that produces form letters. Also called a mail-merge program.

forms control The operational procedure established by an organization to exercise direction in the utilization of documents that are used to collect and/or report information.

forms design The creation of data input forms and source documents.

formula A rule expressed as an equation. For example, $C = 2\pi r$ is the formula for finding the circumference of a circle. It is a way of showing the equal relationship between certain quantities and is especially useful for calculating one quantity when given others.

FORTH A programming language for use in functional programming. Has a specific orientation toward productivity, reliability, and efficiency. Capabilities include structured programming, top-down development, and virtual memory. It is implemented by a series of primitives generated in machine language, and the remainder of the languge is compiled from either source files on disk, or input from a terminal. FORTH was developed by Charles Moore in the early

1970s primarily for use in astronomical observations. Here is a sample program written in FORTH.

```
: FIBONACCI
  1 DUP DUP DUP (SET UP INIT VALUES)
  CR . .         (PRINT FIRST 2 VALUES)
  11 1           (LOOP 10 TIMES)
  DO
     DUP ROT +   (COMPUTE NEXT ELEMENT)
     DUP .       (PRINT IT)
  LOOP
: OK
FIBONACCI
```

FORTRAN An acronym for **FORMULA TRANS**LATOR. A high-level programming language used to perform mathematical, scientific, and engineering computations. FORTRAN has been approved as an American Standard programming language in two versions (FORTRAN and Basic FORTRAN). A widely used programming language. Here is a program written in FORTRAN.

```
C     AIRPLANE DISTANCE COMPUTATION
      S = 1.0
      A = 3.0
      I = 0
  10 I = I + 1
      T = I
      D = SQRT (A**2 + (S*T)**2)
      WRITE (6,20) T, D
  20 FORMAT (F5.0,F10.3)
      IF (I .LT. 60) GOTO 10
      STOP
      END
```

FORTRAN-77 A version of the FORTRAN language that conforms to the ANSI X3.9-1978 standard, with added features for use in microcomputer environments. Includes more sophisticated input-output statements, the ability to process character-string data, and block-structured statements to facilitate structured programming.

FORTRAN translation process The process used to produce computed results from a program written in the FORTRAN language. Includes compiling and executing the program on the computer.

forward chaining An event-driven method of reasoning that proceeds from known conditions to the desired goal.

forward pointer A pointer that tells the location of the next item in a data structure.

FOSDIC An acronym for FILM OPTICAL SENSING DEVICE FOR INPUT TO COMPUTERS. An input device used by the Census Bureau to read completed census questionnaire data into a computer.

fourth generation computer Contemporary digital computers developed from very large scale integrated (VLSI) technology.

FPLA An abbreviation for FIELD PROGRAMMABLE LOGIC ARRAY. An FPLA can be programmed by the user in the field, whereas an ordinary PLA is programmable only by masking at the semiconductor manufacturer's factory.

fractals A branch of mathematics recently codified by Benoit Mandelbrot that deals with curves and surfaces with nonintegral, or fractional, dimension. In computer graphics applications, this relates to a technique for obtaining a degree of complexity analogous to that in nature from a handful of data points.

fragmentation The presence of small increments of unused main memory space spread throughout main storage.

frame (1) The video image produced by one complete scan of the screen of a raster-scan display unit. (2) An area, the length of one recording position, extending across the width of magnetic tape perpendicular to its movement. Several bit positions may be included in a single frame through the use of different recording positions across the width of the tape.

framebuffer In computer graphics, an especially adapted piece of digital memory for storing a computed picture.

Framework™ A software package produced by Ashton-Tate that provides word processing, data base management, spreadsheet, communications, and business graphics. A built-in outline processor lets you organize your thoughts in outline form before expanding the outline into text that can be used in a document. Framework provides "frames" that let the user use more than one program module at the same time. The user can open one frame to work on a word processing document, while another frame shows a spreadsheet, and a third displays a data base. The user can place many frames on the screen, and does not have to stop using one application before beginning another. Framework has a universal set of commands, so many of the commands in the data base or spreadsheet also work in the word processor. Along with a simple menu-style structure, an on-line tutorial program, and help screens, the universal commands make Framework relatively easy to get started with, especially considering the power it offers.

Freedom of Information Act Federal legislation that allows ordinary citizens access to data gathered by federal agencies. See FEDERAL PRIVACY ACT and PRIVACY ACT OF 1974.

free form A type of optical scanning in which the scanning operation is controlled by symbols entered by the input device at the time of data entry.

frequency The number of times that sound pressure, electrical intensity, or other quantities specifying a wave vary from their equilibrium value through a complete cycle in unit time. The most common unit of frequency is the hertz (Hz); 1 Hz is equal to 1 cycle per second.

frequency counter An electronic device capable of counting the number of cycles in an electrical signal during a preselected time interval.

frequency shift keying A method of data transmission in which the state of the bit being transmitted is indicated by an audible tone. Abbreviated FSK.

friction-feed A paper-feed system that operates by clamping a sheet of paper between two rollers. As the rollers rotate, the paper is drawn into the printing device. Typewriters and many printers use this method. Contrast with TRACTOR-FEED MECHANISM.

friendliness How easy a computer or program is to work with. A USER-FRIENDLY program is one that takes little time to learn and is easy to use.

friendly interface A term applied to a combination of terminal equipment and computer programs designed to be easy to operate by casual users of computers.

frob To fiddle with a picking device, such as a joystick or mouse.

front-end processor A computer used to enter, check, or compress data before it is sent to a mainframe computer for further processing.

front panel The collection of switches and indicators by which the computer operator may control a computer system. Same as CONTROL PANEL.

fry To ruin circuitry by subjecting it to excessive heat or current.

fs Abbreviation for FEMTOSECOND.

FSK An abbreviation for FREQUENCY SHIFT KEYING.

full-adder A computer circuit capable of adding three binary bits, one of which is a CARRY from a previous addition.

full-duplex Pertaining to the simultaneous, independent transmission of data in both directions over a communications link. Contrast with HALF-DUPLEX and SIMPLEX.

full-frame Refers to the process by which a display image is scaled to use the entire viewing area of a display device.

full-page display A terminal, used in word processing systems, that displays a standard 8½ x 11 inch (21 x 28 cm) page of text on the screen at one time.

full-screen Condition in which the entire face of the video screen is used for display.

full-screen editing The ability to move the cursor over the entire screen to alter text.

full-text searching The retrieval of certain information by searching the full text of an article or book stored in a computer's auxiliary storage.

fully formed characters Printed characters, such as those of a daisy-wheel printer as opposed to dot-matrix characters.

function (1) A process that generates a value. (2) A precoded routine. (3) In business, a job.

function codes Special codes that help control functions of peripheral devices. For example, a "clear display screen" would be a function code.

function key A special key on a keyboard that can be assigned by a programmer to perform special functions within a program. On the keyboard, these keys are usually labeled F1, F2, F3, and so on.

functional description A phrase used to identify the requirements of a computer system.

functional design The specification of the working relationships between the parts of a system in terms of their characteristic actions.

functional programming Programming that uses function application as the only control structure.

functional specification A set of input, output, processing, and storage requirements detailing what a new system should be able to do. It is the output of the systems analysis function and presents a detailed, logical description of a new system.

functional units of a computer The organization of digital computers into five functional units: arithmetic-logic unit, storage unit, control unit, input device, and output device.

function subprogram A subprogram that returns a single value result.

funware Game programs in firmware.

fuse A safety protective device that opens an electric circuit if overloaded. A current above the rating of the fuse will melt a fusible link and open the circuit. Most computer devices use fuses to protect the equipment from current overloads.

fusible link A widely used PROM programming technique. An excessive current is used to destroy a metalized connection in a storage device, creating a 0, for instance, if a conducting element is interpreted as a 1.

fuzzy logic A method of handling imprecision or uncertainty that attaches various measures of credibility to propositions.

G

gain A general term used to denote an increase in signal power or voltage produced by an amplifier in transmitting a signal from one point to another. The amount of gain is usually expressed in decibels above a reference level. Opposite of ATTENUATION.

gallium arsenide A crystalline material used to make high-grade semiconductors. It is superior to silicon but far more costly.

game playing See COMPUTERIZED GAME PLAYING.

game theory A branch of mathematics concerned with probability, among other things. The term was first used by John von Neumann in 1928 to describe the strategy of winning at poker. A mathematical process of selecting an optimum strategy in the face of an opponent who also has a strategy of her or his own.

gamut The total range of colors that can be displayed on a computer display.

Gantt chart Named after its developer, Henry Gantt, a time-based bar, line, or arrow chart depicting start and end points of activities or tasks. Commonly used to depict scheduled deadlines and milestones for a project.

gap Magnetic memory space between two records (interrecord gap) or two blocks of data (interblock gap). See INTERBLOCK GAP and *interrecord gap*.

garbage (1) A term often used to describe incorrect answers from a computer program, usually resulting from inaccuracies in data entry or a mistake in a computer program, and sometimes from equipment malfunction. (2) Unwanted and meaningless data carried in storage. (3) Incorrect input to a computer. See JUNK and GIGO.

garbage collection Loosely defined, a term for cleaning dead storage locations out of a file.

gas-plasma display A flat-panel display that works on a principle similar to that of neon signs: a narrow gap filled with neon and argon gas separates two glass plates. An alternating-current voltage applied between closely spaced row-and-column electrodes ionizes the gases between the electrodes, causing them to glow. Once initiated, the glow continues at a reduced voltage. See FLAT-PANEL DISPLAY.

gate (1) A Controlling element of certain transistors. (2) A logic circuit with two or more inputs that control one output.

gateway (1) A connection between two dissimilar networks. (2) A computer that connects two distinctly different communications networks together. Used so that one local area network computer system can communicate and share its data with another local area network computer system.

gating circuit Refers to a circuit that operates as a selective switch, allowing conduction only during selected time intervals or when the signal magnitude is within certain limits.

GB An abbreviation for GIGABYTE.

GEM™ An acronym for GRAPHICS ENVIRONMENT MANAGER, a program that adds Macintosh/MacPaint-like qualities to a variety of microcomputers including the IBM Personal Computer and Atari ST. Developed by Digital Research, Inc.

generality The generality of a computer program means its solution of a problem is done in such a way that it will serve a variety of users with the same general kind of problem. A simple example is that of a payroll program that writes a warning message if the net pay it calculates for someone is more than a certain amount. A program with less generality would have a fixed limit; a program with more generality would allow each individual user to specify his/her own limit value, or to turn off the warning feature altogether.

generalized routine A routine designed to process a large range of specific jobs within a given type of application.

general purpose Being applicable to a wide variety of uses without essential modification. Contrast with SPECIAL PURPOSE.

general-purpose computer A computer designed to solve a wide class of problems. The majority of computers are of this type. Contrast with SPECIAL-PURPOSE COMPUTER. See DIGITAL COMPUTER.

general-purpose register A CPU register used for indexing, addressing, and arithmetic and logical operations.

general register A storage device that holds the inputs and outputs of the various functional units of a computing system. Also used for temporary storage of intermediate results.

generate To produce a program by selection of subsets from a set of skeletal coding under the control of parameters; to produce a program by use of a generator. See GENERATOR.

generation (of computers) A term usually applied to the technological progression of computers from those using vacuum tubes (FIRST GENERATION) to those using transistors (SECOND GENERATION), to those using integrated circuits (THIRD GENERATION), and to those using LSI and VLSI circuits (FOURTH GENERATION). See FIFTH GENERATION computers.

generator A software package that contains a number of routines to accomplish specific functions. These routines are capable of accepting input parameters and modifying themselves as the parameters indicate. Generators are used to make the implementation of specific, limited tasks very convenient, such as producing a report. Typically, the user fills out a set of parameter forms defining the task.

generic Pertaining to the next (generally improved) type of an item or device.

geocoding A method of providing a graphic display of data in relation to a geographic area.

geometry The branch of mathematics that deals with the relationships, properties, and measurements of solids, surfaces, lines and angles. It also considers spatial relationships, the theory of space and figures in space. The name comes form Greek words meaning "land" and "to measure." Geometry was first used by the Egyptians to measure land and was later highly developed by the great Greek mathematicians. In computer graphics, geometry refers to the specific physical arrangement of lines that make up the shape of a specific entity.

germanium A chemical element (atomic number 32) used in the manufacture of semiconductor devices (chips). It is the second most popular material (after silicon) for making semiconductor devices.

GERT An acronym for GRAPHICAL EVALUATION AND REVIEW TECHNIQUE, a procedure for the formulation and evaluation of systems using a network approach.

get To obtain a record from an input file. Another name for load.

G flops One billion floating point operations per second.

GI GESELLSCHAFT FUR INFORMATIK, an information processing society in West Germany.

gibberish A term used to describe unnecessary data.

giga A prefix indicating one billion. Abbreviated G.

gigabyte Specifically, 1,073,741,824, or 2^{30} bytes. More loosely, one billion bytes, one million kilobytes, or one thousand megabytes. Abbreviated GB.

gigahertz A frequency of a billion times a second. Abbreviated GHz.

GIGO An acronym for GARBAGE IN-GARBAGE OUT. A term used to describe the data into and out of a computer system; that is, if the input data is bad (Garbage In), then the output data will also be bad (Garbage Out).

glare A reflection from the surface of a display screen.

glitch (1) A popular term for a temporary or random malfunction in hardware. For example, a malfunction caused by a power surge. (2) A hitch of some kind in a program.

global (1) A general term implying a great breadth of scope, as contrasted with local. (2) Pertaining to a variable whose name is accessible by a main program and all its subroutines. **(3)** A computer operation applied to a broad set of data.

global character A character, used in a searching routine, that can stand for any character. It allows the operator to search for a character string of a specified length, by specifying only some of its characters and using global characters to stand for the others. Also called a WILD CARD.

global operation In word processing, an operation performed throughout an entire file.

global search and replace In word processing, the ability to find a string anywhere it appears in a document and to substitute another string for it.

global variable A variable that can be recognized anywhere in a program. Contrast with LOCAL VARIABLE.

gnomon An object representing direction and dimension that facilitates interpretation of a two-dimensional image of a three-dimensional solid.

go down To crash.

GP An abbreviation for GENERAL PURPOSE.

GPSS An abbreviation for GENERAL PURPOSE SYSTEMS SIMULATION. A problem-oriented language used to develop simulation systems.

grabber A fixture on the end of a test equipment lead wire with a spring actuated hook and claw designed to connect the measuring instrument to a pin of an integrated circuit, socket, transistor, and so forth.

graceful degradation The process of undergoing failure in such a way that limited operation can continue. See FAIL-SOFT SYSTEM.

grade Pertaining to the range, or width, of the frequencies available for transmission on a given channel.

gram A metric unit of mass weight equal to 1/1000 kilogram.

grammar Rules prescribing how various elements of a language should be combined. See SYNTAX.

grammatical error An error that results when the rules or syntax of a programming language are not followed. Also called a SYNTAX ERROR.

grammatical mistake See GRAMMATICAL ERROR.

grandfather file A security plan where the three most recent master files (called the grandfather file, father file, and son file) are retained so that, if a malfunction occurs during processing, the most recent error-free file copy can be used to reprocess or recover the data. Sometimes called the grandfather-father-son concept.

graph A diagram showing the relationship of two or more variable quantities. Sometimes called a CHART.

graphical terminal A visual display terminal that has a screen to display a drawing as well as textual information.

graphic-data structure The logical arrangement of digital data representing graphic data for graphic display.

graphic-display mode A mode of operation that allows the computer to print graphics on a special (graphics) screen.

graphic-display resolution The number of lines and characters per line able to be shown on a video screen.

graphic-display terminal A computer terminal that displays information on a screen, usually a cathode-ray tube, TV terminal, or video monitor.

graphic-input device Any device, such as a digitizer, that gives the computer the points that make up an image in such a way that the image can be stored, reconstructed, displayed, or manipulated.

graphic limits The plotting area of a graphics device, such as a digital plotter, as defined by its mechanical limits such as the size of the drum or platen.

graphic output Computer-generated output in the form of visual displays, printouts, or plots.

graphic-output device A device used to display or record an image. A display screen is an output device for soft copy; hard copy output devices produce paper, film, or transparencies of the image.

graphics Any computer-generated picture produced on a screen, paper, or film. Graphics range from simple line or bar graphs to colorful and detailed images.

graphics, business A computer generated chart or graph that represents business related tasks, such as sales, inventory, profits, losses, forecasts, and so on. Common business graphics include bar graphs, pie charts, and scatter graphs.

graphics digitizer An input device that converts graphic and pictorial data into digital inputs for use in a computer. Also called a GRAPHICS TABLET.

graphics display Any output device that can present an image of graphic data derived from a computer system.

graphics-input hardware Peripherals used to put graphics information in the computer, such as a graphics tablet, light pen and mouse.

graphics-output hardware Peripherals on which the computer displays graphics, such as a graphics printer, plotter, visual display terminal and film recorder.

graphics printer An output device that can produce text, charts, graphics and artwork.

graphics program A computer program that lets the computer produce graphics.

graphics resolution A measure of the detail in which graphics can be drawn by output hardware. High resolution pictures have greater detail than low-resolution pictures. See RESOLUTION.

graphics screen A screen that displays graphics information. See DISPLAY, and VIDEO DISPLAY TERMINAL.

graphics tablet An input device that converts graphic and pictorial data into binary inputs for use in a computer. The tablet provides an efficient method of converting object shapes into computer storable information. The device utilizes a flat tablet and a stylus for graphic input. See DIGITIZER.

graphics terminal An output device that displays pictures and drawings.

graph theory A branch of mathematics that belongs partly to combinatorial analysis and partly to topology. Its applications occur in electrical network theory, operations research, statistical mechanics, and sociological and behavioral research.

gray scale In computer graphics systems with a monochromatic display, variations in brightness level (gray scale) are employed to enhance the contrast among various design elements.

greater than A term referring to an inequality between numbers. The symbol is > with the point toward the smaller number. $9 > 5$ means 9 is greater than 5.

grid (1) A network of uniformly spaced points or crosshatched lines displayed on a visual display screen or digitizer and used for exactly locating a position, inputting components to assist in the creation of a design layout, or constructing precise diagrams. For example, coordinate data supplied by digitizers is automatically calculated by the computer from the closest grid point. The grid determines the minimum accuracy with which design entities are described or connected. (2) The display of an electronic spreadsheet model composed of columns and rows. (3) Horizontal and vertical lines on a chart to aid the viewer in determining the value of a point. (4) On a pie chart, the grid is an implied set of lines radiating out from the center representing the degrees of a circle.

grid chart A table that relates input data to its applicable applications program.

gridding A graphic image construction constraint that requires all line endpoints to fall on grid points.

gridsheet Same as GRID, SPREADSHEET, or WORKSHEET.

grounding The process of rendering an electrical current harmless to humans and computers.

grouping Arranging data into groups having common characteristics.

group mark Any indicator signaling the beginning or end of a word or other unit of data.

group printing An operation during which information prints from only the first card of each group passing through an accounting machine.

guest computer A computer operating under the control of another computer (host computer). See HOST COMPUTER.

GUIDE An acronym for **G**UIDANCE OF **U**SERS OF INTE-GRATED **D**ATA **P**ROCESSING **E**QUIPMENT, an international association of users of large-scale IBM computers.

gulp A small group of bytes.

gun The group of electrodes constituting the electron beam emitter in a cathode-ray tube.

gynoid A humanlike female robot. See ANDROID.

H

hacker A person who is not trying to learn about computers in a meaningful manner, but rather by trial and error.

half-adder A computer circuit capable of adding two binary bits.

half-duplex Pertaining to a communications path that can carry a message in either direction but only one way at a time. See FULL-DUPLEX and SIMPLEX.

halftoning Using dot patterns of variable density to simulate gray levels on a display that is strictly black and white.

half-word A contiguous sequence of bits, bytes, or characters that comprises half a computer word and is capable of being addressed as a unit. See WORD.

halt instruction A machine instruction that stops the execution of the program.

hand calculator A small, hand-held calculator suitable for performing arithmetic operations and other more complicated calculations.

hand-held computer A portable, battery-operated, hand-held computer that can be programmed in BASIC to perform a wide variety of tasks. Also called a POCKET COMPUTER.

handler A program with the sole function of controlling a particular input, output, or storage device, a file, or the interrupt facility.

handshaking The procedures and standards (protocol) used by two computers or a computer and a peripheral device to establish communication.

hands-on The process of physically using a computer system.

handwriting recognition Scanning handwritten material with a computer-controlled visual scanning device to determine information content or to verify a signature.

hang-up A nonprogrammed stop in a routine. It is usually an unforeseen or unwanted halt in a machine run. It is often caused by improper coding of a problem, by equipment malfunction, or by the attempted use of a nonexistent or illegal operation code.

hard-clip area The limits beyond which lines cannot be drawn on a digital plotter.

hard contact printing Contact printing in which the mask is pressed against the substrate with appreciable force.

hard copy (1) A printed copy of machine output in readable form; such as reports, listings, or graphic images. (2) A photograph or transparency film of an image displayed on a visual display screen. Contrast with SOFT COPY.

hard disk A fast auxiliary storage device that is either mounted in its own case or permanently mounted inside a computer. A single hard disk has storage capacity of several million characters or bytes of information.

hard error An error caused by a malfunction in the hardware.

hard failure The failure of a piece of equipment. It generally requires repair before the unit can be used again.

hard hyphen A hyphen required by spelling and is always printed, such as in "fourth-generation computer." Contrast with SOFT HYPHEN.

hard sector Sectors on a disk that are hard sectored are identified by some fixed mark on the disk medium. Hard sectored floppy disks have a hole punched in them, marking the beginning of each of the sectors. Contrast with SOFT SECTOR.

hardware The physical components or equipment that make up a computer system, such as a keyboard, floppy disk drive, and visual display. Contrast with SOFTWARE.

hardware configuration The relationships and arrangement of the various pieces of equipment that make up a computer system, including the cables and communications paths that connect them.

hardware dependent See MACHINE DEPENDENT.

hardware description languages (HDL) Languages and notations that facilitate the documentation, design, simulation, and manufacturing of digital computer systems.

hardware key A means to secure software from illegal copying. A hardware key plugs into a port or expansion slot **on** a computer and interacts with a program's antipiracy **soft**ware to allow the program to run only on that machine.

hardware resources CPU time, main storage space, auxiliary storage space, and input/output devices, all of which are required to do the work of processing data automatically and efficiently.

hardware specialist A person who diagnoses, repairs, and maintains the equipment of a computer system. See CUSTOMER ENGINEER, CUSTOMER SERVICE TECHNICIAN and FIELD ENGINEER.

hardwired Pertaining to the physical connection of two pieces of electronic equipment by means of a cable.

harness A group of separate cables that are bound together.

hash Visual static on the screen.

hashing A key-to-address transformation in which the keys determine the location of the data. Sometimes called hash coding.

hash totals The totals of the numbers of identifying fields.

HDBMS See HIERARCHICAL DATABASE MANAGEMENT SYSTEM.

head (1) A device that reads, records, or erases data on a storage medium; for example, a small electromagnet used to read, write, and erase data on a magnetic disk. **(2)** A special data item that points to the beginning of a list.

head-cleaning device A material containing a dirt solvent used to clean the read/write head of a floppy disk drive or a tape drive.

head crash Collision of the read/write head with the recording surface of a hard disk, resulting in loss of data. Usually caused by contamination of the disk, such as from a tiny particle of dust or smoke. Also called DISK CRASH.

header **(1)** The first part of a message containing all the necessary information for directing the message to its destination(s). **(2)** The top margin of a page.

header record A record containing constant, common, or identifying information for a group of records that follows.

headhunter Slang expression for a job placement consultant, someone who finds appropriate personnel for specific job openings within a client corporation.

head positioning Placing a read/write head when data is being read or written by a direct-access storage device.

head slot An opening in a floppy disk jacket that exposes the disk surface to read/write heads.

head switching Activating the read/write head that is to read or write data when data is being read or written by a direct-access storage device.

heap A collection of storage locations that a program can borrow for computations and then return.

heap sort See TREE SORT.

hecto Prefix meaning hundred.

helical wave guide A metal tube containing thin glass fibers and wires capable of transmitting thousands of messages over communications lines.

HELLO A common sign-on message used with terminals in a time-sharing system.

help A handy function available on many systems. It supplies the user with additional information on how the system or program works.

henry A unit of measure of inductance. One henry is the inductance of a circuit in which an electromotive force of 1 volt is produced by a current in the circuit that varies at the rate of 1 ampere per second.

Hertz Cycles per second. Abbreviated Hz.

heuristic Descriptive of an exploratory method of attacking a problem. The solution is obtained by successive evaluations of the progress toward the final results. From the Greek word Eureka, pertaining to the use of empirical knowledge to aid in discovery. Contrast with ALGORITHM. See ARTIFICIAL INTELLIGENCE and MACHINE LEARNING.

heuristic learning A way computers can learn from their mistakes by eliminating unsuccessful or unproductive options from their operations.

Hewlett-Packard A California company that produces a wide range of electronic equipment, including computer and peripherals.

hex See HEXADECIMAL.

hexadecimal Pertaining to a numeral system with a radix of 16. Digits greater than 9 are represented by letters of the alphabet. For example, the binary numeral 1110001011010011 can be represented as hexadecimal E2D3.

hexadecimal number A numeral, usually of more than one digit, representing a sum in which the quantity represented by each digit is based on a radix of 16. The digits used are 0,1,2,3,4,5,6,7,8,9,A,B,C,D,E, and F.

hexadecimal point The radix point in a mixed hexadecimal numeral system. The point that separates the integer part of a mixed hexadecimal numeral from the fractional part. In the hexadecimal numeral 2B.4F3, the hexadecimal point is between the digits B and 4.

hidden line When displaying a three-dimensional object, any line that would normally be obscured from the viewer's sight by the mass of the object itself, visible as a result of the projection.

hidden-line removal The process of deleting line segments from a drawing when they would be obscured if the object was displayed as a solid three-dimensional figure. Many types of computer graphics software and hardware can remove such hidden lines automatically.

hidden objects Distinct graphic entities that would be obscured from view by other entities if they were displayed as solids.

hidden surface The entire surface or plane that would be obscured from view if the graphics figure were displayed as a three-dimensional solid.

hierarchical data base management system (HDBMS) A collection of related programs for loading, accessing, and controlling a data base. In an HDBMS, data are organized like an inverted tree with a series of nodes connected by branches.

hierarchical model A data base model in which each object is of a particular hierarchy in a tree structure.

hierarchical network A computer network in which processing and control functions are performed at several levels by computers specially designed for the functions performed.

hierarchical structure In data base management systems, the simplest form of file organization, in which records of various levels are related by owning or belonging to each other. Also known as TREE STRUCTURE.

hierarchy (1) Order in which arithmetic operations within a formula or statement will be executed. (2) Arrangement into a graded series.

hierarchy plus input-process-output (HIPO) A design and program documentation method that represents functional structure and data flow in a series of three types of diagrams. These diagrams are: visual tables of contents that name the program modules and specify their hierarchical relationships; overview diagrams that describe the input, processing, and output for members of the hierarchy; and detailed diagrams that extend the overview diagrams to include more specific input, processing, and output detail with narrative.

high-level language A programming language that allows users to write instructions in a notation with which they are familiar rather than in a machine code. Each statement in a high-level language corresponds to several machine code instructions. Contrast with LOW-LEVEL LANGUAGE.

highlighting The process of making a display segment more noticeable by causing flickering, blinking, brightening, or reversing the background and the character images (e.g., dark characters on a light background). Most video displays have software controls to accomplish this on a selective basis.

high order Pertaining to the digit or digits of a number that have the greatest weight or significance; for example, in the number 986432, the high order digit is 9. Contrast with LOW-ORDER. See MOST SIGNIFICANT DIGIT.

high-persistence phosphor A phosphor coating used on display monitor screens that holds an image much longer than the coating used on standard TV screens.

high resolution Pertaining to the quality and accuracy of detail that can be represented by a graphics display. Resolution quality depends upon the number of basic image-forming units (called pixels) within a picture image—the greater the number, the higher the resolution. High-resolution pictures are produced by a large number of pixels and therefore are sharper than low-resolution pictures. Contrast with LOW RESOLUTION. See RESOLUTION.

high-speed printer A printer capable of printing from 300 to 3,000 lines per minute.

high storage The upper address range of a computer. In most machines, it is occupied by the operating system.

high volatility A high frequency of changes to a file during a given time period.

HIPO An acronym for HIERARCHY PLUS INPUT-PROCESS-OUTPUT. A technique that provides a graphical method for designing and documenting program logic.

hi-res graphics An abbreviated version of HIGH-RESOLUTION GRAPHICS. A smooth and realistic picture on a display screen produced by a large number of pixels. Contrast with LOW-RES GRAPHICS.

histogram A type of bar graph used to represent a frequency distribution. The bars have for one dimension a distance proportional to a definite range of frequencies and for the other dimension a distance proportional to the number of frequencies occurring within the range.

hit A successful comparison of two items of data. Compare with MATCH.

HKCS An abbreviation for HONG KONG COMPUTER SOCIETY.

HOL An acronym for HIGH-ORDER LANGUAGE, a procedure-oriented programming language such as BASIC, Pascal, or LOGO. See HIGH-LEVEL LANGUAGE and PROCEDURE-ORIENTED LANGUAGE.

holding time In data communications, the length of time a communications channel is in use for each transmission. Includes both message time and operating time.

hologram A three dimensional image produced in thin air by lasers interacting with one another.

holography A method of storing data by making a multidimensional photograph on a storage medium.

home The starting position for the cursor on a terminal screen. It is usually in the top left-hand corner of the screen.

homebrew Refers to early microcomputer systems made by hobbyists, which gave rise to the popularity of the personal computer.

home computer A microcomputer used in the home. It may be used to play games, to control household appliances, to aid students with school homework, to perform business computations, and for a wide variety of other tasks. See DESKTOP COMPUTER, MICROCOMPUTER and PERSONAL COMPUTER.

home-grown software Programs written by users of a computer system.

home key A keyboard function that directs the cursor to its home position, which is usually in the top left portion of the display screen.

home-management software Programs designed for home use to help manage and organize the household, such as check balancing, menu file, and stock portfolio accounting programs.

home record The first record in a chain of records in the chaining method of file organization.

home row The row of keys on the keyboard where keyboard users rest their fingers between keystrokes.

homunculus An infinitely recursive model of the brain. Used in studies of artificial intelligence.

Honeywell A large manufacturer of computer equipment.

horizontal scrolling Refers to the moving of horizontal blocks of data or text, thus allowing users to view more data than can fit on the screen at one time.

host computer (1) The central processing unit (CPU) that provides the computing power for terminals and peripheral devices connected to it. (2) The computer that is in charge during a telecommunications or local area network session. (3) A central controlling computer in a network of computers. See GUEST COMPUTER.

host language A programming language in which another language is included or embedded.

hot site A fully equipped computer center, ready for use in case of emergency.

hot zone On some word processors, a user-defined region beginning at the right margin of a page and extending about seven spaces to the left. If a word ends in the hot zone, the system automatically places the next character entered at the beginning of the next line.

housekeeping Computer operations that do not directly contribute toward the desired results, but are a necessary part of a program, such as initialization, set-up, and clean-up operations. Sometimes called BOOKKEEPING.

housing A cabinet or other enclosure.

HSP An acronym for HIGH-SPEED PRINTER.

hue Color.

huffman tree Tree with minimum values. See MINIMAL TREE and OPTIMAL MERGE TREE.

human engineering Study concerned with designing products that are easier and more confortable for humans to use. Also called ERGONOMICS.

human language The oral or written form of communication.

human-machine interface The boundary at which people interact with machines.

hybrid computer system A system that uses both analog and digital equipment.

hybrids Circuits fabricated by interconnecting smaller circuits of different technologies mounted on a single substrate.

hypercard A kind of programming environment that organizes all forms of information into what appears as stacks of index cards. Users then manipulate those stacks to create applications.

Hz An abbreviation for HERTZ; cycles per second.

I

IBG An abbreviation for INTERBLOCK GAP.

IBI An abbreviation for INTERGOVERNMENTAL BUREAU OF INFORMATICS. An organization consisting of members of the United Nations, UNESCO, or U.N. agencies. The goal is to promote scientific research, computer education and training, and the exchange of information between developed and developing countries. The main focus of IBI is to promote informatics, particularly in developing countries.

IBM Corporation The world's largest manufacturer of computing equipment.

IBM Personal Computer™ The first microcomputer family manufactured by the IBM Corporation. The most popular microcomputer of all time. The IBM PC follows a modular design philosophy; the basic unit consists of a system unit and a keyboard. Other components may be added, such as a monitor or disk unit. The system unit contains space for floppy disks and/or a hard disk. The three members of this family include the IBM PC™, IBM PC-XT™, and IBM PC-AT™.

IBM Personal System/2™ A family of microcomputer systems manufactured by the IBM Corporation.

IC An abbreviation for **INTEGRATED CIRCUIT**, a complex electronic circuit fabricated on a simple piece of material, usually a silicon chip.

ICCA See **INDEPENDENT COMPUTER CONSULTATNS ASSOCIATION**.

ICCE See **INTERNATIONAL COUNCIL FOR COMPUTERS IN EDUCATION**.

ICCP See **INSTITUTE FOR CERTIFICATION OF COMPUTER PROFESSIONALS**.

ICES An abbreviation for **INTEGRATED CIVIL ENGINEERING SYSTEM**. A system developed to aid civil engineers in solving engineering problems. Consists of several engineering systems and programming languages.

icon A tiny on-screen symbol that simplifies access to a program, command, or data file. For example, a wastebasket may represent the command to delete a file. It is activated by moving the cursor onto the icon and pressing a button or key.

ICOT An acronym for **INSTITUTE FOR NEW GENERATION COMPUTER TECHNOLOGY**, the institute conducting Japan's fifth-generation research project.

ICPEM See **INDEPENDENT COMPUTER PERIPHERAL EQUIPMENT MANUFACTURERS**.

ICS An abbreviation for **IRISH COMPUTER SOCIETY**.

identification division One of the four main component parts of a COBOL program.

identifier A symbol whose purpose is to identify, indicate, or name a program, subprogram, or body of data.

idle characters Characters used in data communications to synchronize the transmission.

idle time The time that a computer system is available for use, but is not in actual operation.

IDP An abbreviation for INTEGRATED DATA PROCESSING.

IEEE An abbreviation for INSTITUTE OF ELECTRICAL AND ELECTRONICS ENGINEERS. A professional engineering organization with a strong interest in computer systems and their uses.

IEEECS See INSTITUTE OF ELECTRICAL AND ELECTRONICS ENGINEERS COMPUTER SOCIETY.

IEEE-488 An interface standard mainly used to connect laboratory instruments and other scientific equipment to computers, either for control purposes or to allow the computer to collect data. A type of parallel interface.

IEEE 696/S-100 The identification of a standard, developed by the Institute of Electrical and Electronic Engineers. It ensures the compatibility of all computing products designed to this standard.

IFAC An acronym for INTERNATIONAL FEDERATION OF AUTOMATIC CONTROL. A multinational organization concerned with advancing the science and technology of control.

IFIP See INTERNATIONAL FEDERATION FOR INFORMATION PROCESSING.

I²L An abbreviation for INTEGRATED INJECTION LOGIC. I²L chips are used as control devices for industrial products and computer systems.

illegal character A character or combination of bits not accepted as a valid or known representation by the computer.

illuminate To increase the brightness or luminosity of graphical output at a display screen.

IMACS An abbreviation for INTERNATIONAL ASSOCIATION FOR MATHEMATICS AND COMPUTERS IN SIMULATION. A professional organization to facilitate the exchange of scientific information among specialists, builders, or users interested in analog and hybrid computational methods.

image (1) An exact logical duplicate stored in a different medium. If the computer user displays the contents of memory on a display screen, he or she will see an image of memory. (2) In computer graphics, image refers to the output form of graphics data, i.e., a drawn representation of a graphics file.

image enhancement Any accentuation of all or part of a graphics image through such techniques as coloring, shading, highlighting, zooming, reverse video, or blinking.

image processing A method for processing pictorial information by a computer system. It involves inputting graphic information into a computer system, storing it, working with it, and outputting it to an output device. See VISION RECOGNITION.

Imagewriter A dot matrix printer capable of producing high quality text and graphics output to paper. Used with Apple Macintosh and Apple II microcomputers.

immediate access Ability of a computer to put data in, or remove it from storage without delay.

immediate access storage See MAIN STORAGE.

immediate address Pertaining to an instruction whose address part contains the value of an operand rather than its address. It is not an address at all but rather an operand supplied as part of an instruction.

immediate-mode commands System and editing commands executed as soon as the carriage control key (ENTER, RETURN) is pressed.

impact printer A data printout device that imprints by momentary pressure of raised type against paper, using ink or ribbon as a color medium. See DAISY-WHEEL PRINTER, LINE PRINTER, THIMBLE PRINTER. Contrast with NON IMPACT PRINTER.

impedance The total opposition (resistance) a circuit offers to the flow of alternating current at a given frequency. Measured in ohms.

implementation (1) The process of installing a computer system. It involves choosing the equipment, installing the equipment, training the personnel, and establishing the computing center operating policies. (2) The representation of a programming language on a specific computer system. (3) The act of installing a program.

import To read a file created by another program into a data base system. Contrast with EXPORT.

IMS An abbreviation for INFORMATION MANAGEMENT SYSTEM. A data base management system software package that provides the facilities for storing and retrieving information from hierarchically structured files and data bases.

inactive A transaction that has been loaded into the computer's memory but has not yet been executed.

inactive window A window not in use. See WINDOW.

incidence matrix A two-dimensional array that describes the edges in a graph. Also called a CONNECTION MATRIX.

incident light Light falling on an object. The color of an object is perceived as a function of the wavelengths of incident light reflected or absorbed by it.

inclusive OR The Boolean operator that gives a truth table value of true if either or both of the two variables it connects are ''true.'' If neither is true, the value is false. Abbreviated OR.

increment (1) An amount added to a value or variable. (2) The distance between any two adjacent addressable points on a graphics input/output device.

incremental plotter A digital plotting device that outputs graphic data in discrete movements of the plotting head. See PLOTTER.

incremental spacing A synonym for MICROSPACING.

indegree The number of directed edges that point to a node.

indent To begin or move text a specified number of positions from the left edge or right edge of a page.

indentation White space found at the beginning of a line of text; often denotes the beginning of a paragraph.

Independent Computer Consultants Association (ICCA) A national network of independent computer consultants. Through the national organization and local chapters, members are able to exchange ideas and become part of a collective voice in the computer consulting industry.

Independent Computer Peripheral Equipment Manufacturers (ICPEM)   An organization composed of companies that specialize in manufacturing one or more lines of computer equipment.

independent consultant   A person trained in the information processing field, who works with businesses and organizations on a temporary basis helping them solve problems.

index   (1) A symbol or number used to identify a particular quantity in an array of similar quantities; for example, X(5) is the fifth item in an array of Xs. (2) A table of reference, held in storage in some sequence, that may be accessed to obtain the addresses of other items of data, such as items in a graphics or data file. See INDEX REGISTER.

indexed address   An address that is modified by the content of an index register prior to or during the execution of a computer instruction.

indexed sequential access method (ISAM)   A means of organizing data on a direct-access device. A directory or index is created to show where the data records are stored. Any desired data record can thus be retrieved from the device by consulting the index. The index reveals the approximate location of the record or piece of data on the direct-access device, and the computer searches the area indicated by the index until it locates the desired record or piece of data.

indexer   A program that generates an index for a document.

index hole   A hole punched through a floppy disk that can be read by the electrooptical system in the disk drive to locate accurately the beginning of sector zero on the disk.

indexing   A programming technique whereby an instruction can be modified by a factor called an index. See INDEX.

index register   A register whose contents can be added to or subtracted from an address prior to or during the execution of an instruction.

indicator   A device that registers a condition in the computer.

indirect addressing   Using an address that specifies a storage location that contains either a direct address or another indirect address. Also called MULTILEVEL ADDRESSING.

induce   To produce an electrical charge, current, or voltage by induction. A charge on the gate of a field effect transistor (FET) induces an equal charge in the channel.

inductance   In a circuit, the property that opposes any change in the existing current. Unit of measure is the HENRY.

induction   The process by which a body having electric and magnetic properties produces an electrical charge, a voltage, or a magnetic field in an adjacent body, without physical contact.

industrial data collection device   An input device that can record the time an employee spends on the job. This device can be used to determine wages, costs for jobs being done, and so forth.

industrial robot   A reprogrammable, multifunctional manipulator designed to move material parts, tools, or specialized devices through variable programmed motions for the performance of a variety of tasks. Unlike other forms of automation, robots can be programmed to do a variety of tasks, making them the most versatile of manufacturing tools. Many advantages result from the robot's reprogrammability. Since robots can switch tasks with a minimum of startup and debugging costs, a company is able to maximize its use of a proven design and reduce overall manufacturing costs. Major industries using industrial robots include the auto, aerospace, electronics, home appliances, consumer goods and off-road vehicles industries. Recent developments that give robots added intelligence, such as machine vision, tactile sensing, and mobility, make robots suitable for a wider range of industries. The near future will find robots used increasingly in industries such as textiles, food processing, pharmaceuticals, furniture, construction, and health care. Robots offer substantial gains in manufacturing productivity, particularly when integrated into an automated system. The history of U.S. robot installations indicates that robots increase productivity by 20-30%. Since the majority of robots are applied to existing machinery, companies using robots can accelerate payback on current equipment while reducing the need for new capital investment. For example, it is far more cost-effective to buy robots to make existing stamping presses or machine tools 20-30% more productive than it is to buy one additional piece of machinery at a cost equal to or greater than the robots with less output.

inference The process of drawing a conclusion from an initial set of propositions with known truth value.

inference program A program that derives a conclusion from given facts.

infinite loop A set of instructions that continuously repeat in a program. A loop with no exit condition. Also called an END-LESS LOOP.

infix notation A common arithmetic notation in which operators are embedded within operands. For example, the addition of 8 and 2 would be expressed as 8 + 2.

informal design review An evaluation of system-designed documentation by selected management, systems analysts, and programmers, prior to the actual coding of program modules to determine necessary additions, deletions, and modifications to the system design.

informatics A word used more or less synonymously with IN-FORMATION TECHNOLOGY.

information banks Large data bases that store information pertaining to specific applications.

information bits In telecommunications, those bits that are generated by the data source and do not include error control bits.

information explosion The exponential increase in the growth and diversification of all forms of information. See INFORMATION REVOLUTION.

information networks The interconnection, through telecommunications, of a geographically dispersed group of libraries and information centers for the purpose of sharing their total information resources among more people.

information processing The totality of operations performed by a computer. It involves evaluating, analyzing, and processing data to produce usable information.

information processing center A computer center equipped with devices capable of receiving information, processing it according to human-made instructions, and producing the computed results.

information processing curriculum A course of study, normally offered by a college or university, that prepares students for entry-level jobs as applications programmers, system programmers, or systems analysts.

information processing machine A computer.

information providers The large businesses that supply information to a computer network for a fee, such as The Source or CompuServe.

information resource management A system to manage information as a resource like labor, capital, and raw material.

information retrieval **(1)** That branch of computer technology concerned with techniques for storing and searching large quantities of data and making selected data available. **(2)** The methods used to recover specific information from stored data.

information revolution The name given to the present era because of the impact of computer technology on society. Sometimes called the Computer Revolution.

information science The study of how people create, use, and communicate information in all forms.

information services Broad-based data bases that offer a variety of services, ranging from airline reservation information to stock market quotations. See COMPUSERVE and SOURCE, THE.

information storage and retrieval See INFORMATION RETRIEVAL.

information system A collection of people, procedures, and equipment designed, built, operated, and maintained to collect, record, process, store, retrieve, and display information.

information technology The merging of computing and high speed communications links carrying data, sound, and video.

information theory The branch of learning concerned with the likelihood of accurate transmission or communication of messages subject to transmission failure, noise, and distortion.

information utility See COMPUTER UTILITY.

inherent error A computer error that has incorrect initial values caused by uncertainty in measurements, by outright blunders, or by approximating a value by an insufficient number of digits.

inhibit To prohibit from taking place.

in-house training A program for training individuals within the organization where they work.

initialize (1) To preset a program variable or counter to proper starting values before commencing a calculation. (2) To format a disk. See PRESET.

initiate To start some activity.

ink-jet printer An output device that prints by spraying a thin stream of ink onto the paper.

in-line coding Coding that is located in the main part of a routine.

in-line processing The processing of data in random order, not subject to preliminary editing or sorting.

in-line subroutine A subroutine that is inserted into the main routine as many times as it is needed.

input The introduction of data from an input device or auxiliary storage device into a computer's main storage unit. The information a computer takes in. Contrast with OUTPUT.

input area An area of main storage reserved for input data (data transferred from an input device or an auxiliary storage device). Contrast with OUTPUT AREA.

input data Data to be processed. Often called INPUT. Contrast with OUTPUT DATA.

input device A unit used to enter data into a computer, such as a graphics tablet and keyboard. Contrast with OUTPUT DEVICE.

input job stream See JOB STREAM.

input media The physical substance upon which input data is recorded, such as floppy disks, cassette tapes, and OCR documents.

input/output Pertaining to the techniques, media, and devices used to achieve human/machine communication. Abbreviated I/O.

input/output-bound A situation in which the central processing unit is slowed down because of I/O operations, which are usually extremely slow in comparison to the internal processing operations of the central processing unit.

input/output channel A channel that transmits input data to, or output data from, a computer. See MULTIPLEXER CHANNEL, RS-232C, and SELECTOR CHANNEL.

input/output control system A standard set of routines for initiating and controlling the many detailed aspects of input and output operations. Abbreviated IOCS.

input/output device A unit used to get data from the human user into the central processing unit, and to transfer data from the computer's main storage to some storage or output device. See INPUT DEVICE, OUTPUT DEVICE, and PERIPHERAL EQUIPMENT.

input/output instructions Directions for the transfer of data between peripheral devices and main storage that enable the central processing unit to control the peripheral devices connected to it.

input/output ports The sockets on a computer where the peripherals interface. See PERIPHERAL EQUIPMENT.

input/output processor An auxiliary processor, dedicated to controlling input/output transfers, that frees the central processing unit for non-I/O tasks.

input/output symbol A flowcharting symbol used to indicate an input operation to the procedure or an output operation from the procedure. A parallelogram figure is used to represent this symbol.

input stream The sequence of control statements and data submitted to the operating system on an input unit especially activated for that purpose by the operator. Same as JOB STREAM.

inputting The process of entering data into a computer system.

inquiry A request for data from storage. For example, a request for the number of available airline seats in an airline reservations system.

inquiry processing The process of selecting a record from a file and immediately displaying its contents.

inquiry station The device from which any inquiry is made.

insert In word processing, fitting new characters into already-prepared text.

insertion point The position at which text is entered into a document.

insertion method See SIFTING.

insertion sorting algorithm A sorting algorithm that involves placing the unordered items from one array into a second, ordered array.

install To customize elements of a new program so a specific computer system can use it, such as inserting protocols for communicating with the printer into a specific program.

installation A general term for a particular computing system in the context of the overall function it serves and the individuals who manage it, operate it, apply it to problems, service it, and use the results that it produces.

installation time The time spent installing, testing, and accepting equipment.

instant print A feature of some word processing programs that lets one use the system as a typewriter.

Institute for Certification of Computer Professionals An organization that administers the examinations of four certificate programs: the Certificate in Computer Programming; the Certificate in Data Processing; the Certified Systems Professional designation; and the Associate Computer Professional designation. Examinations are held at different locations several times each year. See CCP, CDP, CSP, and ACP.

Institute of Electrical and Electronics Engineers Computer Society (IEEECS). A computer specialty group within the IEEE. It is one of the leading professional associations in advancing the theory and practice of computer and information processing technology. The society publishes transactions and magazines and promotes cooperation and exchange of current information among its members.

instruction A group of characters, bytes, or bits that defines an operation to be performed by the computer. Usually made up of an operation code and one or more operands. See MACHINE INSTRUCTION.

instructional computing The educational process of teaching individuals the various phases of computer science and data processing.

instruction code Same as OPERATION CODE.

instruction counter A counter that indicates the location of the next computer instruction to be interpreted. Same as PROGRAM COUNTER.

instruction cycle The time required to process an instruction. This includes fetching the instruction from internal storage, interpreting or decoding the instruction, and executing the instruction.

instruction format The makeup and arrangement of computer instructions.

instruction register A hardware register that stores an instruction for execution.

instruction set A set of vendor-supplied codes for a particular computer or family of computers. Synonymous with REPERTOIRE.

instruction time The time it takes for an instruction to be retrieved from main storage by the control unit and interpreted.

instruction word A computer word that contains an instruction.

instrument A document designed as a form, report, questionnaire, or guide to be used in a planned systematic datagathering procedure for the purpose of providing information to the individual, group, or organization initiating the request.

instrumental input Data captured by machines and placed directly into the computer.

instrumentation The application of devices for the measuring, recording, and/or controlling of physical properties and movements.

integer Any member of the set consisting of the positive and negative whole numbers and zero. Examples: -82, -4, 0, 6, 53.

integer BASIC A type of BASIC language that can process whole numbers (integers) only. For example, 1 divided by 3 would yield an answer of 0 rather than 0.33333.

integer variable A quantity that can be equal to any integer and can take on different integer values.

integral controller A communications unit built into a computer.

integrate The process of putting various components together to form a harmonious computer system.

integrated circuit (IC) A complete electronic circuit contained on a minute chip of silicon. Integrated circuits may consist of only a few transistors, capacitors, diodes or resistors, or thousands of them. They are generally classified, according to the complexity of the circuitry, as small scale integration (SSI), medium scale integration (MSI), large scale integration (LSI), very large scale integration (VLSI), and ultra large scale integration (ULSI).

integrated computer package See INTEGRATED SOFTWARE.

integrated data processing (IDP) Data processing in which the coordination of data acquisition with all other stages of data processing is achieved in a coherent system, such as a business data processing system in which data for sales orders and purchasing are combined to accomplish the functions of scheduling, invoicing, and accounting.

integrated injection logic   See I²L.

integrated software   A group of programs that may freely exchange data with each other, a software package that has a word processor, data base manager, electronic spreadsheet, and communications program. Since the information from the electronic spreadsheet may be shared with the data base manager and the word processor (and vice versa), this software is called integrated. Some integrated programs, for instance, split the screen into windows and allow the operator to work with a word processing document and a spreadsheet simultaneously. Examples are APPLEWORKS™, FRAMEWORK™ and SYMPHONY™.

integration   (1) Combining diverse elements of hardware and software, often acquired from different vendors, into a unified system. (2) Combining computer programs into a unified software package so that all programs can share common data.

integrity   The preservation of programs or data for their intended purpose. See DATA INTEGRITY.

Intel Corporation   The company that produced the first microprocessor, the 4-bit 4004, and now makes a wide variety of microprocessors used in many popular microcomputers.

Intel 8088   A 16-bit microprocessor developed by Intel Corporation, used in several microcomputers including the IBM Personal Computer™.

Intel 80286   A 32-bit microprocessor developed by Intel Corporation, used in several microcomputers including the IBM Personal Computer AT™, AT&T PC6300™, Hewlett-Packard Vectra PC™, and Tandy 3000™.

Intel 80386   A 32-bit microprocessor developed by Intel Corporation, used in several microcomputers including the Compaq Deskpro 386.™

intelligence   See ARTIFICIAL INTELLIGENCE.

intelligent language   A programming language that can learn from or be changed by the programmer or user.

intelligent terminal   An input/output device in which a number of computer processing characteristics are physically built

into, or attached to, the terminal unit. See POINT-OF-SCALE
TERMINAL.

intensity The amount of light in a graphics-display device.
The level of brightness emitted by a cathode ray tube. On
most visual-display devices, the intensity can be controlled
by manipulating a switch.

interactive Yielding an immediate response to input. The user
is in direct and continual communication with the computer
system. Denotes two-way communications between a computer system and its operators. An operator can modify or
terminate a program and receive feedback from the system
for guidance and verification.

interactive graphics The general term applied to any graphics
system in which the user and the computer are in active
communication.

interactive graphics system A computer graphics system in
which workstations are used interactively for computer-
aided design, all under full operator control, and possibly
also for text-processing, generation of charts and graphs,
producing graphic images, and generation of 35mm slides
or animation pictures.

interactive processing A type of real-time processing involving a continuing dialog between user and computer; the
user is allowed to modify data and/or instructions. See CON-
VERSATIONAL MODE.

interactive program A computer program that permits data to
be entered or the flow of the program to be modified during
its execution.

interactive query An operation that allows the immediate retrieval of a specific record or records. This mode of processing is essentially a dialogue in which each user input
can elicit a response from the system.

interactive system A system in which the human user or device serviced by the computer can communicate directly
with the operating program. For human users, this is termed
a conversational system.

interblock gap The distance on a magnetic tape or disk between the end of one block of records and the beginning of the next block of records.

interconnection The physical and electrical connection of equipment furnished by different vendors.

interface The point of meeting between a computer and an external entity, whether an operator, a peripheral device, or a communications medium. An interface may be physical involving a connector, or logical involving software. See CENTRONICS INTERFACE, IEEE-488, and RS-232C.

interface card A type of expansion board that permits connection of external devices to computers, such as disk interface cards, serial interface cards, and parallel interface cards.

interference Unwanted signals that degrade the quality of wanted signals.

interlace To assign successive addresses to physically separated storage locations on a magnetic disk or drum in such a way as to reduce the access time.

interleaving A multiprogramming technique in which parts of one program are inserted into another program so that if there are processing delays in one of the programs, parts of the other program can be processed.

interlock A protective facility that prevents one device or operation from interfering with another; for example, the locking of the switches on the control console to prevent their manual movement while the computer is executing a program.

interlude Preliminary housekeeping.

intermittent error An error that occurs intermittently, constantly, and is extremely difficult to reproduce.

internal clock An electronic circuit within the computer system that keeps the time of day.

internal data representation Data representation in registers, storage, and other devices inside the computer.

internal memory Same as MAIN STORAGE.

internal modem A modem that plugs directly into computer expansion slots inside the computer. See MODEM.

internal report A report produced by an organization for people inside the organization, usually concerning inventory, quality control, payroll, and so on.

internal sort The sequencing of two or more records within the central processing unit. The first phase of a multipass sort program.

internal storage Addressable storage directly controlled by the central processing unit. The central processing unit uses internal storage to store programs while they are being executed, and data while they are being processed. Also called IMMEDIATE ACCESS STORAGE, INTERNAL MEMORY, MAIN STORAGE, and PRIMARY STORAGE.

International Business Machines Corporation See IBM CORPORATION.

International Council for Computers in Education (ICCE) A professional organization for people interested in instructional computing at the precollege level.

International Federation for Information Processing (IFIP) A multinational organization representing professional and educational societies actively engaged in the field of information processing. It holds a meeting, at a different location in the world, every three years.

International Standards Organization See ISO.

interpolation A method of finding values between any two known values. In computer graphics, this process is often applied to creating curves by joining a series of straight line segments or to defining smoothing curves between specified points.

interpretation The one-by-one translation of high-level language program statements into machine language instructions. When a program is interpreted, each statement is translated and executed before the next statement is processed. Contrast with COMPILATION.

interpreter A language translator that converts each source language statement into machine code and executes it immediately, statement by statement. A program that performs interpretation. Contrast with *compiler*.

interrecord gap The space between records on magnetic disk and tape. Used to signal that the end of a record has been reached.

interrupt A signal that, when activated, causes the hardware to transfer program control to some specific location in main storage, thus breaking the normal flow of the program being executed. After the interrupt has been processed, program control is again returned to the interrupted program. Can be generated as the result of a program action by an operator activating switches on the computer console or by a peripheral device causing the interrupting signal. Often called TRAPPING.

interrupt driven Pertaining to a computer system that makes extensive use of interrupts.

interval timer A mechanism whereby elapsed time can be monitored by a computer system.

interruption A break in the normal sequence of executing instructions.

interview (1) A fact-gathering method in systems analysis and design. (2) A personal conversation between a job applicant and the person who may offer a job. It is the time a person talks about his or her qualifications for a job opening. During an interview, a person has the chance to give the details about his or her skills, education, and past job experience, as well as to find out more about the job and what will be expected of him or her on the job.

invariant A constant.

inventory control The use of a computer system to monitor an inventory.

inventory management A term applied to the daily and periodic bookkeeping commonly associated with inventory control and with forecasting the future needs for items or groups of items.

inverse video A process that shows dark text on a light background display screen. Normally, light text is shown on a dark background. Same as REVERSE VIDEO.

invert To turn over; reverse. To highlight text or objects by reversing the on-screen display or printout.

inverted file A file organized so it can be accessed by character rather than by record key.

inverted structure A file structure that permits fast, spontaneous searching for previously unspecified information. Independent lists are maintained in record keys that are accessible according to the values of specified fields.

inverter A circuit in which a binary 1 input produces a binary 0 output, and vice versa.

inverting circuit A circuit for changing direct current to alternating current.

invisible refresh A scheme that refreshes dynamic memories without disturbing the rest of the system.

invoice A business paper containing data about the purchase or sale of goods.

I/O An abbreviation for INPUT/OUTPUT.

I/O board A circuit board that controls the input and output of data between the computer and peripheral devices.

I/O-bound The term applied to programs that require a large number of input/output operations, resulting in much central processing unit wait time. Contrast with COMPUTE-BOUND.

I/O channel Part of the input/output system of a computer. Under the control of I/O commands, the channel transfers blocks of data between main storage and peripheral equipment.

IOCS An abbreviation for INPUT/OUTPUT CONTROL SYSTEM. A standard set of input/output routines designed to initiate and control the input and output processes of a computer system.

I/O port A connection to a central processing unit (CPU) that provides for data paths between the CPU and peripheral devices, such as video display terminals, graphics tablets, printers, and floppy disk units.

I/O processor A circuit board or chip that is used only to handle input/output operations between the computer and peripherals.

IPAI A abbreviation for INFORMATION PROCESSING ASSOCIATION OF ISRAEL.

IPSJ An abbreviation for INFORMATION PROCESSING SOCIETY OF JAPAN.

IRG An abbreviation for INTERRECORD GAP.

IRM An abbreviation for INFORMATION RESOURCES MANAGER. The person responsible for operating the company's main computer and for keeping an eye on the numerous employees using it.

ISAM An acronym for INDEXED SEQUENTIAL ACCESS METHOD. A procedure for storing and retrieving data. The procedure uses a set of indexes that describes where the records are located on the disk file.

ISO An abbreviation for INTERNATIONAL STANDARDS ORGANIZATION, an international agency that is responsible for developing standards for information exchange. This agency has a function similar to that of ANSI in the United States.

isolation (1) In a computer security system, the compartmentalization of information so access to it is on a "need to know" basis. (2) The state of being separated or set apart from others.

ISR An abbreviation for INFORMATION STORAGE AND RETRIEVAL. See information retrieval.

I-time See INSTRUCTION TIME.

item (1) A group of related characters treated as a unit. (A record is a group of related items, and a file is a group of related records). (2) A selection within a menu.

iterate To repeat automatically, under program control, the same series of processing steps until a predetermined stop or branch condition is reached. See LOOP and NEWTON-RAPHSON.

iterative Repetitive. Often used when each succeeding iteration, or repetition, of a procedure comes closer to the desired result.

iterative algorithm An algorithm that involves looping; repetitive in nature.

J

jack A connecting device to which a wire or wires of a circuit may be attached and that is arranged for the insertion of a plug.

jacket The plastic container that holds a floppy disk. The disk cannot be removed from the jacket.

jaggies In a computer graphics display, the stairstepped or saw-toothed effect of diagonals, circles, and curves.

jargon The technical vocabulary associated with a specific trade, business or profession.

Jazz™ An integrated software system, developed by Lotus Development Corporation for the Apple Macintosh microcomputer. The program can be used for word processing, data base management, electronic spreadsheet calculations, data communications, and graphics.

JCL An abbreviation for JOB CONTROL LANGUAGE, a special language used to give instructions to the operating system of a computer.

jitter Brief instability of a signal, applied particularly to signals on a video display.

job A collection of specified tasks constituting a unit of work for a computer, such as a program or related group of programs used as a unit.

job control language A language that defines a job and the resources it requires from the computer system, including constraints on the job, such as time limits. The language is more often interpreted than compiled. Abbreviated JCL.

job control statement One statement, written in a job control language, that defines one aspect of a job.

job number   An identification number assigned to a job.

job queue   The set of programs and data currently making its way through the computer. In many operating systems, each job is brought into the queue and is processed (given control of the computer) when it is the "oldest" job within its own priority. An exception to this is a job of higher priority that has not yet obtained sufficient resources to be processed.

job scheduler   A person who aids computer operators in the running of a large computer installation.

job stream   The input to the operating system; it may consist of one or more jobs. Same as INPUT STREAM.

job-to-job transition   The process of locating a program and the files associated with the program and of preparing the computer for the execution of a particular job.

job turnaround   The elapsed time from when a job is given to the computer system until its printed output reaches the person who submitted the job.

joy stick   An electromechanical lever that, when manipulated, moves the display cursor. This device is primarily used to play video games. It is attached to the computer by a cable.

Julian number   A form of calendar representation within a computer system. The Julian date indicates the year and the number of elapsed days in the year; for example, 88-027 was January 27, 1988, the 27th day of 1988.

jump   A departure from the normal sequence of executing instructions in a computer. Synonymous with BRANCH and TRANSFER. See CONDITIONAL TRANSFER and UNCONDITIONAL TRANSFER.

junk   Usually refers to garbled data received over a communications line. If proper communication is not established with a remote system, random, meaningless characters (junk) may appear on the screen. See GARBAGE.

justification   (1) The act of adjusting, arranging, or shifting digits to the left or right to make them fit a prescribed pattern. (2) The alignment of text margins on both right and left sides. Justified text is both flush left and flush right.

justify (1) To align the characters in a field. For example, to left justify, the first character (e.g., the MOST SIGNIFICANT DIGIT) is written in the first or left-hand character position in the field. (2) In word processing, the ability to print with precisely even margins on both the left- and right-hand sides of the copy.

juxtaposition The positioning of items adjacent to each other.

K

K (1) An abbreviation for KILO, or 1000 in decimal notation. For example, "100K ch/s" means "a reading speed of 100,000 characters per second." (2) Loosely, when referring to storage capacity, 2^{10}; in decimal notation, 1024. The expression 8K represents 8192 (8 x 1024).

Kaypro The brand name for a family of portable computers manufactured by Non-Linear Systems of Solana Beach, California.

Karnaugh map A two-dimensional plot of a truth table.

kb An abbreviation for KILOBYTE (1024 bytes).

kc An abbreviation for KILOCHARACTER; One thousand characters per second. Used to express the rate of data transfer operations.

keep-out areas User specified areas on a printed circuit board layout where components or circuit paths must not be located.

Kelvin Temperature expressed on the Kelvin thermodynamic scale, in which measurements are made from absolute zero.

kernel The set of programs in an operating system that implement the most primitive of that system's functions.

kerning The reduction of excess white space between specific letter pairs.

key (1) To enter data into a system by means of a keyboard. (2) Control field or fields that identify a record. (3) The field that determines the position of a record in a sorted sequence. (4) A lever on a manually operated machine, such as a keyboard.

keyboard An input device used to key programs and data into the computer's storage. See DVORAK KEYBOARD, MALTRON KEYBOARD, and QWERTY KEYBOARD.

keyboarding The process of entering programs and data onto input media or directly into the computer by typing on a keyboard, such as using the keyboard of a word processor or computer terminal.

keyboard terminal A typewriter-like keyboard that allows data to be entered into a computer system.

keyboard-to-disk system A data entry system in which data can be entered directly onto a disk by typing the data at a keyboard.

keyboard-to-tape system A data entry system in which data can be entered directly onto a tape by typing the data at a keyboard.

key bounce Characteristic of some poorly designed keyboards where a character registers twice for each time the user presses the key.

key data entry device The equipment, including keyboards, key-to-disk units, and key-to-tape units, used to prepare data so that computer equipment can accept it.

keypad An input device that uses a set of decimal digit keys (0-9) and special function keys. Used as a separate device or sometimes located on devices to the right of a standard keyboard.

key stations Terminals used for data input on a multiuser system.

keystroke The action of pressing a single key or a combination of keys on a keyboard. Speed in many data entry jobs is measured in keystrokes per minute.

key switch The switch part of the input key on a keyboard.

key-to-address See HASHING.

keyboard-to-disk unit A keyboard unit used to store data directly on a floppy disk.

keyboard-to-tape unit A keyboard unit used to store data directly on magnetic tape.

keyword **(1)** One of the significant and informative words in a title or document that describe the content of that document. **(2)** A primary element in a programming language statement (e.g., words such as LET, PRINT, and INPUT in the BASIC programming language). **(3)** A set of words that have special meaning to a computer program. For example, DIR is a command that directs the operating system to produce a DIRECTORY of files stored on a floppy disk.

key-word-in-context See KWIC.

kHz An abbreviation for KILOHERTZ.

kill To delete. To terminate a process before it reaches its natural conclusion. A method of erasing information.

kilo Metric prefix meaning one thousand, or 10^3. Abbreviated K.

kilobaud One thousand bits per second. Used to measure data communications speeds.

kilobit One thousand bits.

kilobyte Specifically, 1024 bytes. It is commonly abbreviated K and used as a suffix when describing memory size. Thus, 24K really means a ($24 \times 1024 =$) 24,576 byte memory system.

kilocycle One thousand cycles.

kilohertz (kHz) One thousand cycles per second—a measure of data transmission frequencies.

kilomegacycle One billion cycles per second.

kinematics A computer-aided engineering process for plotting or animating the motion of parts in a machine or a structure under design on the system.

kludge Makeshift. Pertaining to a collection of mismatched components that have been assembled into a system.

knowledge acquisition Machine learning.

knowledge base A data base of knowledge about a particular subject. The data base contains facts, inferences, and procedures needed for problem solution.

knowledge engineering The engineering discipline whereby knowledge is integrated into computer systems to solve complex problems normally requiring a high level of human expertise.

knowledge industries The industries that perform data processing and provide information products and services.

knowledge representation The structure and organization of the information required for a problem.

knowledge work A term used for occupations where the primary activities involve receiving, processing, and transmitting information.

KoalaPad An inexpensive digitizing tablet for microcomputers.

KWIC An acronym for KEY-WORD-IN-CONTEXT. A method of indexing information by preselected words or phrases, which takes into consideration the context in which the words are used.

L

label An identifier or name used in a computer program to identify or describe an instruction, statement, message, data value, record, item, or file. Same as NAME.

lag The relative difference between two events, mechanisms, or states.

LAN An acronym for LOCAL AREA NETWORK. Hardware and software systems that undertake the job of interdevice communications within limited distances.

land The area of a printed circuit board available for mounting electronic components.

language A set of rules, representations, and conventions used to convey information. See PROGRAMMING LANGUAGE.

language processor A program that translates human-written source language programs into a form that can be executed on a computer. There are three general types of language processors: assembler, compiler, and interpreter.

language prompt   Same as PROMPT.

language statement   A statement coded by a user of a computing system that conveys information to a processing program, such as a language translator program, service program, or control program. A statement may signify that an operation be performed, or it may simply contain data to be passed to the processing program.

language subset   A part of a language that can be used independently of the rest of the language.

language translation   The process of changing information from one language to another, such as from BASIC to Pascal or from FORTRAN to Modula-2.

language translator program   A program that transforms statements from one language to another without significantly changing their meaning (e.g., a COMPILER or ASSEMBLER).

lap top computer   A notebook or briefcase size portable computer, usually weighing less than 10 pounds.

large scale integration   The process of placing a large number (usually over 100) of integrated circuits on one silicon chip. Abbreviated LSI. See INTEGRATED CIRCUIT.

laser   A device that uses the principle of amplification of electromagnetic waves by simulated emission of radiation and operates in the infrared, visible, or ultraviolet region. The term laser is an acronym for LIGHT AMPLIFICATION BY SIMULATED EMISSION OF RADIATION.

laser printer   A nonimpact printing device that places images on a rotating drum using a laser beam. The drum picks up a toner powder on the laser exposed areas. These areas on the drum are pressed and fused into the paper forming the characters. Laser printer output often looks like a good Xerox copy of a document typed with a carbon-ribbon typewriter. See CANON ENGINE.

laser storage   An auxiliary storage device using laser technology to encode data onto a metallic surface.

last in-first out   See LIFO.

last in-last out See LILO.

latency The rotational delay in reading or writing a record to a direct access auxiliary storage device such as a disk.

layer A subset of the data in a graphics file given a logical association.

layering A logical concept that associates subgroups of graphic data within a single drawing. It allows a user to view only those parts of a drawing being worked on, and it reduces the confusion that might result from viewing all parts of a very complex file.

layout The overall design or plan, such as system flowcharts, schematics, diagrams, format for printer output, and makeup of a document (book).

layout sheet Grid paper designed to map the display screen for purposes of program planning. Text and graphics can be sketched in terms of rows and columns or the graphics x-y coordinates.

LCD An abbreviation for LIQUID CRYSTAL DISPLAY. A way to make letters and numbers appear by reflecting light on a special crystalline substance. It features high visibility in high illumination levels but no visibility in low illumination levels. Because of its thin profile, LCD technology is often used in pocket calculators, pocket computers, briefcase computers, keyboards, and other devices.

LDL An abbreviation for LANGUAGE DESCRIPTION LANGUAGE. A metalanguage—a language that describes a language.

leader A blank section of tape at the beginning of a reel of magnetic tape.

leading The vertical distance between the maximum lower limit of a line of type and the maximum upper limit of the next line.

leading edge (1) In optical scanning, the edge of the document or page that enters the read position first. (2) A buzz word implying technological leadership: "on the leading edge of technology."

Leading Edge Model D™ A low-cost microcomputer compatible with the IBM Personal Computer™.

leaf The terminal node(s) of a tree diagram.

lease A method of acquiring the use of a computer system. A lease contract requires no financing and is less expensive than renting the system.

leased line A data communications line for which the user pays a flat monthly charge regardless of usage.

leasing companies Companies that specialize in leasing computer equipment, which they purchase from a computer manufacturer.

least significant digit Pertaining to that digit of a number that has the least weight or significance (e.g., in the number 86423, the least significant digit is 3). Abbreviated LSD. See JUSTIFY and LOW ORDER.

LED An abbreviation for LIGHT EMITTING DIODE, a commonly used alphanumeric display unit that glows when supplied with a specified voltage.

left justify See JUSTIFY.

legend The explanation of the bars, points, symbols, pie segments, or lines used in a graph or chart. Often placed at the side or bottom of a graph or chart.

length The number of characters, bytes, or bits in a computer word. A variable word is made up of several characters ending with a special end character. A fixed word is composed of the same number of bits, bytes, or characters in each word. See FIXED WORD LENGTH and VARIABLE WORD LENGTH.

less than A term referring to an inequality between two numbers. The symbol is <, with the point toward the smaller number. $5 < 9$ means 5 is less than 9.

letter quality A term applied to printed copy of the highest quality. Printing comparable to that obtained on a good typewriter. Contrast with DRAFT QUALITY.

letter-quality printer A printer that produces clear, sharp characters on ordinary paper. The most common type uses a daisy-shaped wheel with characters on the ends of flexible stalks. As the wheel spins at high speed and the print head moves across the page, a hammer strikes the appropriate letters, producing text of higher quality than even a fine typewriter. Some printers of this type use thimble or golf-ball print mechanisms instead of a daisy wheel. Some high-quality dot-matrix printers produce output that is almost letter quality.

letter shift A keyboard key (or the code generated by the key) that signifies that the characters that follow are to be read as letters until a figure shift appears in the message. Same as FIGURE SHIFT.

level The degree of subordination in a hierarchy. A measure of the distance from a node to the root of a tree.

lexicon A language with definitions for all terms.

LF An abbreviation for LINE FEED.

librarian (1) A program or group of programs that maintain the libraries of an operating system. (2) A person responsible for an organization's library of technical documentation, including manuals used by programmers, operators, and other employees. (3) A person responsible for the safe-keeping of all computer files, such as disk packs, magnetic tapes, and floppy disks. Also called a FILE LIBRARIAN and TAPE LIBRARIAN.

library A published collection of programs, routines, and subroutines available to every user of the computer. Same as PROGRAM LIBRARY. See DISK LIBRARY and TAPE LIBRARY.

library automation Application of computers and other technology to library operations and services.

library manager The program that maintains the programs stored in an operating system.

library routine A tested routine maintained in a program library.

license contract A piece of paper that authorizes the purchase of a software product to run the product on his or her computer.

life-cycle The course of a program or system from the inception of the original idea through development, implementation, and maintenance, until it is either replaced or no longer useful.

LIFO An acronym for **LAST IN-FIRST OUT**, the way most microprocessor program stacks operate. The last data or instruction word placed on the stack is the first to be retrieved. See FIFO and PUSH DOWN STACK.

light emitting diode See LED.

light guide A channel designed for the transmission of light, such as a cable of optical fibers.

lightness The amount of light or dark present in a particular color.

light pen An electrical device that resembles a pen and can be used to write or sketch on the screen of a visual display screen to provide input to the computer through its use. A tool for display terminal operators. It is connected to the computer by a cable.

LILO An acronym for **LAST IN-LAST OUT**. A method of storing and retrieving items from a list, table, or stack, such that the last item placed on the stack is the last to be retrieved. Same as FIFO. Contrast with FILO.

limit check An input control technique that tests the value of a data field to determine whether values fall within set limits or a given range.

limiting operation In computer terms, the capacity of a total system with no alternative routing can be no greater than the operation with the least capacity. The total system can be effectively scheduled by simply scheduling the limiting operation. Synonymous with BOTTLENECK.

line (1) In computer graphics, a particular set of points. Lines in geometry extend in two directions without end. In mathematics, unless otherwise stated, lines are always thought to be straight. (2) In a programming language like BASIC, a line begins with a number and contains one or more BASIC statements.

linear list An ordered set of data that makes use of pointers.

linear programming A technique for finding an optimum combination when there may be no single best one. For example, linear programming could be used to solve the problem: What combination of foods would give the most calories and best nutrition for the least money? A computer is often used because such problems would take too long to solve by hand. Abbreviated LP.

linear search A search that begins with the first element and compares until a matching key is found or the end of the list is reached.

linear structure **(1)** In data base management systems, a mode of file organization in which each primary record can own only one secondary record. The latter functions as an overflow record for the primary record. **(2)** A sequential arrangement of data records.

line-at-a-time printer Prints an entire line of information at a time.

line balancing A management technique used in production environments wherein tasks are assigned to computer graphics workstations in equal proportions, thus raising efficiency.

line chart A method of charting business data.

line circuit A physical circuit path, such as a data communications line.

line drawing A drawing where an object's image is represented by a solid-line outline of the surface.

line feed The operation that advances printer paper by one line. Abbreviated **LF**. See FORM FEED.

line filter A device used to correct electromagnetic interference that comes in over the power line.

line generator A hardware or software system that produces lines on a computer graphics system in random configurations.

line height The height of one line of type. It is measured by the number of lines per vertical inch.

line number In programming languages such as BASIC, a number that begins a line of the source program for purposes of identification; a numerical label.

line of code A statement in a programming language usually occupying one line of code.

line per minute Usually used to describe the speed of a line printer. Abbreviated LPM.

line plot A graph with displayed data points and straight lines connecting the points.

line printer An output device that prints output one line at a time.

line printer controller A device that provides character-print buffers and automatic control and timing for a specific printer.

line printing The printing of an entire line of characters as a unit.

line segment A portion of a longer line defined by its two end points.

line speed The maximum rate at which signals may be transmitted over a given channel, usually in baud, or bits per second.

line style In computer graphics, the method of representing a line in a graphics system, such as with dashes, solid lines, or dots.

line surge A sudden high-voltage condition. Short surges of high voltage can cause misregistration, false logic, lost data and even destruction of delicate circuits in computers, data entry terminals, and data communications equipment. These spikes can be a result of inductive load switching of transformers and other types of equipment—even from lightning and static. Equipment can be protected from voltage surges by using surge protectors. See SURGE PROTECTOR.

line voltage The AC voltage that comes out of a standard wall socket.

line width The actual physical thickness of a line in a graphics system.

linguistics The study of language. SYNTAX determines what makes a sentence of a natural language, or a program of a programming language, grammatical. SEMANTICS specifies how the words of a sentence or the statements of a program, work together to give it its overall meaning. PARSING is the process of breaking a string of words into the pieces—such as noun phrase and verb phrase—specified by the syntax.

link In data communications, a physical connection between one location and another whose function is to transmit data. See COMMUNICATIONS CHANNEL.

linkage Coding that connects two separately coded routines, such as the coding that links a subroutine to the program with which it is to be used. See CALLING SEQUENCE.

linker A program that links other programs or sections of programs. It combines separate program modules into one executable program.

linking loader An executive program that connects different program segments so that they may be run in the computer as one unit. A useful piece of software that makes subtasks easily available to a main task.

link register A register of one bit that acts as an extension of the accumulator during rotation or carry operations. Also called carry register.

links Data communications channels in a computer network.

LIPS An acronym for LOGICAL INFERENCES PER SECOND, the unit of measurement of speed for fifth generation computers.

liquid crystal display A visual display made of two sheets of polarizing material sandwiched together with a nematic liquid crystal solution between them. Images are produced when electric currents cause the liquid crystals to align so light cannot shine through. Abbreviated LCD.

LISP An acronym for LIST PROCESSING. A high-level programming language primarily designed to process data consisting of lists. It is especially suited for text manipulation and analysis. It is a popular language used for solving artificial intelligence problems. See PROLOG. Here is a sample program written in LISP.

```
(DEFINE
(FACTORIAL X)
(PROG (F)
(SETQ F 1)
AGAIN
(COND
((ZEROP X)
(RETURN F)))
(SETQ F(TIMES F X))
(SETQ X (SUB1 X))
(GO AGAIN)))
```

LISP machine A computer designed specifically for artificial intelligence applications and especially designed to run LISP software.

list (1) Organization of data using indexes and pointers to allow for nonsequential retrieval. (2) An ordered set of items. (3) To print every relevant item of input data. (4) A command to print program statements; for example, the LIST command in the BASIC language will cause the system to print a listing of the program. (5) An ordered collection of atoms.

listing Generally, any printout produced on a printing device. For example, a source listing is a printout of the source program processed by the compiler; an error listing is a report showing all input data found to be invalid by the processing program. See ASSEMBLY LISTING.

list processing A method of processing data in the form of lists. Usually, chained lists are used so that the logical order of items can be changed without altering their physical locations.

list processing languages Languages designed especially to process data that is in list form. Two popular examples are LISP and PROLOG.

liter A metric unit of liquid capacity equal to one cubic decimeter.

literal Another name for CONSTANT. A symbol that defines itself. Contrast with VARIABLE.

live data The actual data to be processed by the computer program.

load (1) To read information into the storage of a computer. (2) To put a diskette into a floppy disk drive or a tape reel onto a magnetic tape drive.

load-and-go An operating technique in which the loading and execution phases of a program are performed in one continuous run. See COMPILE-AND-GO.

loader A service routine designed to read programs into internal storage in preparation for their execution.

load module A computer program in a form that is suitable to be immediately executed by the circuitry of the computer.

load point A spot at the beginning of a recording area of a magnetic tape.

load sharing The technique of using two or more computers to handle excess volume during peak periods. It is desirable to have one computer handle less than peak loads and the other act as the fallback equipment.

local (1) Pertaining to computer equipment at one's own location. (2) Pertaining to items used only in one defined part of a program. Contrast with GLOBAL.

local area network A network of computer equipment confined to a small area (room, building, site) and interconnected by dedicated communications channels. These computers not only can intercommunicate but also can share resources such as disk storage and printers. Also called a local network. Abbreviated LAN.

local intelligence Processing power and storage capacity built into a terminal so it does not need to be connected to a computer to perform certain tasks. A dumb terminal has no local intelligence. See SMART TERMINAL.

local store A relatively small number of high-speed storage elements that may be directly referred to by the instructions.

local variable A variable that has meaning only within a particular function or subroutine. See GLOBAL VARIABLE.

location A place in the computer's memory where information is to be stored.

lock (1) To permit exclusive use of a computer resource. (2) To protect a disk or tape file from being changed or erased.

lock code A sequence of letters and/or numbers provided by the operators of a time-sharing system to prevent unauthorized tampering with a user's program. Serves as a secret password in that the computer will refuse any changes to the program unless the user supplies the correct lock code.

locked-up keyboard A situation in which the computer does not respond to key presses. Used for computer security purposes.

locking a disk A disk is locked when it has been write protected. This measure ensures that the contents of a disk are preserved from being written over by other data from a computer. See WRITE-PROTECT NOTCH.

lockout (1) Suppression of an interrupt. (2) A programming technique used in a multiprocessing environment to prevent access to critical data by both CPUs at the same time.

lock-up A situation in which no further action may occur.

log A record of operations of a computer system listing each job or run, the time it required, operator actions, and other pertinent data.

logarithm The exponent of the power to which a fixed number is to be raised to produce a given number. The fixed number is called the base and is usually 10 or e. In the example $2^3 = 8$, 3 is the logarithm of 8 to the base 2; this means that 2 must be raised to the third power to produce 8.

logging-in The process of establishing communication with and verifying the authority to use the computer during conversational programming. See CONVERSATIONAL MODE.

logging-off The process of terminating communication between the computer and the user.

logic (1) The science dealing with the formal principles of reasoning and thought. (2) The basic principles and application of truth tables and the interconnection among logical elements required for arithmetic computation in an automatic data processing system.

logical data design Design showing relationships among data; how the data is viewed by applications programs or individual users.

logical decision Generally, a decision as to which two possible courses of action is to be followed, based upon some comparison of values.

logical design The specification of the working relationships among the parts of a system in terms of symbolic logic and without primary regard for hardware implementation.

logical error A programming mistake that causes the wrong processing to take place even though the program is syntactically correct.

logical file A collection of one or more logical records. See logical record.

logical instruction An instruction that executes an operation defined in symbolic logic, such as AND, OR, or NOR.

logical multiply The AND operator.

logical operations The computer operations that are logical in nature, such as logical tests and decisions. This is in contrast with arithmetic operations and data transfer operations, which involve no decision.

logical product The AND function of several terms. The product is 1 only when all of the terms are 1; otherwise it is 0.

logical record A complete unit of information describing something, for example, an invoice, a payroll roster, or an inventory. In an inventory file containing 1,000 different product items, there are 1,000 logical records, one for each item. Contrast with PHYSICAL RECORD.

logical representation A knowledge representation consisting of a collection of logical formulas.

logical sum The inclusive OR function of several terms. The sum is 1 when any or all of the terms are 1; it is 0 only when all are 0.

logical symbol A symbol used to represent a logic operator.

logical unit number A number assigned to a physical peripheral device.

logical value A value that may be either true or false depending on the result of a particular logical decision.

logic card A circuit board that contains components and wiring that perform one or more logic functions or operations.

logic circuits A series of flip-flops and gates that direct electrical impulses to and from the appropriate portions of a computer system.

logic diagram A diagram that represents a logical design and sometimes the hardware implementation.

logic element A device that performs a logic function.

logic error An error caused by a mistake in the algorithm.

logic gates Components in electrical digital circuitry.

logic operator Any of the Boolean operators such as AND, OR, NAND, EXCLUSIVE OR, and NOR.

logic programming An approach to knowledge representation, usually associated with PROLOG, which uses logic and inference to express and solve problems.

logic symbol A symbol used to represent a logic element graphically.

logic theorist An early information processing program able to prove theorems.

logic theory The science that deals with logical operations, which are the basis of computer operations.

log in To sign in on a computer. Same as LOG ON.

log-in name The name by which the computer system knows a user.

LOGO A high-level programming language that assumes the user has access to some type of graphics terminal. The language was designed for school students and seems particularly suited to those in the younger age groups. It is highly interactive, permitting children to learn quickly how to draw geometric patterns and pictures on the screen. It was developed at the Massachusetts Institute of Technology by Seymour Papert. Here is a sample program written in LOGO.

```
TO BOX
10 FORWARD 100
```

```
20 RIGHT 90
30 FORWARD 100
40 RIGHT 90
50 FORWARD 100
60 RIGHT 90
70 FORWARD 100
```

log off To terminate connection with the computer. Same as LOG OUT.

log on The action by which a user begins a terminal session. Same as LOG IN.

log out To stop using the computer. The process of signing off the system. Same as LOG OFF.

look-alike (1) A program that imitates another program so closely that users of the original program can use the look-alike program without learning any new operating instructions. (2) A product that copies another. Often when a vendor produces a successful product, its competitors offer look-alike products.

look-up See TABLE LOOK-UP.

loop A sequence of instructions in a program that can be executed repetitively until certain specified conditions are satisfied. See CLOSED LOOP.

loop code The repetition of a sequence of instructions by using a program loop. Loop coding requires more execution time than would straight-line coding but will result in a savings of storage. Contrast with STRAIGHT LINE CODE.

loophole A mistake or omission in software or hardware that allows the system's access controls to be circumvented.

looping Executing the same instruction or series of instructions over and over again.

loop structure One of three primary structures of a structured flowchart. It provides for repetitive execution of a function until a condition is reached.

loop technology A method of connecting communicating machines together in a computer network.

Lotus 1-2-3™ An integrated software system whose name represents its three functions: electronic spreadsheet, data base functions, and graphics. Users like the ability to move back and forth between these modes—to analyze information both numerically and graphically, and to use the data base functions to sort the rows of a spreadsheet into a new order or to search for entries that meet a particular criterion. While Lotus 1-2-3™ provides all of the features found on any other electronic spreadsheet program, however, it is easy to learn and easy to use. See INTEGRATED SOFTWARE.

low activity   Condition when a small proportion of the total records are processed during an updating run.

lower case   Noncapitalized alphabetic letters. Contrast with UPPER CASE.

lower-level management   First-line supervisors who make the operating decisions to ensure that specific jobs are done.

low-level language   A machine-dependent programming language translated by an assembler into instructions and data formats for a given machine. Same as ASSEMBLY LANGUAGE. Contrast with HIGH-LEVEL LANGUAGE.

low order   Pertaining to the digit or digits of a number that have the least weight or significance; for example, in the number 694312, the low-order digit is 2. Contrast with HIGH ORDER. See LEAST SIGNIFICANT DIGIT.

low-res graphics   Abbreviated version of low-resolution graphics, a blocky and jagged picture on a display screen produced by a small number of pixels. Contrast with HI-RES GRAPHICS.

low resolution   Pertaining to the quality and accuracy of detail that can be represented by a graphics display. Resolution quality depends upon the number of basic image-forming units (pixels) within a picture image—the greater the number, the higher the resolution. Low-resolution pictures are produced by a small number of pixels and, therefore, are not as short and clear as high-resolution pictures. Contrast with HIGH RESOLUTION. See RESOLUTION.

LP   An abbreviation for LINEAR PROGRAMMING and LINE PRINTER. Linear programming is a technique for finding an optimum combination when there may be no single best one. A line printer is a high-speed output device that prints a line at a time, and several hundred or thousand lines per minute.

LPM An abbreviation for **LINES PER MINUTE**.

LSC An abbreviation for **LEAST SIGNIFICANT CHARACTER**.

LSD An abbreviation for **LEAST SIGNIFICANT DIGIT**.

LSI An abbreviation for **LARGE SCALE INTEGRATION**. See **INTEGRATED CIRCUIT**.

luminance Portions of composite video signal controlling brightness.

luminance decay The reduction in screen brightness on a visual display terminal, which inevitably occurs over time.

luminosity Same as **LUMINANCE**.

M

M Abbreviation for mega, meaning one million. Used to represent 1,048,576. Often used to label the capacity of storage devices, such as disks.

MacDraw™ A drawing program designed for artists, architects, engineers, draftsmen and similar professionals in the graphic arts. Used on the Apple Macintosh microcomputer.

machine address Same as absolute address.

machine code An operation code that a machine is designed to recognize.

machine cycle The time period it takes for a computer to perform a given number of internal operations.

machine-dependent Pertaining to a language or a program that works on only one particular type of computer. Synonymous with hardware-dependent.

machine error A deviation from correctness in data resulting from an equipment failure.

machine independent **(1)** Pertaining to a language or program developed in terms of the problem rather than in terms of the characteristics of the computer system. **(2)** Pertaining to the ability to run a program on computers made by different manufacturers or on various machines made by the same manufacturer.

machine instruction An instruction that a computer can directly recognize and execute. See INSTRUCTION.

machine intelligence See ARTIFICIAL INTELLIGENCE.

machine language The basic language of a computer. Programs written in machine language require no further interpretation by a computer. Contrast with SOURCE LANGUAGE.

machine learning Refers to a heuristic process whereby a device improves its performance based on past actions. See ARTIFICIAL INTELLIGENCE and HEURISTIC.

machine operator See COMPUTER OPERATOR.

machine-oriented language A programming language that is more like a machine language than a human language.

machine-readable information Information recorded on any medium in such a way that it can be sensed or read by a machine. Also called MACHINE-SENSIBLE.

machine-run See RUN.

machine-sensible See MACHINE-READABLE INFORMATION™.

Macintosh™ A popular microcomputer system manufactured by Apple Computer, Inc. As sports cars and racing cars have frequently led the way in auto design, the Macintosh has been the trend setter on how a computer and its software should interact with the user. Some of the Macintosh innovations that are now standard tools of the trade are: using a "mouse" for moving the cursor around on the screen, "windows" for displaying various applications at once, and "icons" for indicating a tool or function with a picture instead of words. Newer versions of the Macintosh include the Macintosh II and Macintosh SE.

MacPaint™ A drawing program for the Macintosh microcomputer. A classic program whose features have been included in all popular drawing programs. It allows one to use a mouse to "pick up" paint cans, sprayers, various sized brushes, and geometric shapes, flip them around the screen and create instant art. It is a landmark microcomputer program developed by Apple Computer, Inc. See MACINTOSH.

macro A single, symbolic programming-language statement that when translated results in a series of machine-language statements.

macro assembler An assembler that allows the user to create and define new computer instructions (called MACROINSTRUCTIONS).

macro instruction (1) A source-language instruction that is equivalent to a specified number of machine-language instructions. (2) A machine-language instruction that is composed of several micro instructions.

MacWrite™ A word processing application program for the Macintosh microcomputer, developed by Apple Computer, Inc. This program was bundled with the original Macintoshes to showcase the machines' astonishing graphic talents. Commonly used to create printed documents that contain graphic images created with MacPaint. See MACINTOSH.

macroprogramming Programming with macroinstructions, such as writing control programs for a microprocessor.

mag An abbreviated version of **MAGNETIC**.

magazines, computer-oriented A number of popular magazines contain useful information concerning computers and available hardware and software for them. Most computer stores and larger bookstores carry a good assortment of these magazines.

magnetic Of or producing, caused by, or operated by magnetism.

magnetic bubble memory A memory that uses magnetic "bubbles" that move. The bubbles are locally magnetized areas that can move about in a magnetic material, such as a plate of orthoferrite. It is possible to control the reading in and out of this bubble within the magnetic material, and as a result, a very high-capacity memory can be built. Andrew Bobeck, Richard Sherwood, Umberto Gianola, and William Shockley of Bell Laboratories, invented magnetic bubble memory.

magnetic bubbles Circular magnetic domains having a magnetization opposite that of the substrate that can be shifted about in the substrate material under the inductive influence of surface control electrodes. Under suitable polarized light, the domains are observable as small circular areas, or bubbles.

magnetic card A storage device consisting of a tray or cartridge of magnetically coated cards made of material similar to magnetic tape (although considerably thicker) and with specific areas allocated for storing information. A magnetic card may be visualized as a magnetic tape cut into strips, then placed side by side on a plastic card and mounted on a cartridge. See DATA CELL.

magnetic characters A set of characters, used for checks, insurance billings, utility bills, invoices, and so forth, which permit special character-reading devices (MICR readers) to be employed to read the characters automatically. See MAGNETIC INK CHARACTER RECOGNITION.

magnetic disk A disk made of rigid material (hard disk) or heavy mylar (floppy disk). The disk surface is used to hold magnetized data which is written on the disk and retrieved from the disk by a disk drive.

magnetic disk unit A peripheral storage device in which data are recorded on a magnetizable disk surface. See DIRECT ACCESS, DISK PACK, FIXED-HEAD DISK UNIT, FLOPPY DISK, HARD DISK, and MOVEABLE-HEAD DISK UNIT.

magnetic domain A magnetized spot representing data in bubble memory.

magnetic film storage A storage device that uses 35 mm magnetic film contained on a spool. The spool may be loaded onto a film handler unit.

magnetic head A device used for reading and writing information on devices such as magnetic tapes, disks, or drums.

magnetic ink An ink that contains particles of a magnetic substance whose presence can be detected by magnetic sensors.

magnetic ink character reader An input device that reads documents imprinted with magnetic ink characters.

magnetic ink character recognition   The recognition, by machines, of characters printed with a special magnetic ink. Used primarily in the banking, public utilities and credit card industries. Abbreviated MICR.

magnetic resonance   The phenomenon in which a movement of a particle or system of particles is coupled resonantly to an external magnetic field.

magnetic storage   Any system that utilizes the magnetic properties of materials to store data on such devices and media as disks and tapes.

magnetic strip card   A small card resembling a credit card to which a strip of magnetizable material is affixed. Information can be read from or written on this magnetic strip.

magnetic tape   A plastic tape having a magnetic surface for storing data in a code of magnetized spots. Information may be represented on tape using an 8-bit coding structure. A reel of tape is about 750 meters (2,400 feet) in length. Information is written on the tape and retrieved from the tape by a tape drive. See MAGNETIC TAPE CASSETTE.

magnetic tape cartridge   A magnetic tape contained in a cartridge. The cartridge consists of a reel of tape and the take-up reel. It is similar to a cassette but of slightly different design.

magnetic tape cassette   A magnetic tape storage device, consisting of 1/8-inch magnetic tape housed in a plastic container.

magnetic tape cassette recorder   An input/output and storage device that reads and writes cassette tapes.

magnetic tape code   The system of coding that is used to record magnetized patterns on magnetic tape. The magnetized patterns represent alphanumeric data. See ASCII, BCD and EBCDIC.

magnetic tape deck   Same as MAGNETIC TAPE UNIT.

magnetic tape density   The number of characters that can be recorded on 1 inch (2.5 cm) of magnetic tape. Common densities are 800 and 1,600 characters per inch (cpi), but some devices can record and read 6,250 cpi.

magnetic tape drive A device that moves tape past a head. Synonymous with MAGNETIC TAPE TRANSPORT.

magnetic tape reel A reel used to preserve the physical characteristics of magnetic tape. The tape is usually ½ inch (1.27 cm) wide and 2,400 feet (751.5 meters) in length.

magnetic tape sorting A sort program that uses magnetic tapes for auxiliary storage during a sort.

magnetic tape transport Same as MAGNETIC TAPE DRIVE.

magnetic tape unit A device containing a magnetic tape drive together with reading and writing heads and associated controls. Synonymous with MAGNETIC TAPE DECK. See MAGNETIC TAPE CASSETTE RECORDER.

magnetic thin film See THIN FILM.

magnitude (1) The absolute value of a number. (2) Size.

magstripe A small stripe of magnetic material found on the back of many credit cards. The magstripe contains information such as account number, card holder's name, etc.

magtape A term sometimes used instead of magnetic tape. See magnetic tape.

mail box A set of locations in a storage area. An area reserved for data addressed to specific peripheral devices or other processors.

mailing list program A program that maintains names, addresses, and related data, and produces mailing labels of them.

mail-merging The process of automatically printing form letters with names and addresses from a mailing list file. A mail-merge program merges address information from one file with textual information from another file.

mainframe A large, expensive computer generally used for information processing in large businesses, colleges, and organizations. Originally, the phrase referred to the extensive array of large rack and panel cabinets that held thousands of vacuum tubes in early computers. Mainframes can occupy an entire room and have very large data-handling capacities. They are far more costly than microcomputers or minicomputers. Mainframes are the largest, fastest and most expensive class of computers. (Supercomputers are the largest, fastest and most expensive of the mainframes). See MICROCOMPUTERS, MINICOMPUTERS, and SUPER-COMPUTERS.

main-line program The section of a program that controls the order of execution of other modules in the program.

main memory Same as INTERNAL STORAGE and MAIN STORAGE.

main storage Addressable storage directly controlled by the central processing unit (CPU). The CPU uses main storage to store programs while they are being executed and data while they are being processed. Same as INTERNAL STOR-AGE and PRIMARY STORAGE. Contrast with AUXILIARY STORAGE.

maintainability The characteristic associated with the isola-tion and repair of a failure.

maintenance Any activity intended to eliminate faults or to keep hardware or programs in satisfactory working condi-tion, including tests, measurements, replacements, adjust-ments, and repairs.

maintenance programmer An individual who works with pro-grams that have already been implemented into an infor-mation system, making changes as needed from time to time.

maintenance routine A routine designed to help a customer service technician carry out routine preventive maintenance on a computer system.

major sort key A field containing data (such as a last name) by which most data items can be distinguished and sorted. When duplications occur in this field, a minor sort key (such as a first name) may supply the necessary distinction.

malfunction A failure in the operation of the central process-ing unit or peripheral device. The effect of a FAULT. Contrast with ERROR and MISTAKE. See CRASH.

Maltron keyboard A keyboard layout that allows potentially faster speeds and is easier to learn than the traditional QWERTY layout. The keyboard is designed so that the keys used most frequently are positioned beneath the strongest digits. Thus, the home keys for the right hand are: 't','h','o', and 'r'; and for the left hand 'a','n','i', and 's'. Up to eight keys are assigned to each thumb. Each key is positioned at the correct height for the finger that uses it, thus minimizing unnaturally long finger stretches and making the keyboard less tiring to use than traditional keyboards. Numbers can be typed in sequence. See DVORAK KEYBOARD and QWERTY KEYBOARD.

management graphics Charts, graphs, and other visual representations of the operational or strategic aspects of a business, intended to aid management in assimilating and presenting business data.

management information system An information system designed to supply organizational managers with the necessary information needed to plan, organize, staff, direct, and control the operations of the organization. Abbreviated MIS.

management report A report designed to help managers and decision-makers perform their jobs.

management science A mathematical or quantitative study of the management of a business's resources, usually with the aid of a computer.

manager A person responsible for guiding the operations of a computer center, programming group, software development group, service organization, and so on.

manipulating The act of working on data to put it into a form that has greater meaning to the user.

manpower loading chart A histogram showing the allocation of labor by time period.

mantissa That part of a floating point number that specifies the significant digits of the number. For example, in .82169 x 10^3, .82169 is the mantissa. See CHARACTERISTIC.

manual input Data entered manually by the computer user to modify, continue, or resume processing of a computer program.

manual operation Processing of data in a system by direct manual techniques.

manufacturer's software A set of programming aids that the computer manufacturer supplies or makes available with a computer. See SYSTEMS PROGRAMS.

map A list that indicates the area of storage occupied by various elements of a program and its data. Also called STORAGE MAP.

mapping A transformation from one set to another set; a correspondence. For example, the process by which a graphic system translates graphic data from one coordinate system into a form useful on another coordinate system.

margin The number of spaces between the right or left edge of a page (or window) and the beginning of text.

marginal checking A preventative maintenance procedure in which the unit under test is varied from its normal value in an effort to detect and locate components that are operating in a marginal condition.

mark A sign or symbol used to signify or indicate an event in time or space.

marker A symbol used within a line chart to indicate data points. Styles often used include circles, xs, asterisks, boxes, diamonds, and points.

mark sensing The ability to mark cards or pages with a pencil to be read directly into the computer via a mark sense reader. See OPTICAL MARK READER.

maser An acronym for MICROWAVE AMPLIFICATION BY THE STIMULATED EMISSION OF RADIATION. A device capable of amplifying or generating radio frequency radiation. Maser amplifiers are used in satellite communication ground stations to amplify the extremely weak signals received from communications satellites.

mask (1) A machine word containing a pattern of bits, bytes, or characters used to extract or select parts of other machine words by controlling an instruction that retains or eliminates selected bits, bytes, or characters. (2) In integrated circuit development, the full-sized photographic representation of a circuit designed on the system for use in the production process.

mask design The final phase of integrated circuit design by which the circuit design is realized through multiple masks corresponding to multiple layers on the integrated circuit. The mask layout must observe all process-related constraints, and minimize the area the circuit will occupy.

massage To process data.

mass storage device A device used to supply relatively inexpensive storage for large amounts of data. Examples are hard disks, videodisks, large magnetic disk systems and mass storage cartridge systems holding up to 500 billion characters.

master A device that controls the operation of one or more other devices.

master clear A switch on some computer consoles that will clear certain operational registers and prepare for a new mode of operation.

master clock The device that controls the basic timing pulses of a computer.

master data A set of data that is altered infrequently and supplies basic data for processing operations.

master file A file containing relatively permanent information that is used as a source of reference and generally updated periodically. Contrast with DETAIL FILE.

master file maintenance The process of updating, changing or modifying master files.

master-slave computer system A computer system consisting of a master computer connected to one or more slave computers. The master computer provides the scheduling function and jobs to the slave computer(s).

match To check for identity between two or more items of data. See HIT.

matching (1) A data processing operation in which two files are checked to determine whether there is a corresponding item or group of items in each file. (2) Comparing strings or parts thereof.

material requirements planning Computerized inventory control technique for dependent inventory items.

mathematical functions   A set of mathematical routines that are available in most programming languages. They are usually supplied as part of the language.

mathematical logic   The use of mathematical symbols to represent language and its processes. These symbols are manipulated in accord with mathematical rules to determine whether or not a statement or a series of statements is true or false. See LOGIC.

mathematical model   A group of mathematical expressions that represents a process, a system, or the operation of a device. See SIMULATION.

mathematical software   The set of computer algorithms in the area of mathematics.

mathematical symbols   Symbols used in formulas, equations, and flowcharts and pseudocode.

mathematics   The study of the relationships among objects or quantities, organized so that certain facts can be proved or derived from others by using logic. See APPLIED MATHEMATICS.

matrix   (1) An orderly array of symbols by rows and columns. The symbols comprising the matrix are called elements or entries of the matrix. Subscript are customarily used to indicate the row and column positions of an element in a matrix. Matrices are a way in which complicated mathematical statements can be expressed simply. Computers are often used in work with matrices. (2) A grid composed of vertical columns and horizontal rows; a spreadsheet or portion of a spreadsheet.

matrix notation   Introduced by English mathematician Arthur Cayley in 1858. He used an abbreviated notation, such as $ax = b$, for expressing systems of linear equations.

matrix printer   A printer that uses a matrix of dots to form an image of the character being printed.

mature system   A system that is fully operational and performing all the functions it was designed to accomplish.

mb   An abbreviation for megabyte. One million bytes. 1000kb.

MBASIC An abbreviation for Microsoft BASIC.

MCC An abbreviation for **MICROELECTRONICS AND COMPUTER TECHNOLOGY CORPORATION**; United States consortium of companies formed to conduct research in advanced computers.

means-ends analysis A method of reasoning that looks backward and forward from the initial point to the goal in an attempt to reduce differences.

mechanical data processing A method of data processing that involves the use of relatively small and simple (usually nonprogrammable) mechanical machines.

mechanical translation A generic term for language translation by computers or similar equipment.

mechanization The use of machines to simplify or replace work previously accomplished by human workers.

media The plural form of medium. Media can be classified as source, input, and output. Checks are an example of source media. Diskettes are an example of input media. Output media can be magnetic tape and paper printouts.

media eraser A device designed to demagnetize magnetic tapes and diskettes.

media specialist The person responsible for cataloging and maintaining storage media such as diskettes, disk packs, magnetic tapes, and other related materials.

medium The physical substance upon which data is recorded, such as floppy disks, magnetic tapes, and paper.

medium scale integration The class of integrated circuits having a density between those of large scale integration (LSI) and small scale integration (SSI). Abbreviated MSI. See integrated circuit.

mega A prefix indicating 1,048,576 actually; or roughly one million.

megabit 1,048,576 bits or 1024 kilobits, actually; or roughly one million bits or one thousand kilobits.

megabyte 1,048,576 bytes or 1024 kilobytes, actually; or roughly one million bytes or one thousand kilobytes.

megacycle One million cycles per second.

megaflop One million floating-point operations per second. See MFLOPS.

megahertz A unit of electrical frequency equal to one million cycles per second. A measure of transmission frequency. Abbreviated MHz.

membrane keyboard A keyboard constructed of two thin plastic sheets (called membranes) that are coated with a circuit made of electrically conductive ink. It is an economical, flat keyboard used in several low-priced microcomputers.

memory The storage facilities of the computer, capable of storing vast amounts of data. See AUXILIARY STORAGE, FLOPPY DISK, INTERNAL STORAGE, MAGNETIC BUBBLE MEMORY, MAGNETIC CORE STORAGE, MAGNETIC DISK, MAGNETIC DRUM, MAGNETIC TAPE, PROM, RAM, ROM, SEMICONDUCTOR STORAGE, STORAGE, and VIRTUAL STORAGE.

memory allocation See STORAGE ALLOCATION.

memory board An expansion board that adds RAM to the computer system, making it possible to store and use additional information.

memory chip A semiconductor device that stores information in the form of electrical charges. Memory chips are usually located on memory boards or system boards.

memory cycle The amount of time required to move one byte or word of information into or out of memory.

memory dump A printout showing the contents of memory.

memory management The technique of efficiently controlling and allocating memory resources.

memory map An image in memory of information appearing somewhere else. For example, in a display unit there is a memory map of the screen display, with one memory location corresponding to each character position on the display.

memory protection See STORAGE PROTECTION.

memory sniffing Refers to the continuous testing of storage during processing.

menu A list of options within a program that allows the user to choose which part to interact with. Menus allow computer users a facility for using programs without knowing any technical methods. Menus are usually an on-screen series of program options that allows you to select the course of action you wish to take; for example, print a report or to select a specific program stored on a disk.

menu-display A question-and-answer or multiple-choice interactive method of communicating with a computer system.

menu-driven software Computer programs that make extensive use of menus. Software of this type is designed so it may be used easily by people with minimal computer experience. The menus are used to select tasks to be performed.

menu item A choice in a menu.

merge To combine items into one sequenced file from two or more similarly sequenced files without changing the order of the items. Same as COLLATE.

merge print program A program that lets the user produce personalized form letters.

merge sorting algorithm An algorithm wherein the contents of two ordered arrays are combined to form a third, ordered array.

MESFET An acronym for METAL SEMICONDUCTOR FIELD EFFECT TRANSISTOR, the main active device used in gallium arsenide integrated circuits to provide current gain and inversion.

mesh A set of branches forming a closed path in a network.

message A group of characters having meaning as a whole and always handled as a group. Abbreviated MSSG.

message format Rules for the placement of such portions of a message as message heading, address text, and end of message.

message header The leading part of a message that contains information concerning the message, such as the source of destination code, priority, and type of message.

message queuing In a data communications system, a technique for controlling the handling of messages, allowing them to be accepted by a computer and stored until they have been processed or routed to another destination.

message retrieval The capability to retrieve a message sometime after it has entered an information system.

message switching The switching technique of receiving a message, storing it until the proper outgoing circuit and station are available, and then retransmitting it toward its destination. Computers are often used to perform the switching function.

message switching center A center in which messages are routed according to information contained within the messages themselves.

metacharacter In programming language systems, these characters have some controlling role in respect to the other characters with which they are associated.

metacompiler A compiler for a language used primarily for written compilers, usually syntax-oriented compilers. A special-purpose metacompiler language is not very useful for writing general programs.

metalanguage A language used to describe a language.

metallic oxide semiconductor (MOS) **(1)** A field-effect transistor in which the gate electrode is isolated from the channel by an oxide film. **(2)** A capacitor in which semiconductor material forms one plate, aluminum forms the other plate, and an oxide forms the dielectric. See CMOS.

meta-metalanguage A language that is used to describe a metalanguage.

meter Base unit of length in the SI metric system, approximately equal to 1.1 yards.

method A way of doing something.

methodology A procedure or collection of techniques used to analyze information in an orderly manner. Includes a set of standardized procedures, including technical methods, management techniques and documentation that provide the framework to accomplish a particular function.

metric system Systeme International d'Unites, or SI, the modern version of the metric system currently in use worldwide. It is based on seven base units: meter, kilogram, second, ampere, Kelvin (degrees Celsius), candela, and mole.

metric ton Measure of weight equal to 1,000 kilograms, or about 2,200 pounds.

mflops Acronym for a MILLION FLOATING-POINT OPERATIONS PER SECOND, a measure of computing power: usually associated with large mainframe computers. Short for MEGAFLOP.

MFT An abbreviation for MULTIPROGRAMMING WITH A FIXED NUMBER OF TASKS, the tasks being programs. Sometimes called (jokingly, of course) MULTIPROGRAMMING WITH A FINITE AMOUNT OF TROUBLE.

MHz An abbreviation for megahertz, one million cycles per second.

MICR An acronym for MAGNETIC INK CHARACTER RECOGNITION.

micro (1) A prefix meaning one millionth; for example, a microsecond is a millionth of a second. (2) Computerese for "quite small," for example, as in microprocessor. (3) From the Greek letter mu, meaning very small. See MEGA, one million. (4) Short for microcomputer.

microchart A chart showing the ultimate details of the program's or system's design.

microchip A tiny silicon chip with thousands of electronic components and circuit patterns etched onto its surface.

microcode A sequence of basic subcommands, or pseudocommands, built into the computer and executed automatically by hardware. Generally, these commands are in a special read-only storage unit (firmware) of the computer. These commands define the instruction set of a microprogrammable computer.

microcoding Composing computer instructions by combining basic, elementary operations or subcommands to form higher-level instructions such as addition or multiplication. See MICROINSTRUCTION, MICROPROGRAMMABLE COMPUTER, and MICROPROGRAMMING.

microcoding device A circuit board with fixed instructions for performing standard functions through miniature logic circuits, thus avoiding the need to code these instructions during programming.

microcomputer The smallest and least expensive class of computers. They are fully operational computers that use microprocessors as their CPU. Many microcomputers are used in the home as personal computers. Microcomputers are widely used in schools and businesses. See DESKTOP COMPUTER, HOME COMPUTER, LAP COMPUTER, NOTEBOOK COMPUTER, PERSONAL COMPUTER and PORTABLE COMPUTER.

microcomputer applications Microcomputers are finding applications in business, technology, industry, and the home. They are used in video game machines, traffic control systems, point-of-sale terminals, scientific instruments, blood analyzers, credit card verification, pinball machines, automotive ignition control, and inventory control systems. Industry is using microcomputers and microprocessors in microwave ovens, sewing machines, flow meters, gas station pumps, paint mixing machines, process monitoring, pollution monitoring, and as control units for hundreds of other devices.

microcomputer chip A microcomputer on a chip. Differs from a microprocessor in that it not only contains the central processing unit (CPU) but also includes on the same piece of silicon a RAM, a ROM, and input/output circuitry. Often called a "computer-on-a-chip." See MICROCOMPUTER and MICROPROCESSOR.

microcomputer components The major components of a microcomputer are a microprocessor, memory (ROM, PROM, EPROM, RAM), and input/output circuitry.

microcomputer development system A complete microcomputer system used to test and develop both the hardware and software of other microcomputer-based systems from initial development through debugging of final prototypes. A typical microcomputer development system includes assembler, a text editor, debugging facilities, hardware emulation capabilities, PROM programmer, monitor, and disk/tape I/O system.

microcomputer kit   See COMPUTER KIT.

microcomputer system   A system that includes a microcomputer, peripherals, operating system, and applications programs.

microcontroller   A device or instrument that controls a process with high resolution, usually over a narrow region. A microprogrammed machine (microcomputer or microprocessor) used in a control operation; that is, to direct or make changes in a process or operation. See MICROCOMPUTER and MICROPROCESSOR.

microelectronics   The field that deals with techniques for producing miniature circuits.

microfiche   A sheet of microfilm about 4 by 6 inches (10 by 15 cm) upon which the images of computer output may be recorded. Up to 270 pages of output may be recorded on one sheet of microfiche. See COMPUTER OUTPUT MICROFILM RECORDER and ULTRAFICHE.

microfilm   Photographic film used for recording graphic information in a reduced size. See COMPUTER OUTPUT MICROFILM (COM) RECORDER.

microform   A medium that contains miniaturized images, such as microfiche and microfilm.

micrographics   The use of miniature photography to condense, store, and retrieve graphics information. Involves the usage of all types of microforms and microimages such as microfilm, microfiche and computer output film.

micro instruction   A low-level instruction used to makeup a macro, or machine language instruction. See MICROPROGRAMMING.

microjustification   In some word processing programs, the ability to add small slivers of blank space between words and between letters within words. The result is easier to read than ordinary justified copy, in which the computer merely adjusts space between words.

micrologic   The use of a permanent stored program to interpret instructions in a microprogram.

microminiature chip   An LSI, VLSI or ULSI chip used for computer storage (memory chip) or control (microprocessor chip).

microminiaturization   A term implying very small size, one step smaller than miniaturization.

micron   One millionth of a meter, or approximately 1/25,000 of an inch.

microphone   An electroacoustic device containing a transducer that is actuated by sound waves and delivers essentially equivalent electric waves. Used to input information into a computer.

MicroPro   A California software company that produces programs for microcomputers, including the WordStar word processing program.

microprocessor   The basic arithmetic, logic, and control elements required for processing (generally contained on one integrated circuit chip). Microprocessors are widely used as the control devices for microcomputers, household appliances, business machines, calculating devices, toys, video game machines, and thousands of other devices. See INTEL 8088, INTEL 80286, INTEL 80386, and MOTOROLA 68000 FAMILY.

microprocessing unit   Same as MICROPROCESSOR.

Micro PROLOG   A microcomputer implementation of the PROLOG programming language, available for several microcomputer systems. See PROLOG.

microprogrammable computer   Pertaining to any computer whose instruction set is not fixed but can be tailored to individual needs by the programming of ROMs or other memory devices. Consequently, whether the computer is a mainframe computer, minicomputer, or microcomputer theoretically it can be microprogrammed. See MICROPROGRAMMING.

microprogramming A method of operating the control part of a computer in which each instruction is broken into several small steps (microsteps) that form part of a microprogram. Some systems allow users to microprogram, and hence determine the instruction set of their own machine. See MICRO CODE and MICROPROGRAMMABLE COMPUTER.

MICR reader An input device that reads documents imprinted with magnetic ink characters.

microsecond One millionth of a second (0.000001), abbreviated μs or μsec.

Microsoft A Bellevue, Washington, software company that produces Microsoft BASIC, IBM PC BASIC, IBM PC DOS, MS DOS, Multiplan™, and Microsoft WORD™, as well as many other software systems. The company was formed by William Gates and Paul Allen in 1975.

Microsoft BASIC A popular version of the BASIC programming language used on microcomputers. Abbreviated MBASIC. See BASIC.

Microsoft WORD™ A popular word processing program developed by Microsoft, Inc.

microspacing A feature of some printers that allows them to move extremely small distances. Used to do microjustification and shadow printing.

microwave An electromagnetic wave that has a wavelength in the centimeter range. Microwaves occupy a region in the electromagnetic spectrum that is bounded by radio waves on the side of longer wavelengths and by infrared waves on the side of shorter wavelengths. Used in data communications.

microwave hop A microwave radio channel between two dish antennas aimed at each other.

microwave transmission lines Structures used for transmission of electromagnetic energy at microwave frequencies from one point to another.

middle-level management Those executives who make tactical decisions, and implement the strategies determined at the top level.

milestone   See EVENT.

milli   One thousandth, used as a prefix; for example, a milli-second is a thousandth of a second.

millimicrosecond   Same as nanosecond, one billionth of a sec-ond.

millisecond   One thousandth of a second, abbreviated ms or msec.

mini   Short for minicomputer.

miniaturization   The process of making an object smaller in physical size without decreasing its efficiency.

minicomputer   A computer that is usually more powerful than a microcomputer, and usually less powerful than a main-frame computer.

minimal tree   Tree whose terminal nodes are ordered to make the tree operate at optimum.

minimax   A technique for minimizing the maximal error of a process.

minor sort key   A data field that provides a secondary source of distinctions by which to sort records. It is used only when duplications occur in the MAJOR SORT KEY.

minuend   A number from which another number, called the subtrahend, is to be subtracted. In the subtraction 7 - 3 = 4, 7 is the minuend, 3 is the subtrahend, and 4 is the dif-ference.

mips   An acronym for MILLION INSTRUCTIONS PER SECOND. Refers to the average number of machine language instruc-tions a computer performs in one second.

mirroring   Pertains to the display or creation of graphic data that portrays an image in exactly the reverse orientation it originally had. Many computer graphics systems will au-tomatically create a mirror image of a graphic entity on the display screen by flipping the entity or drawing on its x- or y-axis.

MIS   An abbreviation for MANAGEMENT INFORMATION SYS-TEM.

mistake A human failing that produces an unintended result; for example, faulty arithmetic, use of incorrect computer instructions, or use of incorrect formulas in a computer program. Contrast with ERROR, FAULT, and MALFUNCTION. See BUG.

mixed number A number having both a fractional part and an integer part, such as 48.63 and -182.3.

ML An abbreviation for **MANIPULATOR LANGUAGE**. An IBM Corporation programming language for controlling robots.

mnemonic Pertaining to a technique used to aid human memory. A word or name that is easy to remember and identify.

mnemonic code An easy-to-remember assembly language code; for example, a code that uses an abbreviation such as MPY for "multiply" and ADD for "addition."

mnemonic language A programming language based on easily remembered symbols that can be assembled into machine language by the computer. See MNEMONIC CODE.

mode (1) A method or condition of operation. (2) The form of a number, name, or expression. (3) The most common or frequent value in a group of values.

model A representation of certain key features of an object or system to be studied. Scientific models often make use of complex formulas and involve substantial use of mathematics. If a computer is used to solve the equations and carry out the necessary calculations, the process is called a computer simulation. Modeling and simulation are essential tools in every area of science, business, economics, and a number of other fields. See SIMULATION.

model, geometric A complete, geometrically accurate 3-D or 2-D representation of a shape, a part, or a geographic area, designed on a computer graphics system and stored in the data base.

modeling (1) The process of accurately describing or representing certain parts of a system. (2) Generation of the essence of a problem by a computer. See MODEL and SIMULATION.

modem An acronym for **MODULATOR/DEM**ODULATOR, a device that translates digital pulses from a computer into analog signals for telephone transmission, and analog signals from the telephone into digital pulses the computer can understand. The modem provides communication capabilities between computer equipment over common telephone facilities. Same as DATA SET. See ACOUSTIC MODEM.

modify (1) To alter a portion of an instruction so its interpretation and execution will be other than normal. The modification may permanently change the instruction or leave it unchanged and affect only the current execution. (2) To alter a program according to a defined parameter.

modular coding Pertains to the technique of programming in which the logical parts of a program are divided into a series of individual modules or routines so that each routine may be programmed independently. See TOP-DOWN PROGRAMMING.

modular constraint In computer graphics, a limitation on the placement of images such that some or all points of an image are forced to lie on the intersections of an invisible grid.

modularity The concept of designing computers in a building-block format to promote efficient and economical upgrading of equipment.

modularization The use of independent, self-contained subprograms within a computer program.

modular programming Programming that produces relatively small, easily interchanged, computer routines that meet standardized interface requirements. Modularity is accomplished by breaking the program into limited segments that perform complete functions and are therefore completely understandable in themselves. This technique greatly facilitates development and verification of complex programs and systems. See MODULE and STRUCTURED PROGRAMMING.

modulation In data communications, the process by which some characteristic of a high frequency carrier signal is varied in accordance with another, lower frequency "information" signal. This technique is used in data sets to make

computer terminal signals compatible with communications
facilities.

modulator   A device that receives electrical pulses, or bits,
from a data processing machine and converts them into signals suitable for transmission over a communications link.
Contrast with DEMODULATOR. See MODEM.

Modula-2   A high-level programming language developed by
Niklaus Wirth as a replacement for Pascal. The language is
similar to Pascal and is now being widely used in university
computer science courses. Modula-2 has the potential to become the leading language by the end of the decade. Here
is a sample program written in Modula-2.

```
module Prime; from InOut import writeln,
                  writecard,
                  writestring;
const
  Size = 8190;
var
  Flags        :array[0..Size] of Boolean;
  I, K, Prime  :Cardinal;
  Count, Inter :Cardinal;
  begin
  writeln;
  writestring('10 iterations');
  for Inter := 1 to 10 do
    Count := 0;
    for I := 0 to Size do
      Flags[I] := True
    end;
    for I := 0 to Size do
      if Flags[I] then
        Prime := I + I + 3;
        K := I + Prime;
        while K = Size do
          Flags[K] := False;
          Inc(K, Prime);
        end; (*while*)
        Inc(Count);
      end; (*if*)
    end; (*for I*)
```

```
    end; (*for Iter*)
  writeln;
  writecard(Count, 6);
  writestring(' primes'),
 end Prime.
```

module (1) Specifically, one logical part of a program. A major program may be broken down into a number of logically self-contained modules. These modules may be written (and possibly tested separately) by a number of programmers. The modules can then be put together to form the complete program. This is called MODULAR PROGRAMMING. (2) An interchangeable plug-in item containing components.

modulo A mathematical function that yields the remainder of division. A number x evaluated modulo n gives the integer remainder of x/n. For example, 200 modulo 47 equals the remainder of 200/47, or 12.

monadic Pertaining to an operation that uses only one operand.

monadic Boolean operator A Boolean operator with only one operand, such as the NOT operator.

monitor (1) A control program. See OPERATING SYSTEM. (2) A video display. See COLOR MONITOR and MONOCHROME MONITOR.

monochrome monitor A special display device that displays a single color (white, amber, or green) character set on a contrasting black background. Monochrome monitors produce a sharp, clear display that is easy to read. They are often used in word processing applications, business systems, and educational applications that may require many hours at the computer terminals and that do not require multicolor displays. See COLOR MONITOR.

monolithic (1) The single silicon substrate upon which an integrated circuit is constructed. (2) Complete and all in one piece. For example, a linkage editor combines several fragmentary program modules into a single monolithic program.

monolithic integrated circuit A circuit formed in a single piece of the substrate material, as opposed to a hybrid circuit, in which individual (physically separate) circuit components are electrically interconnected to form the final circuit.

Monte Carlo method A trial-and-error method of repeated calculations to discover the best solution of a problem. Often used when a great number of variables are present with interrelationships so extremely complex as to eliminate straightforward analytical handling.

more than See GREATER THAN.

MOS An abbreviation for **METALLIC OXIDE SEMI-CONDUCTOR**. See METALLIC OXIDE SEMICONDUCTOR.

MOSFET An acronym for **METALLIC OXIDE SEMI-CONDUCTOR FIELD EFFECT TRANSISTOR**, a semiconductor characterized by an extremely high input impedance, a fairly high active impedance, and low switching speeds. When a voltage (negative with respect to the substrate) is applied to the gate, the MOSFET is a conductor; and, if a potential difference is applied between source and drain, there will be current flow.

MOS/LSI See **METALLIC OXIDE SEMICONDUCTOR** and **LARGE SCALE INTEGRATION**.

most significant digit Pertaining to the digit of a number that has the greatest weight or significance (e.g., in the number 84263, the most significant digit is 8). Abbreviated MSD. See HIGH ORDER and JUSTIFY.

motherboard An interconnecting assembly into which printed circuit cards, boards, or modules are connected. The main circuit board of a microcomputer. Also called system board.

Motorola A manufacturer of electronic equipment, including microprocessors.

Motorola 68000 family A family of microprocessors developed by Motorola, Inc: MC 68000 (a 16-bit processor) developed in 1979, MC 68010 (a 16-bit processor) developed in 1983, MC 68020 (a 32-bit processor) developed in 1984, MC 68030 (a 32-bit processor) developed in 1987, and MC 68040 (a 32-bit processor) announced in 1987. The MC 68000 family of microprocessors is used in several popular microcomputers including the Apple Macintosh™, Commodore Amiga™, and Atari ST™.

mouse   A device for moving a cursor or other object around on the display screen. A typical mouse has one or more buttons on the top of a small box that can be moved around on a flat surface. The box is connected to the computer with a long cord. As the mouse moves, the cursor moves correspondingly on the screen, the buttons being used for specific actions. The mouse's main advantage is that it can move a cursor around on the screen with great precision. The mouse is also good at moving the cursor diagonally, such as from the center of the screen to the bottom right-hand corner.

mouse button   A switch on top of the mouse that transmits commands to the computer. See CLICK, and DOUBLE-CLICK.

movable-head disk unit   A storage device or system consisting of magnetically coated disks, on the surface of which data are stored in the form of magnetic spots arranged in a manner to represent binary data. These data are arranged in circular tracks around the disks and are accessible to reading and writing heads on an arm that can be moved mechanically to the desired disk and then to the desired track on that disk. Data from a given track is read or written sequentially as the disk rotates. See MAGNETIC DISK.

move   (1) To transfer data from one location of storage to another location. (2) In computer graphics, to change the current position on a graphics coordinate system.

moving average   A method of averaging out the roughness of random variation in a data series. A moving average uses only the most recent historical data in the series. The method gets its name from the way it slides along the data series, averaging each data point with its immediate predecessors. The average may disclose trends that would otherwise be obscured by the minor fluctuations along a line.

MP/M   An abbreviation for **M**ULTIPROGRAMMING CONTROL **P**ROGRAM FOR **M**ICROCOMPUTERS. It is a multiuser operating system for small computers. MP/M is a CP/M variant. See OPERATING SYSTEM.

MPU   An abbreviation for **M**ICROPROCESSING UNIT. See MICROPROCESSOR.

MPX An abbreviation for MULTIPLEXER.

ms An abbreviation for MILLISECOND.

MSD An abbreviation for MOST SIGNIFICANT DIGIT.

MS/DOS An abbreviation for MICROSOFT DISK OPERATING SYSTEM, the standard operating system used by the IBM Personal Computer™ and compatible computers. Developed by Microsoft, Inc., MS/DOS is marketed by IBM Corporation as PC-DOS for the IBM Personal Computer.™

msec An abbreviation for millisecond, one thousandth of a second.

MSI An abbreviation for MEDIUM SCALE INTEGRATION. See INTEGRATED CIRCUIT.

M68000-M68040 See MOTOROLA 68000 FAMILY.

MSSG An abbreviation for message.

MTBF An abbreviation for MEAN TIME BETWEEN FAILURE. The average length of time a system or component is expected to work without failure.

MTTF An abbreviation for MEAN TIME TO FAILURE. The average length of time in which the system, or a component of the system, works without fault.

MTTR An acronym for MEAN TIME TO REPAIR. The average time expected to be required to detect and correct a fault in a computer system.

Mu The name of the Greek letter μ. The symbol is used to denote the prefix micro.

MUG An acronym for MUMPS USERS GROUP. See MUMPS.

multiaccess computer A computer system in which computational and data resources are made available simultaneously to a number of users, who access the system through terminal devices, normally on an interactive or conversational basis. A multiaccess computer system may consist of only a single central processor connected directly to a number of terminals (star network), or it may consist of a number of processing systems that are distributed and interconnected with one another (ring network) as well as with other terminals.

multiaddress Pertaining to an instruction format containing more than one address part.

multicomputer system A computer system consisting of two or more central processing units.

multidrop line A communications system configuration that uses a single channel or line to service several terminals.

multifile sorting The automatic sequencing of more than one file, based upon separate parameters for each file, without operator intervention.

multifunction board A device that plugs into computers, giving the system more than one new capability, such as a clock/calendar, memory expansion board, or parallel/serial interface.

multijob operation A term that describes concurrent execution of job steps from two or more jobs.

multilayer A type of printed circuit board that has several circuit layers connected by electroplated holes.

multilevel addressing See INDIRECT ADDRESSING.

multilinked list List with each atom having at least two pointers.

multipass The process of running through the same data more than once to accomplish a task too complicated to be accomplished in one pass.

multipass sort A sort program designed to sort more data than can be contained within the main memory of a central computer. Intermediate storage, such as disk or tape, is required.

Multiplan™ An electronic spreadsheet that supplies a large grid for entries, each of which can be text, numbers, or formulas. It has the ability to link spreadsheets and can handle spreadsheets with 4,095 rows and 255 columns for a total of over one million cells. Developed by Microsoft Corporation.

multiple-access network A flexible system by which every station can have access to the network at all times; provisions are made for times when two computers decide to transmit at the same time.

multiple-address instruction An instruction consisting of an operation code and two or more addresses. Usually specified as a two-address, three-address, or four-address instruction.

multiple-address message A message to be delivered to more than one destination.

multiple connector A connector to indicate the merging of several lines of flow into one line, or the dispersal of one line of flow into several lines.

multiple-job processing Controlling the performance of more than one data processing job at a time.

multiple-pass printing A technique used on some dot matrix printers to obtain higher quality characters. The print head makes one pass, the paper is moved slightly, and another pass is made. The end product is a printed character that is easier to read.

multiple regression A statistical technique for predicting the value of a "dependent variable" that is assumed to be dependent upon one or more explanatory or "independent variables."

multiple-user system A computer system designed to allow more than one user on the system at a time.

multiplex To interleave or simultaneously transmit two or more messages over a single channel or other communications facility.

multiplexer A device that allows several communications lines to share one computer data channel. Abbreviated MPX or MUX.

multiplexer channel A special type of input/output channel that can transmit data between a computer and a number of simultaneously operating peripheral devices.

multiplexor An alternate spelling of MULTIPLEXER.

multiplicand The quantity that is being multiplied by another quantity.

multiplication time The time required to perform a multiplication. For a binary number, it will equal the total of all the addition times and all the shift time involved in the multiplication.

multiplier   The quantity that is used to multiply another quantity.

multiprecision arithmetic   A form of arithmetic in which two or more computer words are used to represent each number.

multiprocessing   The simultaneous execution of two or more sequences of instructions by multiple central processing units under common control. See MULTIPROGRAMMING.

multiprocessor   A computer network consisting of two or more central processors under a common control.

multiprogramming   Running two or more programs concurrently in the same computer. Each program is allotted its own place in memory and its own peripherals, but all share the central processing unit. It is made economical by the fact that peripherals are slower than the central processing unit, so most programs spend most of their time waiting for input or output to finish. While one program is waiting, another can use the central processing unit.

multireel sorting   The automatic sequencing of a file having more than one input tape, without operator intervention.

multistar network   A data communications network in which several host computers are connected and where each host computer has its own star network of smaller computers.

multisystem network   A communications network with two or more host computers. It enables a terminal to select the computer with which it wishes to communicate.

multitasking   The ability of a computer to perform two or more functions (tasks) simultaneously. For example, you can do word processing in the foreground (on the screen) while sorting a data base file in the background (off the screen).

multi-user system   A system where two or more people, using different terminals, can access one computer simultaneously.

multiviewports   A screen display that shows two or more viewing screens that are adjacent but independent.

multivolume file A file so large that it requires more than one disk pack, magnetic tape or floppy disk to hold it.

MUMPS An acronym for MASSACHUSETTS GENERAL HOSPITAL UTILITY MULTI-PROGRAMMING SYSTEM, a programming language designed specifically for handling medical records. The language is strong in data management and text-manipulation features.

Murphy's Laws A set of humorous "laws" based on the precept that "if something can go wrong—it will."

musical language A method by which musical notation may be represented in code suitable for computer input. See COMPUTER MUSIC.

musicomp A compositional programming language that provides techniques for generating original musical scores as well as for synthesizing music.

music synthesizer A device that can be linked to a computer for recording music, playing music, and so on.

MUX An acronym for MULTIPLEXER. A channel used to connect low-speed devices to a computer.

MVT An acronym for MULTIPROGRAMMING WITH A VARIABLE NUMBER OF TASKS; the tasks being programs.

mylar A DuPont trademark for polyester film, often used as a base for magnetically coated or perforated information media.

N

naive user A person who wants to do something with a computer but does not have the experience needed to program the computer.

NAK An international transmission control code returned by a receiving terminal to signify that a frame of information has been received but is incorrect. Contrast with ACK.

name An alphanumeric term that identifies a program, a control statement, data areas, or a cataloged procedure. Same as LABEL.

nand A logical operator having the property that if P is a statement, Q is a statement, . . . then the nand of P, Q, . . . is true if at least one statement is false and false if all statements are true.

nano A prefix meaning one billionth.

nanoacre One billionth of an acre, used figuratively to describe the area of an integrated circuit.

nanocomputer A computer capable of processing data in billionths of a second.

nanosecond One billionth of a second, one thousand-millionth of a second; abbreviated ns. Same as millimicrosecond. Light travels approximately one foot per nanosecond, electricity slightly less. The most powerful computers now being manufactured can carry out an instruction in less than a nanosecond. That is, such a machine can execute more than one billion instructions in one second!

narrowband Pertains to a data communications system that handles low volumes of data.

NASA An acronym for **N**ATIONAL **A**ERONAUTICS AND **S**PACE **A**DMINISTRATION.

National Computer Graphics Association (NCGA) A professional organization for people interested in the computer graphics industry. Holds an annual meeting that includes presentations, equipment exhibits, and art show.

National Crime Information Center (NCIC) An FBI computerized network of data related to crimes that have occurred throughout the United States. The network is used by law enforcement agencies throughout the U.S. and Canada.

National Educational Computing Conference (NECC) An annual meeting of educators interested in the use of computers in education.

native compiler A compiler that produces code usable only for a particular computer.

native language A computer language peculiar to the machines of one manufacturer. See MACHINE LANGUAGE.

natural language A language that allows users to prepare programs in an English-like or other natural language.

NBS An abbreviation for **N**ATIONAL **B**UREAU OF **S**TAN-DARDS, a government agency that has the responsibility of establishing standards for the computer industry.

NCC An abbreviation for **N**ATIONAL **C**OMPUTER **C**ONFER-ENCE, a computer trade show held annually.

NCGA See **N**ATIONAL **C**OMPUTER **G**RAPHICS **A**SSOCIATION.

N-channel MOS A circuit that uses current made up of negative charges. It has a higher speed but lower density than PMOS. Abbreviated NMOS.

NCIC An acronym for the FBI's computerized **N**ATIONAL **C**RIME **I**NFORMATION **C**ENTER, the heart of a large law enforcement network.

NCR Corporation A large manufacturer of computer equipment.

NDBMS See **N**ETWORK **D**ATABASE **M**ANAGEMENT **S**YSTEM.

NDRO An acronym for **N**ON-**D**ESTRUCTIVE **R**EAD**O**UT. See NONDESTRUCTIVE READ.

near-letter quality Pertaining to output produced by some printers (dot-matrix) that does not look as readable as that produced by letter-quality printers (daisy wheel or laser).

NECC See **N**ATIONAL **E**DUCATIONAL **C**OMPUTING **C**ONFER-ENCE.

negate To perform the logical operator NOT.

negative true logic A system of logic in which a high voltage represents the bit value 0 and a low voltage represents the bit value 1.

negotiation The art of exchanging services or commitments in an effort to agree on a mutually satisfactory contractual relationship.

nerd A computer amateur.

nest To insert a command between the beginning and end of another command.

nested block A program block inside another program block.

nested loop A loop that is completely contained within another loop. The inner loop executes the specified number of times, and when it has finished, the outer loop then finishes its first execution. This process continues until the outer loop has executed the specified number of times.

nested subroutine A subroutine that is called from another subroutine: the first subroutine is called from the main program and executes until it encounters an instruction that transfers control to the second subroutine. The second subroutine executes until it is finished and then transfers control back to the first subroutine. See SUBROUTINE.

nesting Embedding program segments or blocks of data within other program segments or blocks of data. Algebraic nesting involves grouping expressions within parentheses; for example, (Z * Y * (X - 3)).

network (1) A system of interconnected computer systems and terminals. (2) A series of points connected by communications channels. (3) The structure of relationships among a project's activities, tasks and events.

network chart A chart that depicts time estimates and activity relationships.

network data base management system (NDBMS) A collection of related programs for loading, accessing, and controlling a data base. In an NDBMS, data records are linked by a complex system of pointers that frequently must be updated.

networking (1) A technique for distributing data processing functions through communications facilities. (2) The design of networks. (3) The interconnection of two or more networks.

network, local area See LOCAL AREA NETWORK.

network, ring See RING NETWORK.

network, star See STAR NETWORK.

network theory The systematizing and generalizing of the relationships among the elements of an electrical network.

neural net A mathematical model of some phenomenon associated with neuronal behavior.

neural network A circuit designed to replicate the way neurons act and interact in the brain.

Newton-Raphson A term applied to an interactive procedure used for solving equations. See ITERATE.

nibble One half of a byte; namely, four adjacent bits. Sometimes spelled nybble.

niladic Pertaining to an operation for which no operands are specified.

nil pointer A pointer used to denote the end of a linked list.

nine's complement A numeral used to represent the negative of a given value. A nine's complement numeral is obtained by subtracting each digit from a numeral containing all nines; for example, 567 is the nine's complement of 432 and is obtained by subtracting 432 from 999.

nixie tube A vacuum tube used to display legible numbers.

NMOS An acronym for **N**-CHANNEL **MOS**. Circuits that use currents made up of negative charges and produce devices at least twice as fast as PMOS. See PMOS.

node (1) Any terminal, station, or communications computer in a computer network. (2) A point in a tree structure where two or more branches come together. (3) A connecting point on a component, printed circuit board, or logic element where electrical connections can be made. (4) Any device connected to a network.

noise (1) Loosely defined, any disturbance tending to interfere with the normal operation of a device or system, including those attributable to equipment components, natural disturbance, or manual interference. (2) Spurious signals that can introduce errors. (3) An unwanted signal.

noise immunity A device's ability to accept valid signals while rejecting unwanted signals.

noise pollution Noise, especially office noise that is distracting and cutting into productive work time, such as noise from printers, typewriters and copy machines.

nonconductor A substance through which electricity cannot pass.

nondestructive read A read operation that does not alter the information content of the storage media.

nonerasable storage   A storage device whose information cannot be erased during the course of computation, such as punched cards and photographic film.

nonexecutable statement   A program statement that sets up a program but does not call for any specific action on the part of the program in which it appears. Contrast with EXECUTABLE STATEMENT.

nongraphic character   A character code that when sent to a printer or display unit, does not produce a printable character image, such as carriage control, upper case, and space.

nonimpact printer   A printer that uses electricity, heat, laser technology, or photographic techniques to print output.

nonlinear programming   An area of applied mathematics concerned with finding the values of the variables that give the smallest or largest value of a specified function in the class of all variables satisfying prescribed conditions.

non-numeric programming   Programming that deals with symbols rather than numbers. Usually refers to the manipulation of symbolic objects, such as words, rather than the performance of numerical calculations.

nonoverlap processing   A technique whereby reading, writing, and internal processing occur only in a serial manner. Contrast with OVERLAP PROCESSING.

nonprint   Pertaining to an impulse that inhibits line printing under machine control.

nonprocedural query language   A computer language for interacting with a data base. It specifies what the user wants to know rather than the steps needed to produce the information, which are worked out by the computer. For example, on some systems the user fills out a screen showing a blank record with ranges of values desired for selected fields.

nonreflective ink   Any color of ink that is recognizable to an optical character reader.

nonsequential computer   A computer that must be directed to the location of each instruction.

nonswitched line A communications link that is permanently installed between two points.

nonvolatile storage A storage medium that retains its data in the absence of power, such as ROM.

no-op An abbreviation of the term "no-operation," as in NO-OPERATION INSTRUCTION.

no-operation instruction A computer instruction whose only effect is to advance the instruction counter. It accomplishes nothing more than to advance itself to the next instruction in normal sequence.

NOP An acronym for **NO OP**ERATION. See NO-OPERATION INSTRUCTION.

NOR The Boolean operator that gives a truth table value of true only when both of the variables connected by the logical operator are false.

normalize To adjust the exponent and fraction of a floating-point quantity so the fraction is within a prescribed range. Loosely defined, to SCALE.

Norton Utilities™ A collection of small programs designed to make computing easier. These programs fall into four categories: data recovery, disk management, data security, and miscellaneous functions. Useful for floppy and hard disk users. Developed by Peter Norton Computing, Inc.

NOT A logic operator having the property that if P is a statement, then the NOT of P is true if P is false and false if P is true.

notation See POSITIONAL NOTATION.

notebook computer A briefcase-sized computer that uses a flat panel liquid crystal display. It is about the size of a large book.

NOT-gate A circuit equivalent to the logical operation of negation.

NRZ An abbreviation for **NONRETURN TO ZERO**, one of several methods for coding digital information on magnetic tape.

NS An abbreviation for **NANOSECOND**, one billionth of a second.

NTSC An abbreviation for **NATIONAL TELEVISION SYSTEM COMMITTEE**, a color television standard.

nucleus That portion of the control program that must always be present in internal storage.

null Pertaining to a negligible value or a lack of information, as contrasted with a zero or a blank that conveys information, such as numerical value and a space between words. Empty.

null cycle The time required to cycle through an entire program without introducing new data.

null string String with no characters. See EMPTY STRING.

number (1) A symbol or symbols representing a value in a specific numeral system. (2) Loosely defined, a NUMERAL.

number base See RADIX.

number crunching Pertaining to a program or computer that is designed to perform large amounts of computation and other numerical manipulations of data. See SUPERCOMPUTER.

number representation The representation of numbers by agreed sets of symbols according to agreed rules.

number system An agreed set of symbols and rules for number representation. Loosely, a NUMERAL SYSTEM.

numeral A conventional symbol representing a number; for example, 5, 101, and V are different numerals that represent the same number in different number systems.

numeralization Representation of alphabetic data through the use of digits.

numeral system A method of representing numbers. In computing, several numeral systems, in addition to the common decimal system, are of particular interest. These are the binary, hexadecimal, and octal systems. In each system, the value of a numeral is the value of the digits multiplied by the numeral system radix, raised to a power indicated by the position of the digits in the numeral.

numerator In the expression *a/b*, *a* is the numerator and *b* is the denominator.

numeric Pertaining to numerals or to representation by means of numerals.

numerical analysis The branch of mathematics concerned with the study and development of effective procedures for computing answers to problems.

numerical control A method of controlling machine tools through servomechanisms and control circuitry so the motions of the tools will respond to digital coded instructions on tape or to direct commands from a computer. See APT and PARTS PROGRAMMER.

numerical indicator tube Any electron tube capable of visually displaying numerical figures.

numeric character Same as DIGIT.

numeric coding Coding that uses only digits to represent data and instructions.

numeric constant Data using integer or real numbers.

numeric data Data that consists entirely of numbers.

numeric keypad An input device that uses a set of decimal digit keys (0-9) and special function keys. Used as a separate device or sometimes located on devices to the right of a standard keyboard.

O

oasis A multiuser operating system used on several microcomputer systems.

obey The process whereby a computer carries out an operation as specified by one or more of the instructions forming the program currently being executed.

object code Output from a compiler or assembler that is itself executable machine code or is suitable for further processing to produce executable machine code. Also called OBJECT PROGRAM.

object computer A computer used for the execution of an object program.

objective The ends toward which an organization works.

object language The output of a translation process. Usually, object language and machine language are the same. Contrast with SOURCE LANGUAGE. Synonymous with TARGET LANGUAGE.

object-language programming Programming in a machine language executable on a particular computer.

object-oriented programming A programming approach centered around a collection of data objects, each knowing how to respond to a set of commands that can be given to it.

object program The instructions that come out of the COMPILER or ASSEMBLER, ready to run on the computer. Also called *object code*.

obscure Totally incomprehensible.

OCR An abbreviation for OPTICAL CHARACTER RECOGNITION. Characters printed in a type style that can be read by both machines and people. See OPTICAL CHARACTER RECOGNITION.

octal Pertaining to a number system with a radix of 8. Octal numerals are frequently used to represent binary numerals, with each octal digit representing a group of three binary digits (bits); for example, the binary numeral 110100000010111 can be represented as octal 64027.

octal numeral A numeral of one or more digits, representing a sum in which the quantity represented by each figure is based on a radix of 8. The digits used in octal numerals are 0, 1, 2, 3, 4, 5, 6, and 7.

octal point A radix point in a mixed octal numeral, separating the fractional part from the integer part.

octet A byte composed of eight bits.

OEM An abbreviation for ORIGINAL EQUIPMENT MANUFACTURER. A company or organization that purchases computers and peripheral equipment for use as components in products and equipment that they subsequently sell to their customers.

office automation The application of computers and communications technology to improve the productivity of clerical and managerial office workers.

office computer A term usually applied to a microcomputer system for use in an office environment. The system is likely to include disk units, a printer, and software developed for specific office functions.

office information system A system that can include a variety of data entry terminals, word processors, graphics terminals, printers, and computer systems.

office of the future The office that makes extensive use of computers, data communications, and other electronic technologies. In such an office, numerous clerical, secretarial, and communications tasks are done automatically.

off-line Pertaining to equipment, devices, or persons not in direct communication with the central processing unit of a computer. Equipment not connected to the computer. Contrast with ON-LINE.

off-line storage Storage not under control of the central processing unit.

off load (1) To transfer jobs from one computer system to another that is more lightly loaded. (2) To output data to a peripheral device.

off-page connector A symbol used on a flowchart to link a line of flow on one page with its continuation on a different page.

offset The difference between the value or condition desired and that actually attained.

off-the-shelf Pertaining to a standard, mass-produced hardware or software product readily available from the vendor or supplier.

OMR See OPTICAL MARK RECOGNITION.

on-board computer A computer resident in a vehicle, such as a spacecraft, an automobile, a ship, or an aircraft.

on-board regulation An arrangement in which each board in a system contains its own voltage regulator.

one-address computer   A computer that employs only one address in its instruction format (e.g., ADD *x*, where *x* represents the address in the instruction).

one-address instruction   An instruction consisting of an operation and exactly one address. In special cases, the instruction code of a single address computer may include both zero and multiaddress instructions. Most present-day computers are of the one-address instruction type. See ONE-ADDRESS COMPUTER.

one-chip computer   A complete microcomputer that is implemented on a single chip.

one-dimensional array   An array consisting of a single row or column of elements.

one-for-one   A phrase often associated with an assembler in which one source language statement is converted to one machine language instruction.

one-level memory   Memory in which all stored items are accessed by a uniform mechanism.

one pass compiler   A language processor that passes through a source language program one time and produces an object module.

one's complement   A numeral used to represent the negative of a given value. A one's complement of a binary numeral is obtained by alternating the bit configuration of each bit in the numeral. For example, 01100101 is the one's complement of the binary numeral 10011010.

on-line   Pertaining to describing equipment, devices, and persons who are in direct communication with the central processing unit of a computer. Equipment that is physically connected to the computer. Contrast with OFFLINE.

on-line data base   A data base that can be directly accessed by a user from a terminal, usually a visual display device.

on-line fault tolerant system   A computer system designed to function correctly in the presence of hardware failures.

on-line problem solving   A teleprocessing application in which a number of users at remote terminals can concurrently use a computing system in solving problems on-line. Often in this type of application, a dialogue or conversation is carried on between a user at a remote terminal and a program within the central computer system.

on-line storage Storage under control of the central processing unit.

op An abbreviated version of the term OPERATION.

opacity Pertains to the ease with which light passes through a sheet of paper making it more or less translucent.

op-code See OPERATION CODE.

open The process required to begin work with a file or document.

open-ended Capable of accepting the addition of new programs, instructions, subroutines, modifications, terms, or classifications without disturbing the original system.

open file A file that can be accessed for reading, writing, or possibly both. Contrast with CLOSED FILE.

open shop Pertaining to the operation of a computer facility in which most productive problem programming is performed by each problem originator rather than by a group of programming specialists. Contrast with CLOSED SHOP.

open subroutine A subroutine inserted into a routine at each place it is used. Contrast with CLOSED SUBROUTINE.

operand A quantity or data item that is operated upon.

operating ratio See AVAILABILITY.

operating system Software that controls the execution of computer programs and that may provide scheduling, debugging, input/output control, accounting, compilation, storage assignment, data management, and related services. Abbreviated OS.

operation A defined action. The action specified by a single computer instruction or high-level language statement. Abbreviated OP.

operational management The supervisors or leaders responsible for operating details and the employees who perform them.

operation center A physical area containing the human and equipment resources needed to process data through a computer and produce desired output. Same as DATA PROCESSING CENTER.

operation code The instruction code used to specify the operations a computer is to perform.

operations analysis Same as OPERATIONS RESEARCH.

operations personnel The people responsible for controlling the equipment in a computer center. Operations personnel power up systems, load programs, run programs, report equipment malfunctions, and so on.

operations research A mathematical science devoted to carrying out complicated operations with the maximum possible efficiency. Among the common scientific techniques in operations research are the following: linear programming, probability theory, information theory, game theory, Monte Carlo method, and queuing theory.

operator (1) In the description of a process, that which indicates the action to be performed on operands. (2) A person who operates a machine. See COMPUTER OPERATOR.

optical character A character from a special set of characters that can be read by an optical character reader.

optical character reader An input device that accepts a printed document as input, identifying characters by their shape. See OCR and OPTICAL CHARACTER RECOGNITION.

optical character recognition An information processing technology that converts human readable data into another medium for computer input. Light reflected from characters is recognized by optical character recognition equipment. Abbreviated OCR.

optical communications The transmission of data, pictures, speech, or other information by light. An information-carrying light wave signal originates in a transmitter, passes through an optical channel, and enters a receiver, which reconstructs the original information. Optical fibers and lasers make up a technology that offers the maximum transmitting capacity using devices that occupy little physical space.

optical disk A high-density storage device that uses a laser to burn a pattern of holes into a tellurium film on a disk surface. A single optical disk can hold billions of bytes of data. In fact, one optical disk storage system can store the entire *Encyclopedia Britannica* if necessary.

optical fiber A thread of highly transparent glass that is pulsed very rapidly to carry a stream of binary signals. As well as carrying a high volume of data, optical fibers are immune to the electrical interference that can plague conventional cables. The use of optical fibers is rapidly becoming standard in computer communications.

optical laser disk See OPTICAL DISK.

optical mark reader An input device that reads graphite marks on cards or pages. See MARK SENSING and OPTICAL MARK RECOGNITION.

optical mark recognition An information processing technology that converts data into another medium for computer input. This is accomplished by the presence of a mark in a given position, each position having a value known to the computer that may or may not be understandable to humans. Abbreviated OMR. See OPTICAL MARK READER.

optical page reader An input device that accepts a page of printed manner.

optical printer See ELECTROSTATIC PRINTER.

optical reader See OPTICAL CHARACTER READER and OPTICAL MARK READER.

optical reader wand A device that reads bar codes and enters appropriate information into a computer.

optical recognition device A device that can read symbols or marks that are coded on paper documents and can convert them into electrical pulses. See OPTICAL CHARACTER READER and OPTICAL MARK READER.

optical scanner See OPTICAL CHARACTER READER.

optical scanning Any input method by which information is converted for machine processing by evaluating the relative reflectance of that information to the background on which it appears. See OPTICAL CHARACTER RECOGNITION.

optimal merge tree A tree representation of the order in which strings are to be merged so that a minimum number of move operations occurs.

optimization In its most general meaning, the efforts and processes of making a decision, a design, or a system as nearly perfect, effective, or functional as possible.

optimize To write a program or design a system in such a way as to minimize or maximize the value of some parameter, especially cost, storage, and time.

optimizing compiler A compiler that attempts to correct inefficiencies in a program's logic in order to improve execution times, main storage requirements, and so forth.

optimum Best and most desirable in view of established criteria.

optimum programming Programming to maximize efficiency with respect to some criterion; for example, least storage usage, least usage of peripheral equipment, or least computing time.

optimum tree search A tree search whose object is to find the best of many alternatives.

option key A modifier key on some keyboards. When held down, it gives a different interpretation to characters next typed. A special control key.

opto-electronics The technology concerned with the integration of optics and electronics.

OR See EXCLUSIVE OR and INCLUSIVE OR.

OR circuit See OR-GATE.

order (1) To arrange items according to any specified set of rules. (2) An arrangement of items according to any specified set of rules. (3) A command found in most electronic spreadsheet programs that permits the user to determine the order of calculation.

ordered tree A tree that has the arrangement of its nodes determined by a set of criteria.

ordinal type An ordered range of values, including integer, Boolean, and character values.

ordinate The y-axis of a graph or chart.

organizational control The personnel administrative procedures implemented to protect an information system from infiltration, tampering or sabotage.

organization chart A diagram that shows the organization of a business (how responsibilities are divided up within a business). Pictorial representation of the organizational hierarchy, showing the formal relationships among employees of an organization.

OR-gate A computer circuit containing two switches whose output is a binary 1 if either or both of the inputs are binary. This electrical circuit implements the OR operator.

origin In coding, the absolute memory address of the first location of a program or program segment.

original data Data to be processed. Also called RAW DATA.

original equipment manufacturer A manufacturer who buys equipment from other suppliers and integrates it into a single system for resale. Abbreviated OEM.

originate/answer Pertaining to a modem that can both originate and answer messages. Most telecomputing services are in answer mode, so the user must be in originate mode.

orphan The last line of a paragraph sitting alone at the top of a page of text. Considered undesirable in all forms of printing. Compare with WIDOW.

orthoferrite A naturally occurring substance composed of alternate, snake-like regions of opposite magnetic polarity.

orthographic A type of layout, drawing, or map in which the projecting lines are perpendicular to the plane of the drawing or map.

OS An abbreviation for OPERATING SYSTEM.

oscillating sort An external tape sort that capitalizes on a tape drive's ability to read forward and backward.

oscillography The projection of a pattern of electrical signals on the face of a cathode-ray tube.

oscilloscope An electronic instrument that produces a luminous plot on a flourescent screen showing the relationship of two or more variables. It is used by computer maintenance technicians.

OS/2 An operating system for the IBM Personal System/2 line of computers.

outdegree The number of directed edges leaving a node.

outdent In word processing, a line of text that extends farther to the left than other lines in the same paragraph.

out-of-line Pertaining to statements in a computer program that are not in the main line of the program, such as closed subroutines.

output (1) Data transferred from a computer's internal storage unit to some storage or output device. (2) The final result of data that have been processed by the computer. Contrast with INPUT.

output area An area of a computer's main storage reserved for output data. Contrast with INPUT AREA.

output buffer A buffer used to transfer data to an external device.

output channel A channel that connects peripheral units and the central processing unit, and through which data may be transmitted for output.

output data Data to be delivered from a device or program, usually after some processing. Synonymous with OUTPUT. Contrast with INPUT DATA.

output device A unit that is used for taking out data values from a computer and presenting them in the desired form to the user. Common output devices are printers, visual display devices, and plotters. Contrast with INPUT DEVICE.

output media The physical substance upon which output information is recorded, such as paper, magnetic disk and photographic film.

output stream The sequence of data to be transmitted to an output device.

outputting The process of producing useful information from a computer system.

overflow In an arithmetic operation, the generation of a quantity beyond the capacity of the register or storage location that is to receive the result.

overhead **(1)** A collective term for the factors that cause the performance of a program or device to be lower than it would be in the ideal case. **(2)** Nonproductive effort that takes place when the operating system and programs are performing administrative tasks rather than productive work.

overlap To do something at the same time while something else is being done; for example, to perform an input operation while instructions are being executed by the central processing unit. This approach permits the computer to work on several programs at once.

overlapping A condition in which windows on a screen display are on top of one another, or overlap the borders of each other.

overlap processing The simultaneous execution of input, processing, and output activities by a computer system. Contrast with NONOVERLAP PROCESSING.

overlay To transfer segments of a program from auxiliary storage into main storage for execution so that two or more segments occupy the same storage locations at different times. This technique is used to increase the apparent size of main storage by keeping only the programs or data that are currently being accessed within main storage; the rest is kept on an auxiliary storage device until needed.

overprint The process of printing more than once at the same position in order to emphasize or improve the type.

override To force a preexisting value to change in a program by superseding it.

overrun The condition that occurs when data is transferred to or from a nonbuffered control unit with a synchronous medium and the activity initiated by the program exceeds the channel capacity.

overscan The loss of text at the end of a line if the computer and monitor are not matched properly.

overstriking The ability of a hard-copy printer to strike a character more than once to produce a boldface effect on the printed copy.

overwrite To place data in a location and destroy or mutilate the data previously contained in that location. To blot out information by writing over the top.

P

PABX See PRIVATE AUTOMATIC BRANCH EXCHANGE.

pack To store several short units of data into a single storage cell in such a way that the individual units can later be recovered. For example, to store two 4-bit BCD digits in one 8-bit storage location. Opposite of UNPACK.

package A program or collection of programs to be used by more than one business organization.

packaged software Software which is sold by a vendor (computer store, software developer, mail-order business) in the form of a prepared "package" consisting of the programs and operating instructions.

packet A block of data for data transmission. Each packet contains control information, such as routing, address and error control—as well as data.

packet switching A method of digital communication in which messages are divided into packets of a bit size determined by the needs of the transmission network, and are transferred to their destination over communication channels that are dedicated to the connection only for the duration of the packet's transmission.

packing The process of storing two numbers in a single storage byte.

packing density The number of useful storage cells per unit of area or length. For example, the number of characters per inch.

pad (1) An area of plated copper on a printed circuit board provides a contact for soldering component leads, means of copper-path transition from one side of the printed circuit board to the other, and a contact for test probes. (2) To fill a data field with blanks.

pad character Buffer character used to fill a blank.

padding A technique used to fill out a fixed-length block of information with dummy characters, items, words, or records.

paddle A device, usually held in the hand, which is connected to a computer. By turning a dial on the paddle you can make the display terminal cursor move either up and down or right and left. A paddle is connected to the computer by a cable. It is used in computer graphics and for playing video games.

page (1) Amount of graphics or text material displayed on a screen at one time. (2) A segment of a program or data, usually of fixed length, that has a fixed virtual address but can in fact reside in any region of the computer's internal storage. See VIRTUAL STORAGE.

page frame A location in the storage of the computer that can store one page of commands or data.

page-in The process of swapping programs or data from disk storage to the computer's main storage.

PageMaker™ A powerful desktop publishing application program that lets the user create documents requiring multi-column formatting and text/graphics combinations. The work is displayed on the screen in the form of a page, which can then be printed on some laser printers or typesetting equipment for publication in a report, newsletter, brochure or other printed documents. Developed by Aldus Corporation.

page-out The process of swapping programs or data from the computer's main storage to disk storage.

page printer A printer in which an entire page of characters is composed and determined within the device prior to printing.

page reader A piece of optical scanning equipment that scans many lines of information, with the scanning pattern being determined by program control and/or control symbols intermixed with input data.

page skip A control character that causes a printer to skip the rest of the current page and move to the top of the next page.

pagination (1) The process of numbering pages. (2) The electronic manipulation of graphics and blocks of type for the purpose of setting up an entire page. (3) The breaking up of a printed report into units that correspond to pages.

paging (1) The process of displaying a page of text or graphics on a visual display screen. (2) A technique for moving programs back and forth from real (main) storage to virtual (auxiliary) storage.

paintbrush One of the capabilities found in several computer graphics systems. The paintbrush provides the user with a variety of brush shapes and is used by moving the pointer on the display screen.

painting (1) Displaying the trail of movements of a graphical input device. (2) In computer graphics, filling a selected area with a solid color or pattern. (3) The process of displaying graphic data on a visual display screen.

pair exchange sorting algorithm A sorting algorithm that involves the comparison of data as arranged in pairs.

PAL An acronym for PHASE ALTERNATION LINE, the color television system used in most European countries.

palette The set of available colors in a computer graphics system.

PAM An acronym for PULSE AMPLITUDE MODULATION, in which the modulation wave is caused to amplitude-modulate a pulse carrier.

pane The term for each of the windows that result from splitting a single window.

panel See CONTROL PANEL and PLUGBOARD.

panning The horizontal movement of displayed graphic data across a visual display screen.

paper feed The method by which paper is pulled through a printer. See TRACTOR FEED MECHANISM.

parabola A graphics curve that can be obtained by cutting a right circular cone by a plane parallel to one of the elements. It may also be described as the path of a point which moves so that it remains equidistant from a fixed point and a fixed line.

paradigm A fundamental conception that underlies a possible complex structure. The central kernel within a concept. New paradigms result in new conceptions. A popular buzzword among computer designers. The original Greek word meant merely an example, or pattern.

paragraph A set of one or more COBOL sentences making up a logical processing entity and preceded by a paragraph header or name.

paragraph assembly The process in which a document is assembled on a word processor from paragraphs stored on disks.

parallel (1) Handling all the elements of a word or message simultaneously. (2) In computer graphics it describes lines or planes in a graphics file that are an equal distance apart at every corresponding point. Contrast with SERIAL.

parallel access The process of obtaining information from, or placing information into, storage where the time required for such access is dependent on the simultaneous transfer of all elements of a word from a given storage location.

parallel adder An adder that performs its operations by bringing in all digits simultaneously from each of the quantities involved.

parallel circuit An electric circuit in which the elements, branches, or components are connected between two points with one of the two ends of each component connected to each other.

parallel computer A computer in which the digits or data lines are processed concurrently by separate units of the computer.

parallel conversion The process of changing to a new data processing system that involves running both the old and new systems simultaneously for a period of time.

parallel input/output Data transmission in which each bit has its own wire. All of the bits are transmitted simultaneously, as opposed to being sent one at a time (serially). Contrast with serial INPUT/OUTPUT.

parallel interface An equipment boundary where information is transferred simultaneously over a set of paths.

parallel operation The performance of several actions, usually of a similar nature, simultaneously through the provision of individual, similar, or identical devices for each such action. Contrast with SERIAL OPERATION.

parallel printer A printer that receives information from the computer one character (letter, number, etc.) at a time through eight wires. Additional wires are needed to exchange control signals.

parallel printing Printing an entire row at one time.

parallel processing Pertaining to the concurrent or simultaneous execution of two or more processes in multiple devices, such as processing units or channels. Contrast with SERIAL PROCESSING.

parallel reading Row-by-row reading of a data card.

parallel run The process of running a new system or program parallel with the old system to ensure a smooth transition and error-free conversion.

parallel transmission In data communications, a method of data transfer in which all bits of a character are set simultaneously. Contrast with SERIAL TRANSMISSION.

parameter An arbitrary constant. A variable in an algebraic expression that temporarily assumes the properties of a constant.

parametric Pertaining to the technique by which a line, curve, or surface is defined by equations based on some independent variable. A technique used often in computer-aided design systems.

parent A file whose contents are required (and in some cases the only sources of information available) to create new records. See CHILD.

parent/child relationship The passing of information from one generation to the next. Older information (parent) is necessary to create new information (child).

parentheses A grouping symbol ( ).

parity bit An extra bit added to a byte, character, or word to ensure that there is always either an even number or an odd number of bits, according to the logic of the system. If, through a hardware failure, a bit should be lost in transmission, its loss can be detected by checking the parity. The same bit pattern remains as long as the contents of the byte, character, or word remain unchanged.

parity checking Automatic error detection by using checking bits along with the numerical bits. See PARITY BIT.

Parkinson's law The task expands to meet the time available for its completion.

parser A program or subroutine that determines the syntactic structure of a string of characters. All compilers and interpreters include parsers.

parsing (1) The process of separating statements into syntactic units. (2) Analyzing a character string and breaking it down into a group of more easily processed components. See LINGUISTICS.

partition An area in memory assigned to a program during its execution.

partitioning Subdividing a computer storage area into smaller units that are allocated to specific jobs or tasks.

parts explosion A drawing of all the pieces composing an assembly that illustrates the relation of the pieces to one another.

parts list A collection of the quantities, names, and numbers of all parts used to produce a manufactured item. Most CAD/CAM systems maintain and update such lists automatically during the course of a design and manufacturing process.

parts programmer A programmer who translates the physical explanation for machining a part into a series of mathematical steps and then codes computer instructions for those steps. See APT and NUMERICAL CONTROL.

party-line Used to indicate a large number of devices connected to a single line originating in the central processing unit.

Pascal A high-level programming language, named for Blaise Pascal (a French mathematician, 1623-1662), designed to support the concepts of structured programming, with each program following a precise form. The language provides a flexible set of control structures and data types to permit orderly top-down program design and development. It is easy to use and is taught widely in schools and colleges. See APPLE PASCAL, STANDARD PASCAL, TURBO PASCAL, and UCSD PASCAL. Here is a sample program written in Pascal.

```
PROGRAM SalaryChart;
VAR
  Y      :Integer;(* Yearly salary - looping
  counter *)
  M      :Real;(* Monthly salary *)
  W      :Real;(* Weekly salary *)
BEGIN
  WriteLn('YEARLY        MONTHLY
  WEEKLY');
  WriteLn('SALARY        SALARY
  SALARY');
  WriteLn(' $             $            $');
  Y := 11000;
  REPEAT
    M := Y/12;
    W := Y/52;
    WriteLn(Y,'      ',M:8:2,'        ',W:8:2);
    Y := Y + 500;
  UNTIL Y >= 18000;
END.
```

pass (1) A complete input, processing, and output cycle in the execution of a computer program. (2) A scanning of source code by a compiler or assembler.

passing parameters The process of transferring parameters between a main program and a subroutine.

passive device A device that passes signals without altering them.

passive graphics A computer graphics operation that transpires automatically and without operator intervention.

password A special word, code, or symbol that must be presented to the computer system to gain access to its resources. It is used for identification and security purposes on a computer system. Each user is assigned a specific set of alphanumeric characters to gain entrance to the entire computer system or to parts of the system.

paste To place information previously "cut" from a document into a new position. With some computer systems, areas of text or graphics may be cut from a document, saved, and later pasted into another document. See CUT-AND-PASTE.

patch (1) To modify a computer system by adding post-installation enhancements. (2) A section of coding that is inserted into a program to correct a mistake or to alter the program. (3) A temporary electrical connection. (4) In computer graphics, a piece of curvilinear surface, typically with three or four sides. These are attached together at their edges with at least first-order continuity to form complex 3-D surfaces. The edges of a patch are frequently described with polynomials or ratios of polynomials. For example, if both dimensions are described with cubic polynomials, then the patch is said to be bicubic. If ratios of cubic polynomials are used, then the patch is a rational bicubic patch. Although difficult to deal with, one patch can take the place of hundreds of flat polygons and thus greatly reduce the size of a data base.

patching (1) A makeshift technique for modifying a program or correcting programming errors by changing the object code of the program, usually to avoid recompiling or reassembling the program. (2) Making temporary patches to hardware.

path The hierarchy of files through which control passes to find a particular file. See CHANNEL.

patron A customer or client.

pattern recognition The recognition of forms, shapes or configurations by automatic means.

PC An abbreviation for **P**ERSONAL **C**OMPUTER, **P**OCKET **C**OMPUTER, **P**ORTABLE **C**OMPUTER, **P**RINTED **C**IRCUIT, and **P**ROGRAM **C**OUNTER.

PCB An abbreviation for **P**RINTED **C**IRCUIT **B**OARD, the plastic board into which a computer's various electronic components are soldered. These are linked by thin interconnecting wires printed on its surface.

PC compatibility A property of computers that are able to run software prepared for the popular IBM Personal Computer™. Many levels of compatibility are possible.

PC-DOS A disk operating system for the IBM Personal Computer™. An IBM PC version of MS/DOS, developed by Microsoft, Inc.

PC-File III™ A general-purpose, low-cost data base management system designed for ease of use. It lets the user create and maintain simple data bases, as well as produce simple printed reports based on stored data. Developed by ButtonWare, Inc.

P-channel MOS A relatively old metallic oxide semiconductor technology for large scale integration (LSI) devices. Abbreviated PMOS.

PC/IX An IBM implementation of UNIX on the IBM Personal Computer XT™. See UNIX.

PC Limited 286-8™ A low-cost microcomputer compatible with the IBM Personal Computer AT™, manufactured by PC's Limited.

PCM An acronym for **P**LUG **C**OMPATIBLE **M**ANUFACTURER. A business that makes computer equipment that can be plugged into existing computer systems without requiring additional hardware or software interfaces.

p-code A method of translating a source code to an intermediate code, called p-code, by means of a compiler, then using a special p-code interpreter on a host machine to obtain an executable object code. Several versions of Pascal use p-code. See P-SYSTEM.

PC Paint™   A popular painting and drawing program for microcomputers, developed by Mouse Systems Corporation.

PC Paintbrush™   A popular painting and drawing program for microcomputers, developed by International Microcomputer Software, Inc.

PC-6300   A microcomputer compatible with an IBM Personal Computer XT, manufactured by AT&T Information Systems. It is able to run the MS/DOS and UNIX operating systems simultaneously.

PC-Write™   A popular word processing program for the IBM PC™ and compatibles. Developed by Quicksoft.

PC XENIX   An IBM implementation of UNIX on the IBM Personal Computer AT™. See UNIX.

PDM   An abbreviation for **PULSE DURATION MODULATION**. Pulse time modulation in which the duration of a pulse is varied.

pedestal   A table or other physical support for a terminal.

peek   An instruction that allows the programmer to look at (peek at) any location in a computer's storage. See POKE.

penetration   The act of entering an information or computer system without authorization to do so.

pen plotter   See PLOTTER.

perform   To execute instructions in a computer.

performance   A major factor in determining the total productivity of a system. Performance is largely determined by a combination of the following factors: availability, throughput, and response time.

performance monitor   A program that keeps track of service levels being delivered by a computer system.

perfory   The detachable perforated strips on the two sides of fanfold computer paper.

perfs   Perforations in paper to facilitate removing pin-feed edges and tearing continuous paper into separate pages.

periodic report   A report that provides information to users on a regular basis.

peripheral equipment The input/output units and auxiliary storage units of a computer system, attached by cables to the central processing unit. Used to get data in and data out, and to act as a reservoir for large amounts of data that cannot be held in the central processing unit at one time. Graphics tablets, visual display terminals, and floppy disk drives are examples of peripherals.

peripheral equipment operator In a busy computer room, the computer operator is assigned to the console and rarely leaves it. Additional people assist by mounting and demounting disk packs and tapes, labeling outputs, and operating the various input/output devices as directed. These people are often called peripheral equipment operators.

peripheral slots Empty slots built into the housing of some computers so printed circuit cards can be added to increase capabilities without hardware modification. Motherboard sockets into which circuit boards can be plugged.

permanent storage Same as STORAGE.

persistence In essence, the "staying power" of a lighted phosphor. Since a phosphor begins to dim after it has been excited by the electron guns, a long-persistence screen allows the phosphor to dim more slowly.

personal computer A moderately priced microcomputer system intended for personal use rather than commercial purposes. See DESKTOP COMPUTER, MICROCOMPUTER, and PORTABLE COMPUTER.

personal computing The use of a personal computer (microcomputer) by individuals for applications such as entertainment, home management, and education.

personal identification number A security number that computer systems sometimes require before a user can access the system or before a point-of-sale terminal user can enter or receive information. Commonly used with automated teller machines. Abbreviated PIN.

personalized form letter A computer-generated form letter produced by a word processing system or a merge-print program.

personal microcomputer Same as PERSONAL COMPUTER.

PERT An acronym for **PROGRAM EVALUATION AND REVIEW TECHNIQUE**, a management technique for control of large-scale, long-term projects, involving analysis of the time frame required for each step in a process and the relationships of the completion of each step to activity in succeeding steps. See CRITICAL PATH METHOD.

PERT chart A diagram representing the interdependencies of work elements against time, typically shown graphically as circles and connecting lines.

petri nets A popular and useful model for the representation of systems with concurrency or parallelism.

phased conversion A method of system implementation in which the old information system is gradually replaced by the new one.

phonemes Distinct sounds that make up human speech (speech utterances such as lk, ch, sh, etc.). The smallest component of speech.

phonetic system A system that uses data based on voice information (phonemes) to produce sounds that emulate speech.

phosphor A rare earth material used to coat the inside face of cathode-ray tubes. It holds the light generated by a monitor's electron beam guns. Each dot on the screen is actually a phosphor that glows for a given length of time. The dots are used to create an image.

photocomposition The application of electronic processing to the preparation of print. This involves the specification and setting of type, and its production by a photographic process.

photoelectric devices Devices that give an electrical signal in response to visible, infrared, or ultraviolet radiation.

photo-optic memory A memory that uses an optical medium for storage. For example, a laser might be used to record on photographic film.

photo-pattern generation Production of an integrated circuit mask by exposing a pattern of overlapping or adjacent rectangular areas.

photo-plotter An output device that generates high-precision artwork masters photographically for printed circuit board design and integrated circuit masks.

photoresist The process, utilized in etching semiconductor devices, of selectively removing the oxidized surface of a silicon wafer by masking the part that is to be retained.

phototypesetter A computer controlled device that converts text into professional quality type. Virtually all books, magazines, and newspapers are typeset on phototypesetters.

physical design Refers to how data is kept on storage devices and how it is accessed.

physical record The unit of data for input or output, such as a record on a disk. One or more logical records may be contained in one physical record. Contrast with LOGICAL RECORD.

physical security Guards, badges, locks, alarm systems, and other measures to control access to the equipment in a computer center.

pi (π) The Greek letter representing the ratio of a circle to its diameter. The numerical value of π, calculated to fourteen decimal places, is 3.14159265358979.

pica A type size that fits ten characters into each inch of type. Also, in phototypesetting, a sixth of an inch.

picking device An input device, such as a light pen, mouse, or joystick, used to enter data on a visual display screen.

pico Prefix meaning one trillionth.

picocomputer A computer capable of processing data in trillionths of a second.

picosecond One trillionth of a second, one thousandth of a nanosecond; abbreviated PSEC.

picture element See PIXEL.

picture graph A bar graph that uses symbols instead of bars.

picture processing See IMAGE PROCESSING.

pie chart Graphical representation of information. A charting technique used to represent portions of a whole. Commonly used in business graphics.

piezoelectric A property of some crystals that undergo mechanical stress when subjected to voltages, or that produce a voltage when subjected to mechanical stress.

piggyback board A small printed circuit board mounted on a larger circuit board to add additional features to the larger circuit board.

piggyback file A file capable of having records added at the end, without having to recopy the entire file.

PILOT An acronym for PROGRAMMED INQUIRY, LEARNING OR TEACHING. This is not a general-purpose programming language. It is a specialist tool, designed to aid the development of Computer-Assisted Learning (CAL) software and, in particular, CAL tutorials. The language is composed of powerful and nearly syntax-free conversational-processing statements. Here is a program written in PILOT.

```
PR: U
T: What is the world's highest mountain?
A:
M: EVEREST
TY: Well done - Mount Everest it is.
TN: The correct answer is Mount Everest.
```

pilot method The act of trying a new computer system in one area rather than on a wider range of activities. For example, the implementation of a new information system into an organization whereby only a small part of the business uses the new system until it has proved to be successful.

pin Any of the leads on a device, such as a chip, that plugs into a socket and connect it to a system. Each pin provides a function, such as input, output, control, power, or ground.

PIN An acronym for PERSONAL IDENTIFICATION NUMBER. A security number that computer systems sometimes require before a user can access the system or before a point-of-sale terminal user can enter or receive information.

pin compatible Pertaining to chips and devices that perform identical functions and can be substituted for one another. The devices use the same pins for the same input/output signals.

pin feed A paper-feed system that relies on a pin-studded roller to draw paper, punched with matching holes, into a printer.

pingpong To alternate two or more storage devices so processing can take place on a virtually endless set of files.

pins The small metal connectors on a DIP that fit into sockets on a printed circuit board.

pipeline An overlapping operating cycle function used to increase the speed of computers. It involves decomposing a computer instruction in parts so it can be executed simultaneously.

piracy Refers to the process of copying commercial software without the permission of the originator.

pitch The density of characters on a printed line, usually expressed in terms of characters per inch; for example, 10 pitch means that ten characters are printed in every inch; 12 pitch means that twelve characters are printed per inch.

pixel A picture cell. Shortened version of "picture element." The visual display screen is divided into rows and columns of tiny dots, squares, or cells, each of which is a pixel. The smallest unit on the display screen grid that can be stored, displayed, or addressed. A computed picture is typically composed of a rectangular array of pixels (e.g., 300 by 450). The resolution of a picture is expressed by the number of pixels in the display. For example, a picture with 560 x 720 pixels is much sharper than a picture with 275 x 400 pixels.

PLA An abbreviation for PROGRAMMABLE LOGIC ARRAY. An alternative to ROM (Read-Only Memory) that uses a standard logic network programmed to perform a specific function. PLAs are implemented in either MOS or bipolar circuits.

plaintext A term used by encryption experts to denote an ordinary message in its original meaningful form.

planimeter A peripheral device that measures the surface area of a plane figure when the perimeter of that figure is traced with a stylus.

PLANIT An acronym for PROGRAMMING LANGUAGE FOR INTERACTIVE TEACHING. A programming language designed for use with computer-assisted instruction (CAI) systems.

plansheet Same as SPREADSHEET, WORKSHEET.

plasma display panel A type of visual display utilizing an array of neon bulbs, each individually addressable. The image is created by turning on points in a matrix (energized grid of wires) comprising the display surface. The image is steady, long-lasting, bright, and flicker-free; and selective erasing is possible.

platen A backing, commonly cylindrical, against which printing mechanisms strike to produce an impression, such as the roller in a printer against which the keys strike.

PLATO An acronym for PROGRAMMED LOGIC FOR AUTOMATIC TEACHING OPERATIONS, a computer-based instructional system that uses large computers and plasma display terminals. The system contains thousands of lessons representing 65 fields of study for all levels from kindergarten through graduate school. Examples are courses in subjects such as mathematics, science, English, foreign languages and history. Developed by Control Data Corporation.

platter That part of a hard disk drive that actually stores the information. It is a round, flat, metallic plate covered on both surfaces with a brown magnetic substance. See HARD DISK.

PL/C A version of the PL/I programming language, designed to be used in an educational environment. Here is a program written in PL/C.

```
PROCEDURE OPTIONS(MAIN);
/*                                              *
/*    VARIABLE DICTIONARY:                       *
/*    NEW IS THE VALUE OF THE WORD
CONSTRUCTED                                      *
/*        FROM THREE OTHER INPUT WORDS           *
/*    W1, W2, W3 ARE VALUES OF THREE INPUT
WORDS                                           *
```

```
/*                                                    */
DECLARE (W1,W2,W3,NEW) CHARACTER (20)
VARYING;
GET LIST (W1,W2,W3);
PUT SKIP LIST(W1,W2,W3);
/*   FORM A NEW WORD                                  */
NEW=SUBTR(W1,1,1)||SUBSTR(W2,2,1)||
SUBSTR(W3,3,1);
PUT SKIP(2) LIST (NEW);
END FORM;
```

PL/I A high-level programming language used for communicating with computers. It was developed by the IBM Corporation. The abbreviation comes from the name—**PROGRAMMING LANGUAGE ONE**. PL/I is a good language for developing structured programs. Here is a sample program written in PL/I.

```
1 PAY:PROC OPTIONS (MAIN);
2 DCL PAYNO FIXED(5),
     HOURS FIXED(2),
     RATE FIXED(4,2),
     TAX FIXED(5,2),
     GROSS FIXED(5,2);
3 GET LIST(PAYNO,HOURS,RATE,TAX);
4 GROSS=(HOURS*RATE)-TAX;
5 PUT LIST(PAYNO,HOURS,RATE,GROSS);
6 END;
```

PL/M A programming language used to program microcomputers. The language, developed by the Intel Corporation, is a high-level language that can fully command the microcomputer to produce efficient run-time object code. Designed as a tool to help microcomputer programmers concentrate more on their problem or application and less on the actual task of programming. PL/M is derived from PL/I, a general-purpose programming language.

plot To diagram, draw, or map with a PLOTTER.

plotter An output unit that graphs data by automatically controlled pens. Data is normally plotted as a series of incremental steps. Primary plotter types include: drum, pen, flatbed and electrostatic. Also called DIGITAL PLOTTER, INCREMENTAL PLOTTER, and X-Y PLOTTER.

plotting a curve Locating points from coordinates and connecting these points with a curve that approximates or resembles the actual curve that pictures the relationship existing between variables.

plug The connector on a cable that goes to a jack on a part of the system.

plug compatible A peripheral device that requires no interface modification to be linked directly to another manufacturer's computer system.

plug compatible manufacturer (PCM) A business that makes computer equipment that can be plugged into existing computer systems without requiring additional hardware or software interfaces.

plus sign The sign +, indicating that the operation of addition is to be performed.

PMOS An acronym for P-CHANNEL MOS, the oldest type of MOS circuit, in which the electrical current consists of a flow of positive charges. See NMOS.

PN See POLISH NOTATION.

poaching Accessing files or program listings in search of information to which the user is not entitled.

pocket computer A portable, battery-operated, hand-held computer that can be programmed (in BASIC) to perform a wide number of applications. It is able to process small amounts of data under the control of complex stored programs. Also called a HAND-HELD COMPUTER.

point The smallest unit of graphic information, representing a single location on a coordinate system.

pointer (1) An address or other indication of storage location. (2) A visual display cursor.

point identification A complete description of a graphics point including its coordinate location and any special processing functions implied by it.

point-of-sale terminal A device used in retail establishment to record sales information in a form that can be input directly into a computer. This terminal is used to capture data in retail stores (i.e., supermarkets or department stores). Abbreviated POS. See SOURCE DATA AUTOMATION.

point set curve A curve defined by a series of short lines drawn between points.

Poisson theory A mathematical method for estimating the number of lines needed to handle a given amount of data communications traffic.

poke An instruction used to place a value (poke) into a specific location in the computer's storage. See PEEK.

POL SEE PROCEDURE-ORIENTED LANGUAGE or PROBLEM-ORIENTED LANGUAGE.

polar Pertaining to a situation in which a binary 1 is represented by current flow in one direction and binary 0 by current flow in the opposite direction.

polar coordinates A graphic system for specifying the location of a point by reference to an angle and a distance from a fixed point. Contrast with CARTESIAN COORDINATE SYSTEM.

polarizing filter An accessory for terminal screens to reduce glare.

Polish notation A logical notation for a series of arithmetic operations in which no grouping symbol is used. This notation was developed by a Polish logician, Jan Lukasiewicz, in 1929. For example, the expression $a*(b+c)$ is represented in Polish notation as $*a+bc$, where this expression is read from right to left (the evaluation sequence is c, b, + bc, a, $*a + bc$) See REVERSE POLISH NOTATION.

polling A communications control method used by some computer/terminal systems whereby a computer asks many devices attached to a common transmission medium, in turn, whether they have information to send.

polyphase sort An external tape sort used for six or fewer tapes.

pooler A device for consolidating and/or converting key entry data into a form acceptable to the main computer.

pop To pull or retrieve data from the top of a program pushdown stack. The stack pointer is decremented to address the last word pushed on the stack. The contents of this location are moved to one of the accumulators or to another register. Also called PULL. See PUSH.

pop instruction A computer instruction that executes the *pop* operation.

populated board A circuit board that contains all of its electronic components. Contrast with UNPOPULATED BOARD.

port That portion of a computer through which a peripheral device may communicate. A connection between the CPU and a peripheral device. See INPUT/OUTPUT CHANNEL and INTERFACE.

portability Refers to the ease with which a program can be moved from one computer environment to another. Many programs written in high-level languages may be used on different machines. These programs are, therefore, portable.

portable (1) Pertaining to a computer that can be hand carried from one physical location to another. See HAND-HELD COMPUTER and NOTEBOOK COMPUTER. (2) Pertaining to a program that can be easily executed on several different computers.

portable computer A microcomputer system that can be moved easily from one location to another. See BRIEFCASE COMPUTER, DESKTOP COMPUTER, LAP COMPUTER, MICROCOMPUTER, and NOTEBOOK COMPUTER.

portable program Software that can be used on compatible computer systems.

POS An abbreviation for POINT-OF-SALE terminal.

positional notation A method for expressing a quantity by using two or more figures wherein the successive right-to-left figures are to be interpreted as coefficients of ascending integer powers of the radix.

POS systems Department stores and supermarkets are currently using POS systems, in which the cash register is actually a special-purpose computer terminal that can monitor and record transactions directly in the store's data files for inventory control, check on credit card validity, and other data handling functions. See POINT-OF-SALE terminal.

positive true logic A logic system in which a lower voltage represents a bit value of 0 and a higher voltage represents a bit value of 1.

post To enter a unit of information on a record.

post edit To edit output data from a previous computation.

postfix A notation system whereby the operator follows the operands. The addition of 9 and 4 would be expressed as $94+$. See REVERSE POLISH NOTATION.

post-implementation review Evaluation of a system after it has been in use for several months.

post mortem Pertaining to the analysis of an operation after its completion.

post mortem dump A storage dump taken at the end of the execution of a program. See STORAGE DUMP.

PostScript A page description language developed by Adobe Systems for designing page layouts on microcomputer systems.

potentiometer A device used to develop electrical output signals proportional to mechanical movement.

power A symbolic representation of the number of times a number is multiplied by itself. The process is called EXPONENTIATION. For example, 5 to the power of 4 means 5 x 5 x 5 x 5 and is written as 5^4.

power amplifying circuit An electronic circuit that converts an input AC voltage into an output DC voltage.

power down (1) To turn off a computer or peripheral device. (2) The steps a computer may take to preserve the state of the processor and to prevent damage to it or to connected peripherals when the power fails or is shut off. Contrast with POWER UP.

power fail/restart A facility that enables a computer to return to normal operation after a power failure.

powerful Hardware is considered powerful if it is faster, larger, and can accomplish more work than comparable machines. Software is considered powerful if it is efficient and provides a wide range of options.

power on To turn the power switch to the ON position or otherwise supply electric current to a device.

power supply The electrical circuit that changes power from the 110 volt AC current supplied by your local electric utility into low-voltage current used internally by most microcomputers.

power surge A sudden, brief increase in the flow of current that can cause problems in the proper operation of computer equipment.

power up **(1)** To turn on a computer or peripheral device. **(2)** The steps taken by a computer processor when the power is turned on, or restored after a power failure. The processor and peripherals are initialized so that program execution may be started. Contrast with POWER DOWN.

pph An abbreviation for PAGES PER HOUR.

PPM An abbreviation for PULSE POSITION MODULATION, pulse time modulation in which the value of each instantaneous sample of the wave modulates the position in time of a pulse.

pragmatics An investigation of the relationship between symbols and the use of those symbols.

precanned routines See CANNED SOFTWARE.

precedence Rules that state which operators should be executed first in an expression. See HIERARCHY.

precision The degree of exactness with which a quantity is stated. The result of calculation may have more precision than it has accuracy; for example, the true value of pi to six significant digits is 3.14159; the value of 3.14162 is precise to six digits given six digits but is accurate only to about five. See ACCURACY.

precompiler A computer program that processes the source code of another computer program immediately before that program is to be compiled. It may provide the programmer with: **(1)** The ability to use convenient abbreviations that are not acceptable to the compiler itself—the precompiler expands ("transcribes") the shorthand version into source code that is acceptable to the compiler. **(2)** The ability to use nonstandard programming statements that are not acceptable to the compiler. This may be done to aid structured programming in a language that is not well suited to it. The added statements are translated into standard language statements (called a structured programming precompiler). (3) The ability to enforce standards. The source statements written by a programmer can be edited for usages that violate the standards the programmer is supposed to be following. See COMPILER.

predefined function   A standard mathematical procedure available to the user for inclusion in a program.

predefined process   (1) A process identified only by name and defined elsewhere. (2) A CLOSED SUBROUTINE.

predefined process symbol   A flowcharting symbol that is used to represent a subroutine.

predictive reports   Business reports that are used for tactical and strategic decision making.

pre-edit   See EDIT.

prefix notation   A method of forming mathematical expressions in which each operator precedes its operands. For example, in prefix notation, the expression "x plus y multiplied by z" would be represented by "+ xy × z." Polish notation is a form of prefix notation.

p-register   A program counter register in which the location of the current instruction is kept.

preprinted forms   Forms that can contain computer-produced output but that enter a computer system with headings and identifying information already imprinted.

preprocessor   A program that performs conversion, formatting, condensing, or other functions on input data prior to further processing.

presentation graphics   High-quality business graphics intended to visually reinforce points made in the presentation of proposals, plans, and budgets, to top management.

preset   To establish an initial condition, such as control values of a loop or initial values in index registers. See INITIALIZE.

press   The act of pushing down and holding the button on a mouse. See CLICK.

pressure sensitive keyboard A keyboard constructed of two thin plastic sheets coated with a circuit made of electrically conductive ink. It is an economical, flat keyboard used in low-priced microcomputers.

pressure sensitive pen A stylus used with a digitizer. It contains a pressure transducer that detects and transmits writing pressure as z-axis data.

PRESTEL A commercial videotex service in Great Britain.

preventive maintenance The processes used in a computer system that attempt to keep equipment in continuous operating condition by detecting, isolating, and correcting failures before their occurrence. It involves cleaning and adjusting the equipment as well as testing the equipment under both normal and marginal conditions. Contrast with CORRECTIVE MAINTENANCE.

primary cluster A buildup of table entries around a single table location.

primary colors The set of colors from which all others can be derived, but which cannot be produced from each other. The additive primaries (light) are blue, green, and red. The subtractive primaries (colorant) are cyan, magenta, and yellow. The psychological primaries are the pairs red/green, yellow/blue, and black/white.

primary key A unique field for a record. It is used to sort records for processing or to locate a particular record within a file.

primary storage See MAIN STORAGE.

prime shift A working shift that coincides with the normal business hours of an organization, as opposed to a night shift.

primitive (1) A basic or fundamental unit, often referring to the lowest level of a machine instruction or the lowest unit of language translation. (2) In computer graphics, the most basic graphic entities available, such as points, line segments, or characters.

primitive data type The simplest data form.

primitive element A graphics element, such as a line segment or point, that can be readily called up and extrapolated or combined with other primitive elements to form more complex objects or images.

print chart A form used to describe the format of an output report from a printer.

print control character A control character for operations on a printer, such as carriage return, page ejection, or line spacing.

print controller A device that provides print buffers and automatic control and timing for a specific printer.

printed circuit An electronic circuit that is printed, vacuum deposited, or electroplated on a flat insulating sheet. Abbreviated PC.

printed circuit board A thin board on which electrical components such as integrated circuit chips, resistors and switches, are mounted.

print density The number of printed characters per unit of measurement, such as the number of characters on a page.

print element That part of a printer that actually puts the image on paper. Popular print elements are daisy wheels, thimbles, and type balls.

printer An output device that produces hard copy output. See ELECTROSTATIC PRINTER and LINE PRINTER.

printer stand A wood or metal stand designed to support a printer. The stand has an opening in the top for fanfold printer paper.

print head The part of a printer that actually puts the image on paper. Also called a print element.

print layout sheet A chart used for establishing margin and spacing requirements for a printed report.

printout Computer output printed on paper.

print position Any of the various positions on a form where a character may be printed.

print quality The quality of a printout produced on a printer. See DRAFT QUALITY and LETTER QUALITY.

Print Shop™ A simple graphics package that performs several useful printing services easily and well. It prints standard and customized signs, greeting cards, posters, and letter heads, as well as multipage banners on fan-fold paper with a wide selection of fonts, icons, borders, and graphics. Developed by Broderbund Software.

print wheel A single element providing the character set at one printing position of a wheel printer.

priority interrupt An interrupt that is given preference over other interrupts within the system.

priority processing The processing of a sequence of jobs on the basis of assigned priorities. See JOB QUEUE.

privacy Those personal aspects a person chooses to shield from public scrutiny. The right of individuals to select the time and circumstances where information about them is to be made public. See *Freedom of Information Act* and *Privacy Act of 1974*.

Privacy Act of 1974 An act passed by the U.S. Congress to regulate the storage of data in federal-agency data bases and to give individuals the right to see their records, correct errors, and remove data that should not be on the file.

private automatic branch exchange A private automatic telephone switching system that provides telephone communications within a business and controls the transmission of calls to and from the public telephone network. Abbreviated PABX.

private line A channel or circuit furnished to a user for exclusive use.

privately leased line A communications line intended for the use of a single customer.

privileged instruction A computer instruction not available for use in ordinary programs written by users; its use is restricted to the routines of the operating system. See STORAGE KEY and STORAGE PROTECTION.

probabilistic model A model that makes use of the mathematics of probability. It is used to analyze data whose individual values are unknown but whose long-range behavior can be predicted.

probability Probability measures the odds of a given event taking place. For example, on a coin flip the probability is 1/2 that it will show heads and 1/2 that it will show tails.

probability theory A measure of the likelihood of occurrence of a chance event. It is used to predict the behavior of a group.

problem analysis The use of a plan to solve a problem. First step in the program developmental cycle.

problem definition The formulation of the logic used to define a problem. A description of a task to be performed.

problem description In information processing, the statement of a problem. May also include a description of the method of solution, the solution itself, the transformation of data, and the relationship of procedures, data, constraints, and environment.

problem-oriented language A programming language designed for the convenient expression of a given class of problems. Abbreviated POL. Contrast with ASSEMBLY LANGUAGE, MACHINE LANGUAGE, and PROCEDURE-ORIENTED LANGUAGE. See APT, COGO, GPSS, and RPG.

problem program A program executed when the central processing unit is in the "problem state." Any program that does not contain privileged instructions.

problem solving While a problem that can be solved by a computer need not be described by an exact mathematical equation, it does need a certain set of rules that the computer can follow. If the solution to a problem depends upon intuition or guessing, or if the problem is badly defined, the computer cannot be used to solve it. A computer cannot perform tasks properly unless problems are specified correctly in every detail. The instructions must also list in complete detail each step of the solution. Here is an overview of the steps taken to solve a problem:

A computer user studies the problems and prepares a plan of action, perhaps with the aid of an analyst.

The programmer, or the analyst, decides which steps the computer must take to obtain the desired results and specifies the form of input and output.

This plan of action is then coded into a set of steps in a programming language.

These instructions are prepared for input by keying them directly into the computer's memory via a keyboard or by keying them onto a magnetic disk or magnetic tape.

Once in the computer's memory, the program is translated into machine language (the only language the computer understands) by a translating program called an interpreter, compiler, or assembler.

The program is now ready to be executed by the computer.

The steps of the program are carried out on the data used with the program, and the output is generated.

procedure (1) The course of action taken for the solution of a problem. (2) A portion of a high-level language program that performs a specific task necessary for the program. (3) Another name for a computer program. (4) A form of subprogram.

procedure division One of the four main component parts of a COBOL program.

procedure manual A manual that describes the job functions required in a certain organization or department.

procedure-oriented language A high-level, machine-independent, programming language designed for the convenient expression of procedures used in the solution of a wide class of problems. Examples include Pascal, BASIC, and Modula-2. Abbreviated POL. Contrast with ASSEMBLY LANGUAGE, MACHINE LANGUAGE, and PROBLEM-ORIENTED LANGUAGE. See ADA, ALGOL, APL, BASIC, C, COBOL, FORTH, FORTRAN, LOGO, MODULA-2, PASCAL, PILOT, PLANIT, PL/I, SIMSCRIPT, SNOBOL, WATFIV and WATFOR.

process A systematic sequence of operations to produce a specified result. To transform raw data into useful information.

process-bound A situation in which the computer system is limited by the speed of the processor.

process control The use of the computer to control industrial processes such as oil refining and steel production.

process control computer   A computer used in a process control system. Generally limited in instruction capacity, word length, and accuracy. They are designed for continuous operation in nonairconditioned facilities.

process conversion   Changing the method of running the computer system.

processing   The computer manipulation of data in solving a problem. See DATA PROCESSING.

processing symbol   A rectangular-shaped flowcharting symbol used to indicate a processing operation (e.g., a calculation).

processor   A device or system capable of performing operations upon data, such as a central processing unit (hardware) or compiler (software). A compiler is sometimes referred to as a language processor.

processor-bound   Refers to processes that are slowed down by the time it takes the central processing unit to perform the actual processing or computations. Contrast with I/O-BOUND. Same as COMPUTE BOUND.

ProDOS   An Apple II operating system designed to support mass storage devices and floppy disk storage devices. ProDOS stands for **PRO**FESSIONAL **D**ISK **O**PERATING **S**YSTEM.

product   The quantity that results from multiplying two quantities.

production   Actual work done by a computer to produce output for users.

production run   The execution of a debugged program that routinely accomplishes its purpose. For example, running a payroll program to produce weekly paychecks is a production run.

productivity   A measure of the work performed by a software/hardware system. Productivity largely depends on a combination of two factors: the facility (ease of use) of the system and the performance (throughput, response time, and availability) of the system.

ProFile Apple Computer's personal mass storage system. A ProFile holds the equivalent of dozens of floppy disks.

program A series of instructions that will cause a computer to process data. It may be in a high-level source form, which requires intermediate processing before the computer can execute it, or it may be in an object form directly executable by the computer. Here is a sample program.

```
program add (input, output);
var
  first, second, sum: integer;
begin
  read (first, second);
  sum := first + second;
  write (sum)
end.
```

program chaining A process of linking programs or program sections together. This allows programs that are larger than main memory to be executed through sequential loading and execution of successive sections or modules of that program.

program coding The process of writing instructions in a programming language.

program control Descriptive of a system in which a computer is used to direct the operation.

program correctness See PROGRAM TESTING.

program counter A counter that indicates the location of the next program instruction to be executed by the computer. Same as INSTRUCTION COUNTER.

program development cycle The steps involved in the solution of a problem with a computer; problem analysis, algorithm development, coding, program execution, program debugging, program testing, and documentation.

program file A file containing computer programs.

program flowchart A diagram composed of symbols, directional lines, and information about how the computer will be used to solve a problem. Contrast with SYSTEM FLOWCHART. See FLOWCHART.

program generator See GENERATOR.

program graph A graphical representation of a program.

program ID Program identification.

program language See PROGRAMMING LANGUAGE.

program library A collection of available computer programs and routines, or portions of programs. The contents of the library are stored for reuse. If they are complete programs, they may be simply reused as is. Parts of programs may be copied into other programs to reduce labor and standardize the use of those copied parts in new programs.

program listing See LISTING.

program maintenance The process of keeping programs up to date by correcting errors, making changes as requirements change, and altering the programs to take advantage of equipment changes.

programmable Designing a device whose operation can be controlled by a program.

programmable communications interface An interface board used for communications control.

programmable function key A keyboard key whose function changes with the programs within the computer.

programmable logic array A device that provides the sum of a partial product with outputs for a given set of inputs.

programmable memory A content-changeable memory, where most computer programs and data are stored. It is usually RAM. Contrast with ROM. See STORAGE.

programmable read-only memory A memory that can be programmed by electrical pulses. Once programmed, it is read-only. A special machine (called a PROM programmer) is used to write in the new program. Abbreviated PROM.

programmed check A check consisting of tests inserted into the programmed statement of a problem and performed by the use of computer instructions.

programmed label To make the identification of disk and tape files more reliable, most programs include a built-in routine that creates a label record at the beginning of the file.

programmer A person whose job is to design, write, and tes[t] programs and the instructions that cause a computer to d[o] a specific job. Also called COMPUTER PROGRAMMER. Se[e] CODER and PARTS PROGRAMMER.

programmer/analyst A person whose major tasks involv[e] combining system analysis and design functions with pr[o]gramming activities.

programmer board A board that allows a user to progra[m] PROM or EPROM memories for use in computer syster[ms] See PROM PROGRAMMER.

programming The process of translating a problem from i[ts] physical environment to a language that a computer ca[n] understand and obey. Planning the procedure for solving [a] problem. This may involve, among other things, the analys[is] of the problem, coding of the problem, establishing inp[ut] output formats, establishing testing and checkout proc[e]dures, allocation of storage, preparation of documentatio[n] and supervision of the running of the program on a co[m]puter.

programming aids Computer programs that aid comput[er] users, such as compilers, debugging packages, editors, a[nd] mathematical subroutines.

programming language A scheme of formal notation [in] which a programmer specifies computer programs to [a] computer hardware. There are hundreds of programmi[ng] languages in existence, ranging from machine-oriented l[an]guages that are very difficult for a human to follow or [use] to high-level languages that require intermediate translat[ion] before they can be used by the machine.

programming librarian A person who is one of the three [nu]cleus members of the Chief Programmer Team. This pers[on] maintains and operates the development support libra[ry.] Duties include code creation, submission of computer ru[ns,] and filing and logging of all outputs.

programming linguistics Three interconnected concepts[:] syntax, semantics, and pragmatics that can be used to [de]scribe languages for communication between any two s[ys]tems, whether mechanical, electrical, or human.

programming team A group of individuals assigned to a programming project. See CHIEF PROGRAMMER.

program specifications A document that identifies the data requirements of a system, the files required, the input/output specifications, and the processing details.

program stack An area of computer memory set aside for temporary storage of data and instructions, particularly during an interrupt. See POP, PUSH, PUSH DOWN LIST, PUSH DOWN STACK, and STACK.

program stop A stop instruction built into the program that will automatically stop the computer under certain conditions, upon reaching the end of the processing, or upon completing the solution of a problem.

program storage A portion of main storage reserved for the storage of programs, routines, and subroutines. In many systems, protection devices are used to prevent inadvertent alteration of the contents.

program switch A point in a programming routine at which two courses of action are possible, the correct one being determined by a condition prevailing elsewhere in the program or by a physical disposition of the system.

program testing Executing a program with test data to ascertain that it functions as expected.

progress reporting Input of actual time, resource utilization, and task/activity completions.

project An undertaking, having a definite objective and specific start and completion points, that is the composite of tasks and activities set up in a logical order to achieve the objective.

project control The phase of a project management cycle that compares actual performance with the planned schedule, and implements corrective measures to avoid project completion delays.

projecting Producing a two-dimensional graphics display of a three-dimensional scene.

projection An extension of past trends into the future. Computer supplied information can be invaluable in this technique.

project library A data base of projects, tasks, and activities that can be modified and applied when planning new projects.

project manager A person responsible for the enforcement of a project's goals. Sometimes called a project team leader.

project plan The phase of a project management cycle that involves the development and organization of the work plan.

project schedule The phase of a project management cycle that details the start and completion times for each task and activity.

PROLOG An acronym for **PRO**GRAMMING IN **LOG**IC; a high-level logic-based programming language used in the field of artificial intelligence. PROLOG is designed to manipulate knowledge instead of numbers. It is composed mainly of common English words and uses these words to describe facts, relationships, and patterns in a logical, concise fashion. What distinguishes PROLOG from more traditional procedure-oriented programming languages is that each line of PROLOG includes both instructions to and data to be managed by the computer. Developed by Alain Colmerauer at the University of Marseilles. See MICRO PROLOG and TURBO PROLOG. Here is a program written in PROLOG.

```
X is-route-between (y z) if
                    X begins-with y &
                    X ends-with Z &
                    X is-connected

(x1Y) begins-with x

X ends-with y if
                    X reverses-to Z &
                    Z begins-with y

(x) is-connected
(x1 x21Y) is-connected if
```

```
                    x1 Linked-to x2 &
                    (x2|Y) is-connected

   x Linked-to y if x joined-to y
   x Linked-to y if y joined-to x
```

PROM An acronym for **PROGRAMMABLE READ ONLY MEM-ORY.** A memory that can be programmed by electrical pulses. Once programmed, it is read-only. The PROM chips can be purchased blank and then programmed by using a special machine (PROM PROGRAMMER).

PROM burner See PROM PROGRAMMER.

PROM programmer A device used to program PROMs (Programmable Read Only Memories) and reprogram EPROMs (Erasable PROMs) by electrical pulses. Sometimes called PROM burner.

prompt A character or message provided by the computer to indicate that it is ready to accept keyboard input. Usually an on-screen question or instruction that tells the user which data to enter or what action to take, such as "Enter name:" or "Enter diameter of circle:".

proofing program Same as DICTIONARY PROGRAM or SPELL-ING CHECKER.

propagated error An error or mistake occurring in one operation and affecting data required for subsequent operations so the error or mistake is spread through much of the processed data.

propagation delay A time delay in a satellite communications system.

proportional spacing If the horizontal space allotted to a printed character is proportional to the width of that character, the spacing is said to be proportional. Since this book is typeset in proportional spacing, the "w" in the word "write" consumes more space than the "i." The standard typewriter style, in contrast, allots equal space to all characters.

proposition A statement in logic that can be true or false.

proprietary An adjective meaning "held in private ownership."

proprietary software A program that is owned by an individual or business because it is either copyrighted or not yet released to the public. One cannot legally use or copy this software without permission. Compare with PUBLIC DOMAIN SOFTWARE.

protect To prevent unauthorized access to programs or a computer system. To shield against harm. Often means write-protecting a disk.

protected storage Storage locations reserved for special purposes in which data cannot be stored without undergoing a screening procedure to establish suitability for storage therein.

protocol Set of rules or conventions governing the exchange of information between computer systems. See HANDSHAKING.

prototype The first version or model of a software package or computer hardware device or system ready for preproduction testing.

proving Testing a machine in order to demonstrate that it is free from faults, usually after corrective maintenance.

psec An acronym for picosecond; one trillionth of a second.

pseudocode An intermediate form of writing program instructions—instructions that approach the computer programming language but are written in an English-like language instead of a true programming language so that programming logic can be checked more easily. An example of a pseudocode sequence follows.

```
For every coin in the cup
    Pull out a coin
        If it is a 50 cent piece
            Put it in the half-dollar pile
        Else if it is a 25 cent piece
            Put it in the quarter pile
        Else if it is a 10 cent piece
            Put it in the dime pile
        Else if it is a 5 cent piece
```

```
            Put it in the nickel pile
      Else if it is a 1 cent piece
            Put it in the penny pile
      Else discard it
Do next coin until cup is empty.
```

pseudolanguage A language, not directly understandable by a computer, that is used to write computer programs. Before a pseudoprogram can be used, it must be translated into a language that the computer understands (machine language). See HIGH-LEVEL LANGUAGE.

pseudooperation An operation that is not part of the computer's operation repertoire as realized by hardware; hence, an extension of the set of machine operations.

pseudorandom number A number generated by a computer in a deterministic manner. These numbers have been subjected to many statistical tests of randomness and, for most practical purposes, one can be used as a random number.

p-system A microcomputer operating system, with a principal advantage that programs written for it will work on a wide variety of machines. It translates p-code into the machine language appropriate to a specific computer. See P-CODE and UCSD P-SYSTEM.

publication language A well-defined form of a programming language suitable for use in publications. A language such as this is necessary because some languages use special characters that are not available in common type fonts.

public domain software Software not protected by copyright laws and is therefore free for all to reproduce and trade without fear of legal prosecution. It is any computer program that is donated to the public by its creator. See FREE-WARE. Compare with PROPRIETARY SOFTWARE.

public network A communications service open to anyone, usually on a fee basis.

puck A handheld, manually controlled, graphics input device used to pinpoint coordinates on a graphics tablet. A puck has a transparent window containing cross hairs, allows coordinate data to be digitized into the system from a drawing placed on the tablet surface.

pull See POP.

pull-down menu A menu that can be displayed by moving the mouse pointer to a title, then pressing the mouse button.

pull instruction An instruction that pulls or retrieves data from the top of the program push-down stack. Same as POP IN-STRUCTION.

pulse An abrupt change in voltage, either positive or negative, that conveys information to a circuit.

pulse modulation Use of a series of pulses that are modulated or characterized to convey information. Types of pulse modulation include amplitude (PAM), position (PPM), and duration (PDM) systems.

punched card A cardboard card, used in data processing operations in which tiny rectangular holes at hundreds of individual locations denote numerical values and alphanumeric codes.

pure procedure A procedure that never modifies any part of itself during execution.

purge To erase a file.

push Putting data into the top location of a program stack. The stack pointer is automatically incremented to point to the next location, which becomes the top of the stack. Also called put. See POP.

push-down list A list written from the bottom up, with each new entry placed on the top of the list. The item to be processed first is the one on the top of the list. See LIFO (LAST IN-FIRST OUT).

push-down stack A set of memory locations or registers in a computer that implements a push-down list.

push instruction A computer instruction that implements a push operation.

push-pop stack A register that receives information from the program counter and stores the address locations of instructions on a last-in-first-out basis. Two operations are involved in stack processing: "pushing" describes the filling of the stack from registers; "popping" involves emptying the stack for transfer to registers.

push-up list A list of items in which each item is entered at the end of the list and the other items maintain their same relative position in the list.

put See PUSH.

Q

quad-density A term used to specify the data storage density of a computer disk system. Quad-density systems can store up to four times the data that can be stored on single-density disks. Double-sided double-density disks are quad-density disks.

quadratic quotient search A hashing algorithm that uses a quadratic offset when probing subsequent table locations.

quality control A technique for evaluating the quality of product being processed by checking it against a predetermined standard and taking the proper corrective action if the quality falls below the standard.

quality engineering The establishment and execution of tests to measure product quality and adherence to acceptance criteria.

quantify To assign numeric values to nonnumeric objects.

quantity A positive or negative real number in the mathematical sense.

quantum The smallest unit of measure employed in a system.

quasilanguage See PSEUDOLANGUAGE.

Quattro™ A spreadsheet program developed by Borland International, Inc.

QUBE An information utility that is part of an advanced cable-TV system providing viewers everything from first-run movies to special programs for doctors and lawyers. It is an interactive Viewdata-type service.

query To ask for information. To make a request for information from a database system.

query by example To ask for information from a database system by defining the qualifications for selected records on a sample record, rather than decribing a procedure for finding the information.

query language A high-level natural language that allows the user to make inquiries of a computer system without knowing any codes or keywords. Special software analyzes the user's request, interprets its likely meaning, and responds on the display screen.

question-answer The process of interacting with the computer. The computer asks the user a question, and the user provides the answer.

queue A group of items waiting to be acted upon by the computer. The arrangement of items determines the processing priority. Queues are nothing more than the waiting lines that have become an accepted and often frustrating fact of modern life. For example, customers at a supermarket checkout counter or messages to be transmitted in a data communications system.

queued access method Any access method that automatically synchronizes the transfer of data between the program using the access method and the input/output devices, thereby eliminating delays for input/output operations.

queuing A method of controlling the information processing sequence.

queuing theory A form of probability theory useful in studying delays or lineups at servicing points. A research technique concerned with the correct sequential orders of moving units. May include sequence assignments for bits of information or whole messages.

quibinary code A binary coded decimal code used to represent decimal numbers in which each decimal digit is represented by seven binary digits.

quick disconnect A type of electrical connector that allows rapid locking and unlocking of the mating connector halves.

quicksort A sorting algorithm making use of pivot values.

QWERTY keyboard The keyboard arrangement that is standard on most keyboards found on typewriters, word processors and computers. It was developed more than a century ago to slow down swift typists and prevent jamming of the old mechanical typewriters. The design is called QWERTY after the first six letters on the top alphabetic line of the keyboard. Now that electronics can accommodate high-speed typing, QWERTY is no longer efficient. Many businesses are replacing the QWERTY keyboards with the more efficient Dvorak keyboard. Some computer companies now offer keyboards with a switch that will change from one keyboard to the other. See DVORAK KEYBOARD and MAL-TRON KEYBOARD.

R

R An abbreviation for REGISTER, REQUEST, and RESET.

race condition The indeterminate state that results when two computer instructions are operating concurrently and it is not possible to know which one will finish first.

rack A metal frame or chassis on which panels of electrical, electronic, or other equipment such as amplifiers, and power supply units may be mounted.

radian A central angle subtended in a circle by an arc whose length is equal to the radius of the circle. Thus the radian measure of an angle is the ratio of the arc it subtends to the radius of the circle in which it is the central angle (a constant ratio for all such circles). A straight line (180-degree angle) has an angle of π radians; a 90-degree angle is 1.5707963 radians, or $\pi/2$. Trigonometric functions in many high-level programming languages work on radians rather than degrees.

Radio Shack A manufacturer and distributor of electronic equipment, including microcomputer systems sold under the name of TRS-80 or Tandy. A division of the Tandy Corporation.

radix The base number in a number system (e.g., the radix in the decimal system is 10). Synonymous with BASE.

radix complement See COMPLEMENT.

radix point In a number system, the character (a dot) or implied character that separates the integral part of a numeral from the fractional part. See BINARY POINT, HEXADECIMAL POINT, and OCTAL POINT.

radix sorting algorithm A sorting algorithm based on the radix of the items being sorted.

ragged left Refers to text printed with a straight right margin and an uneven left margin. Also called flush right.

ragged right Text printed with a straight left margin and an uneven right margin. Also called flush left.

raised flooring Elevated flooring used in computer rooms so connecting cables can be laid directly between equipment units.

RAM An acronym for RANDOM ACCESS MEMORY, a memory into which the user can enter information and instructions (write), and from which the user can call up data (read). RAM is the "working memory" of the computer, into which applications programs can be loaded from outside and then executed.

RAM card A printed circuit board containing RAM chips. By plugging such a board into some computers, their main storage can be expanded.

random access The process of obtaining data from or placing data into a storage location in which access is independent of the order of storage. Another name for DIRECT ACCESS.

random access memory A memory whose contents can be read or written on directly without regard to any other memory location. See RAM.

random files Files not organized in any sequence. Data are retrieved based on the address of the record on the direct access device.

random logic design Designing a system by using discrete logic circuits.

random number A patternless sequence of digits. An unpredictable number, produced by chance, that satisfies one or more of the tests for randomness. See PSEUDO RANDOM NUMBER.

random number generator A computer program or hardware designed to produce a pseudo random number or series of pseudo random numbers according to specified limitations

random processing Processing of data randomly. Same as DI-RECT ACCESS PROCESSING. Contrast with SEQUENTIAL PROCESSING.

range The span of values that an element may assume.

range check A check usually applied to a numeric element to verify that it falls within a particular range, such as the months of the year being in the range of 1 to 12.

rank (1) To arrange in an ascending or descending series according to importance. (2) A measure of the relative position in a group, series, array, or classification.

raster display A video display that sweeps a beam through a fixed pattern, building up an image with a matrix of points. See RASTER GRAPHICS and VECTOR DISPLAY.

raster fill The process used by a graphics camera to fill in the spaces between the raster lines of a video screen to give a screen picture a more finished appearance.

raster graphics Manner of storing and displaying data as horizontal rows of uniform grid or picture cells (pixels). Raster scan devices recreate or "refresh" a display screen thirty to sixty times a second in order to provide a clear image for viewing. Raster display devices are generally faster and less expensive than vector tubes and are therefore gaining popularity for use with graphics systems.

raster scan The generation of an image on a display screen made by refreshing the display area line by line.

rat's nest A feature on printed circuit design systems that allows users to view all the computer-determined internections between components. This makes it easier to determine whether further component-placement improvement is necessary to optimize signal routing.

raw data Data that has not been processed. Such data may or may not be on machine-readable media.

RDBMS See RELATIONAL DATA BASE MANAGEMENT SYSTEM.

read To get information from any input or file storage media, such as reading a magnetic disk by sensing the patterns of magnetism. Contrast with WRITE.

reader Any device capable of transcribing data from an input medium.

read head A magnetic head designed to read data from the media. Contrast with WRITE HEAD.

reading wand A device that senses marks and codes optically, such as a device that reads price tags in a point-of-sale terminal.

read ink See NONREFLECTIVE INK.

read-only memory A special type of computer memory, permanently programmed with one group of frequently used instructions. Read-only memory does not lose its program when the computer's power is turned off, but the program cannot be changed by the user. In many microcomputers, the BASIC language interpreter and operating systems are contained in read-only memory. Several microcomputers use plug-in read-only memory modules that contain special programs, such as game programs, educational programs, and business programs. Abbreviated ROM. See EPROM, FIRMWARE, PROM, ROM, and SOLID STATE CARTRIDGE.

read-only storage See READ-ONLY MEMORY.

readout The manner in which a computer represents the processed information, such as by visual display, printer, plotter, and photographic film.

read-write head A small electromagnet used to read, write, or erase data on a magnetic storage device, such as disk or tape. See READ HEAD and WRITE HEAD.

real constant A number that contains a decimal point, such as 843.22 or -67.3. Also called floating-point constant.

real number Any rational or irrational number.

real storage The main storage in a virtual memory system.

real time Descriptive of computer processing systems that receive and process data quickly enough to produce output to control, direct, or affect the outcome of an ongoing activity or process. For example, in an airline reservations system, a customer-booking inquiry is entered into the computer to see whether space is available. If a seat is booked, the file of available seats is updated immediately, thus giving an up-to-date record of seats reserved and seats available.

real-time clock A clock in the computer that keeps track of time.

real-time image generation Performance of the computations necessary to update an image is completed within the refresh rate, so the sequence appears correctly to the viewer. An example is flight simulation, in which thousands of computations must be performed to present an animated image, all within the rate of 30-60 cycles per second at which the frames change.

real-time output Output data removed from a system at a time of need by another system.

reasonableness check A technique whereby tests are made on processed data to indicate whether a gross error exists. Programming instructions would check if the data lies within preset upper and lower limits and initiate some action if the data are not reasonable.

reboot To stop and boot the operating system again. Usually occurs by human intervention as the result of a problem. It is similar to "reset" on a home appliance. To RESTART.

receive To capture messages transmitted by a sender.

receive-only A designation used to indicate the read-only capabilities of equipment lacking keyboards and other input facilities.

receiver The recipient of messages dispatched by a sender.

recompile To compile a program again, usually after debugging or because the program needs to be run on a different type of computer.

reconstruction Restoring the data base system to a previous state after data has been tampered with or destroyed.

record A collection of related items of data treated as a unit. The description of an item in a data base. Each item is represented by a record that consists of one or more fields. Everyday examples of a record include an entry in a dictionary or a listing in a phone book.

recording density The number of useful storage cells per unit of length or area. For example, the number of characters per inch on a magnetic tape or the number of bits per inch on a single track of a disk. Also called packing density. The most common magnetic tape densities are 800, 1,600, and 6,250 characters per inch (cpi). A recording density of 6,250 cpi on tape means that there are 6,250 characters per inch.

record layout The arrangement and structure of data elements in a record, including the size and sequence of its components.

record length A measure of the size of a record, usually specified in units such as words, bytes, or characters.

record manager Another term for FILE MANAGER.

record number A number automatically assigned to each new record as it is created. Serves as a reference number and may be transparent to the user.

records management Concerned with the creation, retention, and scheduled destruction of an organization's paper and film documents.

recover To continue program execution after a failure. To overcome a problem.

recoverable error An error condition that can be sensed and corrected thereby allowing continued operation of a program.

rectangular coordinate system A system in which every point in a plane is given an address in the form of a pair of numbers called the coordinates of the point. Same as CARTESIAN COORDINATE SYSTEM.

rectifier An electrical device that changes alternating current into direct current.

recurring costs Budgeted items that are not one-time expenditures, such as personnel, supplies, equipment rental, and overhead costs associated with a computer system.

recursion A set of operations or program statements in which one of the operations or statements is specified in terms of the entire set. The continued repetition of the same operation(s).

recursive Pertaining to a process that is inherently repetitive. The result of each repetition is usually dependent upon the result of the previous repetition.

recursive algorithm An algorithm that involves recursion.

recursive procedure A procedure which, while being executed, either calls itself (*A*) or calls another procedure (*B*), which in turn calls back procedure *A*.

recursive subroutine A subroutine capable of calling itself, or a subroutine that invokes another subroutine, which in turn invokes the original subroutine.

red-green-blue monitor A high-resolution color display unit. See RGB MONITOR.

reduction The process of saving computer storage by eliminating empty fields or unnecessary data to reduce the length of records.

redundancy (1) The duplication of a feature in order to prevent system failure in the event of the feature's malfunction. (2) Repetition of information among various files.

redundancy check A check based on the transfer of more bits or characters than the minimum number required to express the message itself, the added bits or characters having been inserted systematically for checking purposes. See PARITY BIT and PARITY CHECKING.

redundant code A binary coded decimal value with an added check bit.

redundant information A message expressed in such a way that the essence of the information occurs in several ways.

reel A mounting for magnetic tape.

reentrant Pertaining to a routine that can be used by two or more independent programs at the same time.

reentrant code Assembly generated machine language programs that may be shared simultaneously by any number of users.

reentrant subroutine In a multiprogramming system, a subroutine of which only one copy resides in main storage, shared by several programs.

reference edge   See ALIGNING EDGE.

reference manual   A manual designed to describe how a piece of equipment or a program works.

reference parameter   A parameter not accessed by name, but through a pointer variable.

reflectance   In optical scanning, a relative value assigned to a character or color of ink when compared with the background.

reflectance ink   In optical scanning, ink that has a reflectance level that very nearly approximates the acceptable paper reflectance level for a particular optical character reader.

Reflex™   An analytical data base program that can be used to build and manage information in list format. One of its strengths is an ability to use information created by such programs as Lotus 1-2-3™, dBASE III™, and PFS:File™. Developed by Borland International, Inc.

reformat   To change the representation of data from one format to another.

refresh circuitry   The electronic circuitry necessary to restore (1) the information displayed on a visual display screen, and (2) the data stored in dynamic RAM, which steadily lose their charge.

refresh display cycle   The time between scans of the electron beam on a display screen. The phosphors on the face of a CRT are excited and glow as the result of each pass of the electron beam in each refresh cycle. The refresh rate usually occurs at a level fast enough to eliminate the flicker from the brightening and fading of the phosphors each time they are struck. Typically, the image must be regenerated at a rate of 1/30th or 1/60th of a second.

refreshing   The process of constantly reactivating or restoring information that decays or fades away when left idle. For instance, the phosphor on a CRT screen needs to be constantly reactivated by an electron beam to remain illuminated. Typically, the image must be regenerated at a rate of 30 to 60 hertz to avoid flicker. Likewise, cells in dynamic memory elements must be repeatedly accessed to avoid losing their contents.

refresh memory The area of computer memory that holds values indicating whether a particular dot of a graphics raster is on or off. The memory may also contain information on brightness and color.

refresh rate The rate at which the graphic image on a CRT is redrawn in a refresh display; time needed for one refresh of the displayed image.

regenerate The process of renewing some quantity. Used in storage devices to write back information that has been read in a destructive manner.

region In multiprogramming with a variable number of tasks, a term often used to mean the internal storage space allocated.

register A high-speed device used in a central processing unit for temporary storage of small amounts of data or intermittent results during processing.

registration The accurate positioning relative to a reference.

regression analysis (1) A technique in model-building used to define a dependent variable in terms of a set of independent variables. (2) The construction of a "line of best fit" to best illustrate the pattern of a set of data points.

regression testing Tests performed on a previously verified program whenever it is extended or corrected.

relation (1) The equality, inequality, or any property that can be said to hold (or not hold) for two objects in a specified order. (2) In a relational data base model, a table, the basic form of information storage. (3) In a network/hierarchical data base model, a named association among sets of entities.

relational data base A data base in which some data items in one type of record refer to records of a different type. Relational data bases give the user the flexibility to link (join, or create a relationship between) information stored in many disk files. It allows you to interchange and cross reference information between two different types of records, such as comparing the information in a group of invoices to the information in an inventory. Most people do not need relational data bases. If you merely want to keep track of a mailing list, you don't require a relational data base. If you want to keep a simple inventory of something, you don't need a relational data base. However, if you want to print out a mailing list of people who ordered products from your inventory, you will need a relational data base. Relational data bases are more powerful, more complex, more difficult to use, and more expensive than other data base systems.

relational data base management system A collection of hardware and software that organizes and provides access to a relational data base. See RELATIONAL DATA BASE.

relational expression An expression that contains one or more relational operators.

relational model A data base model in which items are functionally related.

relational operator A symbol used to compare two values. It specifies a condition that may be either true or false, such as = (equal to), < (less than), and > (greater than).

relational structure A form of data base organization in which all data items are contained in one file and are linked together by a trail of logical pointers. The relationships between these data items can be altered at will, and the information can be obtained by interactive query or batch processing.

relative address An address to which a base address must be added in order to form the absolute address of a particular storage location.

relative coding Coding that uses machine instructions with relative addresses.

relative movement Movement of an object on the screen to a new position in terms of the last position rather than from 0, 0. For example, "move 4, 8" would move a marked point four units to the right and eight units up from the last recorded point.

relay A magnetically operated switch used in preelectronic computers.

release version The version of a program currently available for purchase.

reliability A measure of the ability of a program, system, or individual hardware device to function without failure.

relocatable addresses The addresses used in a program that can be positioned at almost any place in main storage.

relocatable program A program existing in a form that permits it to be loaded and executed in any available region of a computer's main storage.

relocate A program coded so that it may be executed anywhere in computer storage.

remainder The dividend minus the product of the quotient and divisor.

remark Verbal messages inserted into a source language program that do not cause any computer processing steps but are helpful notes for future users who may attempt to understand or alter the program.

remote Physically distant from a local computer, such as a video display terminal or printer.

remote access Communication with a computer facility by a station (or stations) distant from the computer.

remote batch processing The processing of data in batches at the remote location by using a small computer system. See BATCH PROCESSING.

remote computing services Services offered to customers by computer service centers. Examples are batch processing, interactive problem solving, and consulting.

remote job entry Refers to the computer programs used to submit processing jobs from remote terminals. Abbreviated RJE.

remote processing The processing of computer programs through an input/output device remotely connected to a computer system. See REMOTE BATCH PROCESSING.

remote site An outpost in a distributed computer network.

remote station See REMOTE TERMINAL.

remote terminal A device for communicating with a computer from sites that are physically separated from the computer, often distant enough so that communications facilities such as telephone lines are used rather than direct cables. See TERMINAL.

removable media Diskettes, hard disk cartridges, or tape cassettes that can be removed from the device that reads data from them or writes data to them.

reorder point The lowest amount of stock that can be on hand before ordering more of an item.

repagination A process in which a word processor adjusts a multipage document as it is revised to ensure uniform page length and appearance.

repaint The redrawing of an image on a visual display device to reflect updated graphic or textual data. A feature on many graphics systems that automatically redraws a design displayed on the visual display screen.

repeat counter A program counter that records the number of times an event takes place in a program for later comparison.

repeating decimal number A nonterminating decimal number, such as .3333333 . . . or .31282828 . . . .

repeat key A keyboard key that can be held down so it repeatedly makes contact without need for additional pressing.

repertoire A complete set of instructions that belongs to a specific computer or family of computers.

repetition instruction An instruction that causes one or more instructions to be executed an indicated number of times.

repetitive Being done over and over.

replacement theory The mathematics of deterioration and failure, used to estimate replacement costs and determine optimum replacement policies.

report Usually associated with output data; involves the grouping of related facts so as to be easily understood by the reader. A common means of presenting information to users. Most reports are on-screen display or printed listings showing selected information extracted form a data base.

report file A file generated during data processing, usually used to print out or display desired output.

report generation The manipulation and organization of data to create an on-screen or hard copy document from all or part of a data base file.

report generator A program that converts machine-readable data into a printed report organized for a specific purpose. See RPG.

reporting by exception A report containing only items outside normal ranges that require management attention.

report program generator See RPG.

report writer A utility program that generates standard and custom reports from information stored in data files.

reproduce To copy information on a similar medium, such as to obtain a duplicate floppy disk from a specific floppy disk.

reprogramming Changing a program written for one computer so that it will run on another.

reprographics The technology that includes reproduction and duplication processes for documents, written materials, pictures, drawings, and films, as well as methods of their mass reproduction, such as photocopy, offset printing, microfilming, and offset duplicating.

request for proposal (RFP) A document sent to hardware/software vendors requesting them to propose equipment and software to meet system specifications.

request for quotation (RFQ) A document sent to hardware/software vendors requesting them to quote prices for equipment and/or software that meets system requirements.

requirements list Formal written statements that specify what the software must do or how it must be structured.

rerun To repeat all or part of a program on a computer, usually because of a correction, a false start, or an interrupt.

reserve accumulator An auxiliary storage register allied to the main accumulator in a central processing unit. See ACCUMULATOR.

reserved words Certain words that, because they are reserved by operating systems, language translators, and so on for their own use, cannot be used in an applications program. For example, READ, FOR, and LET in the BASIC programming language. See KEYWORD.

reset (1) To return computer components to a specified static state. (2) To place a binary cell into the zero state.

reset key A key on a keyboard that normally is used to reset the parts of a computer to the way they were before the program was executed.

reside To be recorded in. For example, a program may reside on a floppy disk or in RAM.

resident program A program that occupies a dedicated area of a computer's main memory (ROM or RAM) during the operating session. See TRANSIENT PROGRAM.

residual value The value of a piece of equipment at the end of a lease term.

resilient Pertaining to a system capable of continuing execution despite failure.

resistor A component of an electrical circuit that produces heat while offering opposition, or resistance, to the flow of electric current.

resizing The process of scaling a graphics file or entity according to predetermined parameters.

resolution A term used to describe the amount of information that a video display can reproduce. A pixel is the smallest unit on the display screen grid that can be stored, displayed, or addressed. The resolution of a picture is expressed by the number of pixels in the display. A high-resolution picture looks smooth and realistic. It is produced by a large number of pixels. A low-resolution picture is blocky and jagged. It is produced by a small number of pixels. Low-resolution pictures represent surfaces with ragged edges, while high resolution produces a finely defined image.

resolution, plotter A measure of the quality of a plotted image. The number of addressable points on a digital plotter determines the resolution: the more points, the higher the resolution.

resource Any component of a computer configuration. Memory, printers, visual displays, disk storage units, software, materials, and operating personnel are all considered resources.

resource allocation The sharing of computer resources among competing tasks or activities.

resource file Programs or data, stored on disk or tape, for use by applications programs.

resource leveling The scheduling of activities with float time to optimize the use of resources, thereby avoiding large fluctuations in resource requirements.

resource sharing The sharing of one central processor by several users as well as several peripheral devices.

response position In optical scanning, the area designated for marking information on an optical mark recognition form.

response time The time it takes the computer system to react to a given input. It is the interval between an event and the system's response to the event.

restart To resume execution of a program. To REBOOT.

results The product of computer processing.

resumé An inventory of a person's goals, education, background, employment history and qualifications. It is an important document usually used when applying for a new job. It should highlight those factors that distinguish a person from other applicants.

reticle The photographic plate used to create an integrated circuit mask.

retrieval The extraction of data from a data base or files.

retrieving The process of making stored information available when needed.

retrofit To update or add to an existing system in order to improve it.

return A set of instructions at the end of a subroutine that permits control to return to the proper point in the main program.

RETURN key A key on a computer keyboard that means "execute a statement or command." Same as ENTER key on some keyboards.

reusable The attribute of a routine that permits the same copy of the routine to be used by two or more tasks.

reverse Polish notation A form of postfix notation in which the operands are entered before the operators. For example, the expression a*(b+c) is represented in reverse Polish notation as abc +*, where this expression is read from left to right. See POLISH NOTATION and POSTFIX.

reverse video A term used to indicate, in some video terminals, the ability to display dark characters on a light background. The inverse of the normal foreground and background colors on a video screen. For example, the reverse video of light characters on a dark background would be dark characters on a light screen background.

review An evaluation of a new system's performance.

rewind To return a magnetic tape to its starting position.

rewrite To erase and reset.

RF An abbreviation for RADIO FREQUENCY, the general term for a broad spectrum of electromagnetic radiation ranging in frequency from 10,000 to 40 billion cycles per second. RF radiation has been used primarily for the purpose of communication.

RFP An abbreviation for REQUEST FOR PROPOSAL. A document that describes one's requirements, sent to vendors to elicit their design of a hardware or software system that meets those requirements.

RF modulator A device that lets a microcomputer use any ordinary television set for output.

RFQ An abbreviation for REQUEST FOR QUOTATION.

RGB monitor A color monitor that uses color "guns" for red, green, and blue to produce a high-quality picture. See COLOR MONITOR, COMPOSITE VIDEO, MONOCHROME MONITOR, and RGB VIDEO.

RGB video A form of color video signal (red, green, blue), distinctly different from the composite color video used in standard television sets. RGB can be displayed only on a color monitor that has a separate electron gun for each of these primary colors. Ordinary color television sets use only one gun. RGB monitors are noted for their crisp, bright colors and high resolution. See COMPOSITE VIDEO.

ribbon cable A group of attached parallel wires; a flat cable containing a number of wires side by side. Often used to connect computers with peripherals.

ribbon cartridge A plastic holder that contains a printer ribbon.

right justify See JUSTIFY.

rigid disk Same as HARD DISK.

ring A cyclic arrangement of data elements. See CIRCULAR LIST.

ring network A computer network in which each computer is connected to other computers, forming a continuous loop, or circle. Usually employed when the computers are geographically close.

ripple sort See BUBBLE SORT.

RI/SME An abbreviation for ROBOTICS INTERNATIONAL OF THE SOCIETY OF MANUFACTURING ENGINEERS. This professional organization is directed toward engineers interested in the design and use of robots.

RJE An abbreviation for REMOTE JOB ENTRY. Refers to the programs used to submit processing jobs from terminals.

RO An acronym for RECEIVE-ONLY. A designation used to indicate the read-only capabilities of equipment lacking keyboards and other input facilities.

roam To move a display window around on a visual display screen.

robot A computer-controlled device equipped with sensing instruments for detecting input, signals, or environmental conditions. It is also equipped with a calculating mechanism for making decisions and with a guidance mechanism for providing control.

robot-control languages Languages for programs that are designed to control robots. VAL, AL, ML, and ROBOTLAN are examples of these languages.

robotics An area of artificial intelligence related to robots. The science of robot design and use.

Robotics International opf the Society of Manufacturing Engineers (RI/SME) A professional organization directed toward engineers interested in the design and use of robots.

robustness The quality that causes a software program or set of programs to be able to handle, or at least avoid disaster in the face of, unexpected circumstances, such as when given improper data. An example is the deliberate inclusion of program logic to process anticipated errors in the input, such as testing for the presence of alphabetic data that was accidentally keyboarded into a location reserved for numbers. When such an error is detected, the record containing it is shunted aside from further processing.

rollback A system that will restart the running program after a system failure. Snapshots of data and programs are stored at periodic intervals, and the system rolls back to restart at the last recorded snapshot.

roll out To record the contents of internal storage in auxiliary storage.

rollover A buffer that can store typed characters and commands when they are entered faster than the computer system can process them.

roll paper Printer paper in continuous form on a spool.

ROM An acronym for READ-ONLY MEMORY. Generally, a solid state storage chip that is programmed at the time of its manufacture and that cannot be reprogrammed by the computer user. Also called firmware, since this implies software that is permanent or firmly in place on a chip.

ROM cartridge A read-only memory module that contains a preprogrammed function, such as a game, an educational program, or a business system. The module is plugged into the computer. See FIRMWARE and READ-ONLY MEMORY.

ROM simulator A general purpose device used to replace ROMs or PROMs in a system during program checkout. Because it offers real-time in-circuit simulation, it can be used in the engineering prototype or reproduction model to find and correct program errors or in the production model to add new features.

root The first node of a tree.

rotating memory A magnetic information storage device in the form of a round platter that is spun like a phonograph record. See FLOPPY DISK and MAGNETIC DISK.

rotation In computer graphics, the turning of a computer-modeled object relative to an origin point on a coordinate system. In three-dimensional graphics, an object can be rotated in space, usually around the axis, to provide different views.

rotational delay The time it takes for a record contained on one of the sectors of a disk to rotate under the read/write head.

RO terminal A data communications machine capable only of receiving and not of transmitting.

round See ROUND OFF.

rounding The process of dropping the least significant digit or digits of a numeral, and adjusting the remaining numeral to be as close as possible to the original number.

round off To truncate the far right digit of a number, and to increase by one the remaining far right digit if the truncated digit is greater than or equal to half of the number base. For example, the base 10 number 823.1067 could be rounded to 823.107, or 823.11 or 823.1, depending upon the precision desired, and the number 23.602 would be rounded to 23.60.

round-off error The error resulting from rounding off a quantity by deleting the less significant digits and applying the appropriate rule of correction to the part retained. For example, 0.2751 can be rounded to 0.275 with a round-off error of 0.0001, or rounded to 0.28 with a round-off error of 0.0049. Contrast with TRUNCATION ERROR.

round robin A scheduling method that engages each device and process at its turn in a fixed cycle.

routine A short set of program codes that perform a specific task. Typically used in reference to assembly language programs. Sometimes used as a synonym for PROGRAM.

routing The assignment of a path for the delivery of a message.

row (1) The horizontal members of one line of an array. (2) One of the horizontal lines of punching positions on a punched card. (3) Horizontal divisions of an electronic spreadsheet. Together with columns, rows serve to form the spreadsheet matrix. Contrast with COLUMN.

RPG An abbreviation for REPORT PROGRAM GENERATOR. A popular business-oriented programming language, highly structured and relatively easy to learn. Allows users to program many business operations as well as to generate reports. A fairly simple RPG program can perform rather sophisticated business tasks.

RPROM An acronym for REPROGRAMMABLE PROM. See EPROM.

RS-232C An industry standard for asynchronous serial data communications between terminal devices, such as printers, computers, and communications equipment, such as modems. This standard defines a 25-pin connector and certain signal characteristics for interfacing a terminal or computer with a modem. Most popular microcomputers provide for RS-232C interfaces.

RS-422 A recently adopted standard for a very high-speed serial port.

rubber banding A CAD capability that allows a component to be tracked across the visual display screen, by means of an electronic pen or mouse, to a desired location, while simultaneously stretching all related interconnections to maintain signal continuity.

ruggedized computer A computer designed to be used in special environments, such as, aboard a space vehicle, on a ship, in a missile, in a submarine, in a tank, or in farm equipment.

ruled-based deduction A technique of obtaining conclusions in which knowledge is represented as a set of simple rules that guide the dialogue between the system and the user.

run The execution of a program by a computer on a given set of data.

run manual A manual or book documenting the processing system, program logic, controls, program changes, and operating instructions associated with a computer run.

running in parallel The process of running a new program together with the existing system of programs.

run time (1) The time during which data is fetched by the control unit and actual processing is performed in the arithmetic-logic unit. (2) The time during which a program is executing.

R/W READ/WRITE MEMORY.

S

salami technique The theft of small amounts (slices) of assets from a large number of sources. An embezzlement technique that gets its name from taking a "slice" at a time, such as a few cents from many bank accounts.

sales forecasting model A model used to simulate annual sales for each period of a forecast. The input factors can include market size, selling price, market growth rate, share of the market, measures of competitors' actions, and other factors. Such forecasts often use equations estimated with regression analysis and then placed in a spreadsheet program.

sales representative A person who sells computers and related equipment and software. Most representatives work for computer manufacturers, service organizations, or computer stores.

SAM An acronym for SEQUENTIAL ACCESS METHOD. A method for storing and retrieving data on a disk file.

sample data A set of hypothetical data used to see if an algorithm is logical or if a program works. See TEST DATA.

sampling Obtaining a value of a variable at regular or intermittent intervals.

sampling rate The frequency at which sampling occurs.

sans serif Letters of typefaces without serifs—the ornate, widened bases and tops seen on some characters of some type fonts.

sapphire A material used as a substrate for some types of integrated circuit chips.

satellite An earth-orbiting device capable of relaying communications signals over long distances.

satellite communications The use of orbiting transponders or microwave relays to transmit information around the world.

satellite computer (1) An additional computer, usually smaller, that supports a larger computer system. An economy of processing can be effected if the satellite computer handles lower-level functions such as remote terminal coordination, data validity checking, code conversion, and input/output functions. (2) An off-line auxiliary computer.

saturate To reach maximum capacity, beyond which nothing else can be absorbed or retained. For example, a floppy disk is saturated when all of its tracks are full of data.

save To store information somewhere other than in the computer's main memory, such as on a tape or disk, so it can be used again.

SBC (1) An abbreviation for SMALL BUSINESS COMPUTER, a small-size computer capable of performing a variety of basic business applications. (2) An acronym for SINGLE BOARD COMPUTER, a board with CPU, ROM, RAM, and peripheral interfaces.

scalar value An integer declared as such in a programming language and possessing a value within a fixed range.

scale (1) To adjust the magnitude of a quantity so as to fit in the available storage location. (2) To change the size of a graphics file by a specified quantity to make it fit a specified boundary. (3) The quantity by which graphic data are multiplied or divided to fit size limitations.

scale factor One or more factors used to multiply or divide quantities occurring in a problem and to convert them into a desired range, such as the range from +1 to -1.

scaling The process of changing the size of an image. For example, scaling by a factor of four multiplies all dimensions of an image by 4.

scan (1) To examine point by point in logical sequence. (2) An algorithmic procedure for visiting or listing each node of a data structure. (3) The operation required to produce an image on a visual display screen.

scan area That area of a form or document that contains information to be scanned by an optical character reader.

scan line A horizontal line on a raster display screen.

scanner Any optical device that can recognize a specific set of visual symbols.

scanner channel A device that polls individual channels to see if they have data ready to be transmitted.

scanning The rapid examination of every item in a computer's list of data to see whether a specific condition is met.

scan path In optical scanning, a predetermined area within the clear area where data to be read must be located. The position of the scan path and the amount of data that can be read will generally depend upon the machine involved.

scatter plot Plot showing a two-variable frequency distribution by plotting a dot or symbol at each data point. Sometimes a line or curve is added to show the correlation (if there is one) between the variables represented on the two axes. Also called scatter diagram.

scatter read-gather write "Scatter read" refers to placing information from an input record into nonadjacent storage areas. "Gather write" refers to placing information from nonadjacent storage areas into a single physical record.

SCDP See SOCIETY OF CERTIFIED DATA PROCESSORS.

scenario An imagined sequence of events that determine key system inputs and parameters to a decision-making model. For each scenario, one can then run the model on a computer, observing how system variables interact over time.

schedule A list of events in the order they should occur.

scheduled report A report produced at regular intervals to provide routine information to users.

schedule maintenance Maintenance of a computer system at fixed intervals to maintain its reliability.

scheduler A program that schedules jobs for processing.

scheduling (1) The task of determining what the succession of programs should be in a multiprogramming computer center. (2) Allocating a nonsharable resource, such as CPU time, or an I/O device to a particular task for a period of time.

schema (1) The overall logical organization of a data base. (2) A person's point of view on some set of issues, which greatly determines the way the person responds to them.

schematic A diagram of an electronic circuit showing connections and identification of components.

schematic symbols Symbols used in schematic diagrams.

scientific applications Tasks that are traditionally numerically oriented and often require advanced engineering, mathematical or scientific capabilities.

scientific notation A notation in which numbers are written as a "significant digits" part times an appropriate power of 10. For example, 0.82649×10^7, or $0.82649E+07$, stands for 8,264,900.

scissoring The automatic erasing of all portions of a design on the visual display device that lie outside user-specified boundaries. See CLIPPING.

SCM An abbreviation for SOCIETY FOR COMPUTER MEDICINE, an organization that brings together physicians and computer scientists, emphasizing the use of automation for medical applications.

SCR An acronym for SILICON CONTROLLED RECTIFIER, a semiconductor device useful in controlling large amounts of DC current or voltage. Basically, it is a diode turned on or off by a signal voltage applied to a control electrode called the gate. Its characteristics are similar to the old vacuum tube thyratron, which is why it is sometimes called a THY-RISTOR.

scrapbook A function that stores text and pictures for frequent use in documents.

scratch To delete data from memory.

scratch file Temporary file created during the processing of substantial files of data by copying all or part of a data set to an auxiliary storage device.

scratch pad A small, fast storage used in some computers in place of registers. See CACHE MEMORY.

screen A surface on which information is displayed, such as a video display screen. See CATHODE-RAY TUBE, DISPLAY, and VIDEO DISPLAY TERMINAL.

screen dump The process of transferring the information currently appearing on a display screen to a printer or other hard-copy device.

screen generator A special utility program used to create customized screen displays.

screen position The physical location of graphic data on a visual display screen.

screen size A measure of the amount of information that a video display screen can display. Screens can be measured diagonally, as TV sets (usually a diagonal measure in inches), or by the number of vertical and horizontal dot or character positions.

screen update Process of changing screen contents to reflect new information.

Scripsit™ A software package used for word processing on Radio Shack TRS-80™ microcomputer systems. See SUPER-SCRIPSIT and WORD PROCESSOR.

scripts Schema-like structures for representing sequences of events.

scrolling The movement of data on a video display. This movement of text is repeated until the desired spot in the text has been reached. If the scroll is upward, a new line must appear at the bottom of the screen as an old one disappears at the top. May also refer to the ability to move data from right to left and left to right, as well as downward.

SCS An abbreviation for **S**OCIETY FOR **C**OMPUTER **S**IMULATION and **S**HANGHAI **C**OMPUTER **S**OCIETY.

S-curve A curve plotting personnel versus time; used to smooth out resource allocation. The goal is to develop a gradual build-up and subsequent cutback of personnel by rearranging resources utilized for activities with slack time

search To examine a set of items for those that have some desired property or predetermined criterion, such as a particular name or part number.

search and replace A software feature that finds a designated character sequence and replaces it with a new one. An important feature in word processing systems.

searching time The amount of time that is required to examine a set of data and return the desired information.

search key Data to be compared to specified parts of each item for the purpose of conducting a search.

search memory See ASSOCIATIVE STORAGE.

search string In word processing, the number of characters that can be specified for a search and replace function. This is usually less than one line, but enough to permit names, phrases, and technical terms to be located and changed.

second Base unit of time in the SI metric system; also used in the customary English system.

secondary key A field that is used to gain access to records in a file, however, it is not required to be unique.

secondary storage A memory device that supplements the primary main memory of a computer. Same as AUXILIARY STORAGE.

second-generation computers Computers, prominent from 1959 to 1964, made with transistors.

second source A manufacturer who produces a product that is interchangeable with the product of another manufacturer.

sector (1) A portion of the track on a magnetic disk surface that is numbered and can hold a specified number of characters. (2) A pie-shaped section on the surface of a magnetic disk.

secure kernel A protected segment of a systems program.

security The state achieved by hardware, software or data as a result of successful efforts to prevent damage, theft, or corruption.

security controls Methods to ensure that only authorized users have access to a computer system and its resources.

security files Back-up files for important and critical data and information.

security program A program that controls access to data in files and permits only authorized use of terminals and other equipment.

security specialist A person responsible for the physical security of the computer center and logical security for data resources.

seed A constant used to initiate a pseudo random number generator. The seed is used to generate the first number; all subsequent numbers are based on previous results.

seek To position the access mechanism of a direct access device at a specified location.

seek time The time required to position the access mechanism of a direct access storage device at a specified position, such as the time needed to position the read/write head in a drive over the specified track of the disk. See ACCESS TIME and TRANSFER RATE.

segment (1) To divide a program into parts such that some segments may reside in internal storage and other segments may reside in auxiliary storage. Each segment will contain the necessary instructions to jump to another segment or to call another segment into main storage. (2) The smallest functional unit that can be loaded as one logical entity during execution of an overlay program. (3) As applied to the field of telecommunications, a portion of a message that can be contained in a buffer of specified size.

segmentation A technique for dividing computer programs into logical, variable-length blocks.

segmented bar chart A bar chart made up of two or more segments positioned atop each other to represent elements of a whole. Similar to a pie chart, except that varying sizes of bars can be used to allow comparisons of the whole as well as its constituent parts.

select To pick out a group of records from a data base according to specifications provided by the user. For example, to select all records with the year greater than "1988."

selection Choosing between alternatives.

selection sort A sort that selects the extreme value (smallest or largest) in a list, exchanges it with the last value in the list, and repeats with a shorter list.

selection structure One of three primary structures of a structured flowchart. It provides a choice between two alternative paths, based upon a certain condition.

selector channel In certain computer systems, an input/output channel that can transfer data to or from only one peripheral device at a time. Contrast with MULTIPLEXER CHANNEL.

self-adapting Pertaining to the ability of a system to change its performance characteristics in response to its environment.

self-checking code See ERROR-DETECTION CODE.

self-compiling compiler A compiler written in its own source language and is capable of compiling itself.

self-complementing code A code with the property that the binary one's complement of the weighted binary number is also the number nine's complement in decimal notation.

self-correcting code A numerical coding system in which transmission errors are automatically detected and corrected. Same as ERROR-CORRECTING CODE.

self-validating code A code that makes an explicit attempt to determine its own correctness and proceed accordingly.

semantics The relationships between the words and symbols in a programming language and the meanings assigned to them. See LINGUISTICS.

semaphores Synchronization primitives used to coordinate the activities of two or more programs or processes running at the same time and sharing information.

semiconductor A solid material, usually germanium or silicon, with an electrical conductivity that lies between the high conductivity of metals and the low conductivity of insulators. Depending on the temperature and pressure, a semiconductor can control a flow of electricity. It is the material from which integrated circuits are made.

semiconductor device An electronic element fabricated from crystalline materials such as silicon or germanium which, in the pure state, are neither good conductors nor good insulators and are unusable for electronic purposes. When certain impurity atoms, such as phosphorus or arsenic, are diffused into the crystal structure of the pure metal the electrical neutrality is upset, introducing positive or negative charge carriers. Diodes and transistors can then be implemented.

semiconductor storage A memory device whose storage elements are formed as solid state electronic components on an integrated circuit chip.

semirandom access The method of locating data in storage that combines in the search for the desired item some form of direct access, usually followed by a limited sequential search.

sense (1) To examine, particularly relative to a criterion. (2) To determine the present arrangement of some element of hardware.

sense probe An input mechanism that activates sensitive points on a visual display screen and thereby provides input to a computer.

sense switch A computer console switch that may be interrogated by a program. Sense switches are very useful when debugging a large, complex program.

sensitivity The degree of response of a control unit to a change in the incoming signal.

sensors Devices to detect and measure physical phenomena, such as temperature, stress, heartbeat, wind direction, and fire. These devices translate physical stimuli into electronic signals that may, for example, be input into computers.

sequence (1) An arrangement of items according to a specified set of rules. (2) In numeric sequence, normally in ascending order.

sequence check A check used to prove that a set of data is arranged in ascending or descending order.

sequence structure One of three primary structures of a structured flowchart, in which instructions are executed in order.

sequential Pertaining to the occurrence of events in time sequence, with little or no simultaneity or overlap of events.

sequential access A term used to describe files, such as magnetic tape, that must be searched serially from the beginning to find any desired record. May also be used with magnetic disk storage, which is more commonly accessed randomly. Contrast with DIRECT ACCESS.

sequential algorithm An algorithm that does not involve loops.

sequential computer A computer in which events occur in time sequence with little or no simultaneity or overlap of events.

sequential data set A data set whose records are organized on the basis of their successive physical positions, such as on magnetic tape.

sequential data structure A data structure in which one atom is immediately adjacent to the next atom. Also called CONTIGUOUS DATA STRUCTURE.

sequential device A peripheral device from which data is read or into which data is written in order; nothing can be omitted.

sequential file organization The organization of records in a specific sequence based on a key, such as part number or employee ID. The records in sequential files must be processed one after another.

sequential list A list stored in contiguous locations. Also called dense list and linear list.

sequential logic A circuit arrangement in which the output state is determined by the previous state of the input. See COMBINATION LOGIC.

sequential machine A mathematical model of a certain type of sequential switching circuit.

sequential processing The processing of files ordered numerically or alphabetically by key. Contrast with DIRECT ACCESS PROCESSING and RANDOM PROCESSING.

sequential search A search whereby each item in a list is examined until the item sought is either found or the end of the list is encountered. The search begins at the beginning of the list and progresses through the list in a FIFO manner.

sequential storage Auxiliary storage where data is arranged in ascending or descending order, usually by item number.

serial (1) Pertaining to the sequential occurrence of two or more related activities in a single device. (2) The handling of data in a sequential fashion. Contrast with PARALLEL.

serial access Descriptive of a storage device or medium in which there is a sequential relationship between access time and data location in storage; that is, the access time is dependent upon the location of the data. Contrast with DIRECT ACCESS. See SERIAL PROCESSING.

serial adder An adder that performs its operations by bringing in one digit at a time from each of the quantities involved.

serial computer A computer in which each digit or data word bit is processed serially by the computer.

serial data Data transmitted sequentially, one bit at a time.

serial input/output Data transmission in which the bits are sent one by one over a single wire. Contrast with PARALLEL INPUT/OUTPUT.

serial interface An interface on which all the data moves over the same wire, one bit after the other.

serializability When several users access data at the same time, the result must be equivalent to that which occurs when they access the data one at a time. This effect is called serializability.

serial operation A computer operation in which all digits of a word are handled sequentially rather than simultaneously. Contrast with PARALLEL OPERATION.

serial port An input/output port in a computer through which data is transmitted and received one bit at a time. In most cases, in personal computers, serial data is passed through an RS-232C serial interface port.

serial printer A printer that receives information from the computer one bit at a time through a single wire. (One character equals eight bits). One or more additional wires may be necessary to exchange control signals. Prints one character at a time at speeds up to 600 cps. Contrast with PARALLEL PRINTER.

serial processing Reading and/or writing records on a file, one by one, in the physical sequence in which they are stored. Contrast with PARALLEL PROCESSING. See SERIAL ACCESS.

serial transmission A method of data transfer in which the bits composing a character are sent sequentially. Serial transmission is required for telephone data transfer. Contrast with PARALLEL TRANSMISSION.

service bureau An organization that provides data processing services for other individuals or organizations. Sometimes called COMPUTER SERVICES COMPANY. See COMPUTER UTILITY.

service contract A contract with a computer dealer, computer store, or service company that ensures immediate repair of a computer system.

service programs Programs that supplement the control programs of an operating system, such as language translators, utility routines, and programming aids.

servicer A service bureau that provides computer services to other organizations for a fee.

servomechanism   A feedback control system.

session   (1) The period of time during which a computer system operator works from a terminal at one sitting. (2) A complete set of interchanges between a user and a remote computer.

set   (1) To place a binary cell into the 1 state. (2) To place a storage device into a specified state, usually other than denoting zero or blank. (3) A collection of related items. (4) In a relational data base model, a collection of things. (5) In a network/hierarchical data base model, a one-to-many relationship, the path by which one record type is connected to another.

SETL   A high-level language designed to facilitate the programming of algorithms involving sets and related structures.

setup   An arrangement of data or devices to solve a particular problem.

setup time   The time between computer runs or other machine operations that is devoted to such tasks as changing disk packs and moving forms and other supplies to and from the equipment.

shade   In computer graphics, the quantity of black mixed with a pure color.

shading symbols   Refers to block graphics characters that are part of some computer graphics built-in character set. These symbols provide different dot densities, giving the appearance of different levels of shading.

shadow printing   Printing of a bold character by backing up the print head to within 1/120 inch of its previous position and restriking. The slight amount of misregistration between the initial impression and the overstrike produces a fatter, bolder character.

shared file   A direct access device that may be used by two systems at the same time. A shared file may link two computer systems.

shared logic   The concurrent use of a single computer by multiple users.

shared resource Computer resource shared by several users

shareware Software that can be used and copied withou charge. However, shareware is copyrighted and the copy right holder often asks that the user send a donation if th software is to be used regularly. See PUBLIC DOMAIN SOFTWARE.

sharpness Refers to the clarity and quality of an image pro duced on a visual display device, plotter, printer, film re corder, and other devices.

sheet feeder A device that attaches to the printer, designe to automatically insert and line up single sheets of paper o envelopes in much the same way as an operator would per form the task. The sheet feeder usually sits above the printe platen and is operated either mechanically or electrically b the printer.

shielding Protection against electrical or magnetic noise.

shift To move the characters of a unit or information colum to the right or left. For a number, this is equivalent to mul tiplying or dividing by a power of the base of notation.

shift-click To click the mouse button while depressing the shif key on the keyboard.

shift key The key on a computer keyboard that, when presse makes letters print as capitals instead of lower case letter and allows some special characters to be printed. On man keyboards, acts as a shift lock and must be pressed agai to return to lower case.

shortest operating time A scheduling procedure that sched ules those jobs that take the shortest amount of compute time first.

short precision See SINGLE PRECISION.

SHRDLU The first natural language program that integrate syntactic and semantic analysis with knowledge of th world.

shutdown The termination of electrical power to all or part o the computer system components.

SI Standard abbreviation of the worldwide International Metric System. (From French, **S**YSTEME **I**NTERNATIONAL D'UNITES, or International System of Units).

sibling Two nodes coming off the same previous node in a tree.

side effect A consistent result of a procedure that is in addition to the basic result.

SideKick™ A desktop accessory program that provides a computerized calculator, notepad, appointment calendar, and automated phone dialer. These features can be used alone or in combination with each other; some features can also be used with other software. For example, if you use dBASE III™, PFS:File™, or another data base to keep track of names and phone numbers, SideKick™ can automatically dial phone numbers from these other data bases. Developed by Borland International Inc. See DESKTOP ACCESSORY.

sift To extract certain desired items of information from a large amount of data.

sifting A method of internal sorting by which records are moved to permit the insertion of other records. Also called INSERTION METHOD.

SIG Abbreviation for **S**PECIAL **I**NTEREST **G**ROUP. Often a subunit of a professional organization or user club. Made up of members with common interests, e.g., a "Computers in Medicine" SIG.

sign Used in the arithmetic sense to describe whether a number is positive or negative.

signal In communications theory, an intentional disturbance in a communications system. Contrast with NOISE.

signal-to-noise ratio In data communications, the ratio of the (wanted) signal to the (unwanted) noise.

signaling rate The rate at which signals are transmitted over a communications link.

sign digit The digit in the sign position of a word.

sign extension The duplication of the sign bit in the higher-order positions of a register. This extension is usually performed on one's complement or two's complement binary values.

sign flag   A flip-flop that goes to position 1 if the most significant bit of the result of an operation has the value of 1.

significant digit   A digit that contributes to the precision of a number. The number of significant digits is counted beginning with the digit contributing the most value, called the most significant digit, and ending with the one contributing the least value, called the least significant digit.

signing-on   The process of establishing a user/computer interface.

sign position   The position at which the sign of a number is located.

silicon   A nonmetallic **chemical** element used in the manufacture of integrated circuits, solar cells, and so forth. It is a chemical element (atomic number 14, symbol Si) widely found in sand and clay. Next to oxygen, silicon is the most abundant element in the Earth's crust. It was discovered by Swedish chemist Baron Jons Jakob Berzelius in 1823. Silicon grows with a native oxide on its surface. It is perfect for delivering and protecting an exact wiring pattern of millions of integrated circuits that make up a chip. Also, it is cost-attractive and easy to handle environmentally. The chip manufacturing process starts with common sand, or quartz, that is purified into polycrystalline silicon. In its raw form, the "poly" looks very similar to a lump of coal, only shinier. A complex process and advanced technologies convert this raw material into computer chips. Building a chip of a particular design requires several months in a series of 150 to 200 chemical and physical processes. The various steps of chip fabrication are grouped into nine broad categories—oxidation, photolithography, diffusion, metalization, sputtered quartz, terminal metals, dicing, chip placement and module encapsulation. Adding to the complexity, chips must be fabricated in ultra-clean environments that are about 1,000 times cleaner than a hospital operating room. This is necessary to assure their quality and reliability.

silicon chip A tiny portion of a silicon wafer with thousands of electronic components and circuit patterns etched onto its surface. See SILICON.

silicon-controlled rectifier A semiconductor device which, in its normal state, block a voltage applied in either direction. Abbreviated SCR.

Silicon Valley A heavily industrialized area south of San Francisco, California, which accounts for much of the U.S. integrated circuit production and houses the largest concentration high-technology companies in the country.

silicon wafer A silicon slice on which integrated chips are fabricated. After fabrication, the wafer is cut into many individual chips, which are then mounted in Dual In-line Packages (DIPS). See SILICON.

simplex Pertaining to a communications link capable of transmitting data in only one direction. Contrast with FULL DUPLEX and HALF DUPLEX.

SIMSCRIPT A high-level programming language specifically designed for simulation applications.

simulation (1) The modeling of a real problem by a computer. (2) The representation of certain features of the behavior of a physical or abstract system by the behavior of another system, such as the representation of physical phenomena by means of operations performed by a computer, or the representation of operations of a computer by those of another computer.

simulator A device, computer program, or system that represents certain features of the behavior of a physical or abstract system. For example, a computer-controlled aircraft simulator is used by most airline companies to train pilots.

simultaneous input/output The process in which some computer systems allow new information to be input while other information is being output.

simultaneous processing The performance of two or more data processing tasks at the same instant. Contrast with CONCURRENT PROCESSING.

single address See ONE-ADDRESS INSTRUCTION.

single-board computer A computer that contains all of its circuitry on one board.

single density A method of storing data on a floppy disk. See DOUBLE DENSITY.

single precision Pertaining to the use of one computer word to represent a number. Contrast with DOUBLE PRECISION.

single-sided disk Magnetic disk with only one side used for reading and writing information. Contrast with DOUBLE-SIDED DISK.

single step The operation of a computer in such a manner that only one instruction is executed each time the computer is started.

SI units Units of measure in the international metric system. See SI.

sixteen-bit chip A microprocessor chip that processes information sixteen bits at a time.

sketching A computer graphics technique in which a trail of lines is drawn or sketched along the path of the cursor.

sketch pad A working storage area displayed on a visual display screen that permits the operator to add and delete graphic or textual information easily before it is entered into permanent storage.

skew In computer graphics and optical scanning, a condition in which a character, line, or reprinted symbol is neither parallel with nor at right angles to the leading edge.

skip To ignore one or more instructions in a sequence of instructions.

SLA An abbreviation for SPECIAL LIBRARIES ASSOCIATION. This international organization of libraries and information specialists promotes the establishment of resource centers for interest groups such as banks, museums, law firms, and other businesses.

slab A part of a WORD.

slack time See FLOAT.

slave A device controlled by another device.

sleeve The protective envelope for storing a floppy disk.

slew To move paper through a printer.

slewing Pertaining to the speed at which numerically controlled machine tools move from one position to another.

slice A special type of chip architecture that permits the cascading of devices to increase word bit size.

slide A photographic representation of a visual screen display.

slide show package A computer graphics software package that displays the graphics in a timed sequence on the video display screen; similar to a slide show.

slope The rate at which a curve rises or falls per horizontal unit.

slot A socket in a microcomputer designed to accept a plug-in circuit board.

SLSI An abbreviation for SUPER LARGE SCALE INTEGRATION. Refers to ultra-high density chips that contain one million or more components per chip.

slug A metal casting that carries the image of a printable character. The slug prints by striking the paper.

small-business computer A stand-alone data processing system built around a digital computer system dedicated to the processing of standard business applications such as payroll, accounts receivable and payable, order entry, inventory, and general ledger.

small scale integration The class of integrated circuits that has the fewest number of functions per chip. Abbreviated SSI. See INTEGRATED CIRCUIT.

SMALLTALK A language and software system designed to make computer use as easy as possible for the layperson. It presents possible choices of operation in the form of pictures, or "icons," on the screen. The user selects one by moving a pointer with the aid of a mouse to the appropriate position and then presses a button on top of the mouse to inform the computer of the choice. SMALLTALK systems are characterized by a high degree of pictorial interaction.

smart Having some computational ability of its own. Smart devices usually contain their own microprocessors or microcomputers.

smart card A credit card with a built-in computer.

smart machines Industrial and consumer products with "intelligence" provided by built-in microprocessors or microcomputers that significantly improve the performance and capabilities of such products.

smart terminal A terminal that contains some capacity to process information being transmitted or received. See LOCAL INTELLIGENCE.

smash To destroy an area of storage by overwriting with another program.

SMIS An acronym for SOCIETY FOR MANAGEMENT INFORMATION SYSTEMS. A professional organization for fostering improved management performance and information exchange.

smooth To apply procedures that decrease or eliminate rapid fluctuations in data.

smooth scrolling The ability to scroll text without it jerking from one line to the next.

SNA An acronym for SYSTEMS NETWORK ARCHITECTURE

snapshot dump A dynamic dump of the contents of specified storage locations and/or registers performed at specified points or times during the running of a program.

SNOBOL An acronym for STRING ORIENTED SYMBOLIC LANGUAGE, a high-level programming language used for string manipulation, pattern recognition, and the like needed in such areas as linguistics, the compiling of indexes and bibliographies, text editing, compiling, and symbolic manipulation of algebraic expressions. It is a unique language that provides complete facilities for the manipulation of strings of characters. Developed at Bell Laboratories.

SO An acronym for SEND ONLY, a designation used to indicate the send-only capabilities of equipment.

Society for Computer Medicine (SCM) An organization that brings together physicians and computer scientists, emphasizing the use of automation for medical applications.

Society for Computer Simulation (SCS) A technical society devoted primarily to the advancement of simulation and allied technologies, notably those dealing with management, social, scientific, biological, and environmental problems. It has a worldwide membership.

Society of Certified Data Processors (SCDP) An organization that represents the interests and wishes of certified computer professionals. SCDP members control which positions, actions, and directions the organization takes.

soft clip area The limits of the area where data can be presented on a plotting device.

soft copy Data presented as a video image, in audio format, or in any other form that is not hard copy. See HARD COPY.

soft fails Noise bursts in microelectronic circuits caused by cosmic-ray particles that result in spontaneous changes in the information stored in computer memories. These changes are called soft fails. This sensitivity to cosmic rays is one of the unanticipated results of the ever-decreasing size of the components of integrated microelectronic circuits, and it present new considerations in the development of very large scale integrated circuits.

soft hyphen A conditional (nonrequired) hyphen. It is printed only to break a word between syllables at the end of a line. See HARD HYPHEN.

soft keys Keys on a keyboard that can have a user defined meaning. Some systems allow the user to specify the meaning of special keys. These keys are called soft keys because their meaning can change from user to user or program to program.

soft return A combination line feed/carriage return command, entered by a program containing the word-wrap feature to begin a new line within a paragraph. Unlike a hard return, it is conditional—the computer executes the command only when the current word doesn't fit in the line in progress.

soft sector A method of marking sectors or sections on a disk using information written on the disk. When a soft-sectored disk is formatted, the computer writes a magnetic pattern onto the disk to mark the boundaries of each sector. Contrast with HARD SECTOR.

software The programs or instructions that tell a computer what to do. Software may be built into the computer's ROM or may be loaded temporarily into the computer from a disk or tape. Contrast with HARDWARE. See APPLICATION PROGRAMS, CANNED SOFTWARE, COURSEWARE, FIRMWARE, SHAREWARE, and SYSTEM SOFTWARE.

software base The software available for a particular computer system. The broader the software base, the more versatile the computer system.

software broker An individual who specializes in marketing software packages.

software company (1) A company that writes programs for users on a contract basis. (2) A business that offers both general software packages and specific software packages for sale to computer system owners.

software compatability Refers to the ability to use programs written for one system on another system with little or no change.

software development The creation of sets of programs that meet the requirements of a user.

software documents The written or printed material associated with computer equipment and software systems.

software encryption The encoding or decoding of computerized data using programming techniques rather than hardware devices such as scramblers.

software engineer A name given to systems analysts, designers, and programmers.

software engineering A term coined in 1967 by the Study Group on Computer Science of the NATO Science Committee to imply the need for software manufacture based on the types of theoretical foundations and practical disciplines traditional in established branches of engineering. Software engineering is concerned with the development and impl mentation of large-scale software systems on production-model computers. Encompasses a broad range of topics related to the controlled design and development of high-quality computer software, including programming methodology (structured programming, egoless programming, software quality assurance, programming productivity aids) and management of software projects (structured walk-throughs, chief programmer teams, program support library, HIPO technique). See COMPUTER ENGINEERING.

software ergonomics The technology concerned with relating computer programs to the needs and functions of those individuals using the specified programs, exemplified in the term "user friendly" and in meaningful and easy-to-understand documentation.

software flexibility A property of software that enables it to change easily in response to different user and system requirements.

software house (1) A company that offers both general software packages and specific software packages for sale to computer systems owners. (2) A company that develops software for customers on a contrast basis.

software librarian A person in charge of a large collection of software (usually on floppy disks, disk packs or magnetic tapes) in a company.

software license A contract signed by the purchaser of a software product in which the purchaser is usually made to agree not to make copies of the software for resale.

software maintenance The ongoing process of detecting and removing errors from existing programs.

software monitor A program used for performance measurement purposes.

software package A prewritten program that can be purchased for use with a specified computer to perform a specific task, such as word processing, graphics, inventory control, simulation, statistical analysis, language translation, etc. A package usually includes the program stored on a floppy disk and an operating manual.

software piracy The copying of commercial or proprietary software without the permission of the originator.

software portability Refers to the ease with which a program can be moved from one computer environment to another. As third-party software becomes more prevalent in the computer industry, portability becomes a more valuable attribute of that software.

software product A vendor package comprising programs, operating manual, and sometimes vendor assistance. Also called programming product.

software protection Resistance to unauthorized copying of software.

software publisher A business that publishes and sells software packages.

software resources The program and data resources that represent the software associated with a computing system.

software science A discipline concerned with the measurable properties of computer programs.

software security The protection of software assets such as user application programs, data base management software, and the operating system.

software system The entire set of computer programs and their documentation, as used in a computer system.

software transportability The ability to take a program written for one computer and run it without modification on another computer.

solar cell A semiconductor electrical junction device that absorbs and converts the radiant energy of sunlight directly and efficiently into electrical energy.

solicitation A request to vendors to submit bids for hardware, software, or services. See REQUEST FOR PROPOSAL (RFP) and REQUEST FOR QUOTATION (RFQ).

solid state Descriptive of electronic components whose operation depends on the control of electric or magnetic phenomena in solids such as integrated circuits and transistors.

solid state cartridge A preprogrammed plug-in module used with several microcomputer systems. See CARTRIDGE, FIRMWARE, and ROM CARTRIDGE.

solid state device A device built primarily from solid state electronic circuit elements.

S-100 bus A standard means of interconnection between some microcomputers and peripheral equipment.

son file See FATHER FILE and GRANDFATHER FILE.

SOP An acronym for **S**TANDARD **O**PERATING **P**ROCEDURE, the status quo.

sort (1) To arrange records according to a logical system. On a computer, most sorting is done by using magnetic disks or tapes. (2) A utility program that sorts records held on disk or tape.

sort effort The number of steps needed to order an unordered list.

sort generator A program that generates a sort program for production running.

sorting The arranging of data into a specified order.

sort/merge program A generalized processing program that can be used to sort or merge records in a prescribed sequence.

SOS An abbreviation for **S**ILICON **O**N **S**APPHIRE, the process of fabricating integrated chips on layers of silicon and sapphire.

sound hood A device that fits over a printer during use to dampen noise.

source One of three terminals or electrodes of a field effect transistor (FET). The source is the origin of the charge carriers that flow past the gate to the drain.

Source (The) An information utility service available to subscribers. It allows users with microcomputers and modems to play games, access data bases, check flight schedules, post messages, receive and send electronic mail, read newspaper wire services, and a host of other things. Personal computer users can use The Source network via a common telephone hookup. It is operated by The Source Telecomputing Corporation. See COMPUSERVE.

source code Symbolic coding in its original form before being processed by a computer. The computer automatically translates source code into a code the computer can understand.

source/computer A computer used to translate a source program into an object program.

source data automation A process whereby data created while an event is taking place are entered directly into the system in a machine-processable form. See POINT-OF-SALE TERMINAL.

source disk The disk from which a file or program is copied. See TARGET DISK.

source document An original document from which basic data is extracted, such as an invoice, a sales slip, or an inventory tag.

source language The original language in which a high-level program (BASIC, Pascal, Modula-2, COBOL) or an assembly language program is written.

source program A computer program written in a source language, such as BASIC, Pascal, LOGO, or assembly language. It is converted to machine code by a special processing program, such as a compiler or assembler.

source register The register that contains a data word that is being transferred.

SPA An abbreviation for SYSTEMS AND PROCEDURES ASSOCIATION, a professional organization whose purpose is to promote advanced management systems and procedures through seminars, professional education, and research.

space (1) One or more blank characters. (2) The state of a communications channel corresponding to a binary zero.

spacebar The long, narrow key at the bottom of a keyboard that generates spaces. When pressed once, it causes a space to be placed into text at the insertion point.

spaghetti code A program that contains excessive GOTO statements.

span The difference between the highest and lowest values in a range of values.

spanning tree A subgraph of a graph with two properties: (a) it is a tree; and (b) it contains all the nodes of the original graph.

sparse array An array in which most of the entries have a value of zero.

spatial data management A technique that allows users access to information by pointing at pictures on a display screen, representing data bases, document files, or any category of information.

spatial digitizer A device often used in computer graphics to simulate three-dimensional objects.

spec An abbreviated version of SPECIFICATION.

special character A graphics character that is neither a letter, a digit, nor a blank; for example, a plus sign, equal sign, asterisk, dollar sign, comma, period, and so on.

special interest groups A special group within an organization that holds meetings, sponsors exhibits, and publishes documents related to some special interest, topic, or subject. The Association for Computing Machinery (ACM) has more than thirty special interest groups (SIGs). These groups elect their own officers, set their own dues, and are self-supporting.

Special Libraries Association (SLA) This international organization of libraries and information specialists promotes the establishment of resource centers for various interest groups, such as banks, museums, and law firms.

special purpose Being applicable to a limited class of uses without essential modification. Contrast with GENERAL PURPOSE.

special-purpose computer A computer designed for solving only a few selected types of numerical or logical problems. User range from cameras, microwave ovens, automobiles to monitoring space vehicle flights. Contrast with GENERAL-PURPOSE COMPUTER.

special-purpose programming language A programming language designed to handle one specific type of problem or application.

specification A detailed description of the required characteristics of a device, process, or product. Also called SPEC.

specification sheet A form used for coding RPG statements.

specs An abbreviated version of specifications.

speech recognition The recognition of speech wave patterns by a computer that matches them with stored speech patterns of words. Currently used as a technique for orally entering data and inquiries into a computer. See VOICE RECOGNITION.

speech synthesis The arranging of coded speech components into real words and sentences. A technique that converts computer data into sounds that imitate human speech.

speech synthesizer A device that converts numerical code into recognizable speech, which is played over a loudspeaker. In other words, a peripheral that converts output signals into an artificial human voice that "speaks."

speed of light The speed at which light travels—186,284 miles per second. A limiting factor in the speed of data transmissions within and between computers and peripherals.

spelling checker A computer program, usually associated with a word processing package, that compares typed words against a word list and informs the user of possible spelling mistakes.

spider configuration A type of distributed system in which a central computer system is used to monitor the activities of several network computer systems.

spike A sharp-peaked, short-duration voltage transient. A brief sudden surge of electricity. See SURGE.

spinwriter A particular type of high-quality computer printer. See THIMBLE PRINTER.

spline In computer graphics, a piecewise polynomial with at least first-order continuity between the pieces. A mathematically simple and elegant way to connect disjoint data points smoothly, hence, it is used not only for generating smooth curves and surfaces between sparse data points, but also for smooth motions between parameters sparsely located in time, such as those used to describe the keyframes in an animation.

split screen A display screen that can be partitioned into two or more areas (called windows) so that different screen formats can be shown on the screen at the same time.

splitting a window The act of dividing a window into two or more panes.

split window Same as SPLIT SCREEN.

spool (1) A reel of magnetic tape. (2) To wind a magnetic tape.

spooler A program or peripheral device that allows a computer to produce hard copy on a printer while doing something else.

spooling (1) The process by which various input/output devices appear to be operating simultaneously, when actually the system is inputting or outputting data via buffers. (2) Temporarily storing data on disk or tape files until another part of the system is ready to process it.

spreadsheet Any one of a number of programs that arranges data and formulas in a matrix of cells.

sprites Small, high-resolution objects that can be moved independently of other text or graphics on the monitor. They can change color and size and move in front of or behind other objects on the monitor. Used to create animated sequences.

sprocket holes Equally spaced holes on both edges of continuous forms for use by a tractorfeed mechanism to feed paper through a printer.

squeezer The person who lays out a circuit in its original "large" form.

SSI An acronym for SMALL SCALE INTEGRATION. See INTEGRATED CIRCUIT.

stack A sequential data list stored in main storage. Rather than addressing the stack elements by their memory locations, the computer retrieves information from the stack by "popping" elements from the top (LIFO) or from the bottom (FIFO). See PROGRAM STACK and STACK POINTER.

stack pointer A register that is used to point to locations in the stack. A stack pointer is incremented by one before each new data item is "pulled" or "popped" from the stack, and decremented by one after a word is "pushed" onto the stack. See STACK.

staffing To make people available for organizations.

stair-stepping A technique used on raster displays to represent a line drawn at any angle other than 45 degrees, horizontal or vertical.

stand-alone Descriptive of a single, self-contained computer system, as opposed to a terminal that is connected to and dependent upon a remote computer system. A stand-alone device will operate by itself, requiring no other equipment.

stand-alone graphics system A graphics system that includes a microcomputer or minicomputer, storage, video display terminal, graphics tablet, and other input/output devices.

stand-alone system A self-contained computer system that can work independently, not connected to or under the control of another computer system.

stand-alone word processor A single word processor that contains its own operating capability and control logic.

standard (1) A rule established to improve the quality of various aspects of information systems development and operation. (2) A guide used to establish uniform practices and common techniques. (3) A yardstick (meterstick!) used to measure performance of any computer system function. A standard may be laid down by a statutory body or simply created by a major manufacturer's practice.

standard function In many programming languages, these are built-in mathematical operations, such as square root, absolute value, sine of an angle, and random number.

standard interface A standard physical means by which peripheral devices are connected to the central processing unit, such as a standard form of plug and jack.

standardize To establish standards or to cause conformity with established standards.

Standard Pascal A version of the Pascal programming language that is described in the *Pascal User Manual and Report* by Kathleen Jensen and Niklaus Wirth. See APPLE PASCAL, PASCAL, TURBO PASCAL, and UCSD PASCAL.

standards enforcer A computer program used to determine automatically whether prescribed programming standards and practices have been followed.

standby equipment A duplicate set of equipment to be used as backup if the primary unit becomes unusable because of malfunction.

standby time (1) The period between placing an inquiry into the equipment and the availability of the reply. (2) The period between the setup of the equipment for use and its actual use. (3) The period during which equipment is available for use.

star bit A bit used in asynchronous transmission to precede the first bit of a character transmitted serially, signaling the start of the character.

star network A network configuration consisting of a central host computer and satellite terminals that connect to the computer to form a star pattern. Also called a centralized network.

start bit (1) A bit or group of bits that identifies the beginning of a data word. (2) A bit indicating the beginning of an asynchronous serial transmission.

startup The process of setting computer system devices to proper initial conditions and applying appropriate electrical power.

start-up disk A floppy disk that contains the information to start the computer system.

stat An abbreviated version of **STAT**ISTICAL or PHOTO**STAT**.

state Used most often to refer to the condition of bistable devices used to represent binary digits. By definition, such devices can have only two states; the state of a switch describes whether it is on or off.

statement An expression of instruction in a computer language.

statement label The line number of a statement in a source language program.

state-of-the-art A phrase that implies being up-to-date in technology. Pertaining to the latest technology.

static Not moving or progressing, stationary, at rest.

static analysis Analysis of a program that is performed without executing the program.

static dump A storage dump performed at a particular point in time with respect to a machine run, often at the termination of a run.

static memory A memory that retains its programmed state as long as power is applied. It does not need to be refreshed, and does not require a clock.

static RAM A memory that doesn't need to be refreshed many times a second, as is required with dynamic RAM. It does not lose its contents as long as power to the computer is on. Once the computer puts a value into a static memory location, it remains there.

static refresh A method of processing data stored temporarily in a remote intelligent terminal rather than in the central processing computer. It permits faster editing of data because data need not be transferred back and forth between the remote terminal and the central processing computer.

static storage A specific type of semiconductor memory that does not require periodic refresh cycles. Data is held by changing the position of an electronic "switch," a transistor flip-flop, contained in integrated circuits.

station One of the input or output points on a data communications system. Synonymous with WORKSTATION. See TERMINAL.

statistics The branch of mathematics that collects information and tabulates and analyzes it.

statitizing The process of transferring an instruction from computer storage to the instruction registers and holding it there, ready to be executed.

status The present condition of a system component.

status report An analysis of actual project costs and time expended against the plan, with variances calculated and displayed.

step **(1)** To cause a computer to execute one instruction. **(2)** One instruction in a computer routine.

stepped motor A mechanical device that rotates by a fixed amount each time it is pulsed. Often used in disk drives and digital plotters.

stochastic procedures Trial and error, as opposed to algorithmic procedures.

stochastic process Any process dealing with events that develop in time or cannot be described precisely, except in terms of probability theory.

stop bit **(1)** A bit or group of bits that identifies the end of a data word and defines the space between data words. **(2)** A bit indicating the end of asynchronous serial transmission.

stop code A specific control character.

storage Descriptive of a device or medium that can accept data, hold them, and deliver them on demand at a later time. The term is preferred over memory. See AUXILIARY STORAGE, INTERNAL STORAGE, MAIN STORAGE, PROM, PROTECTED STORAGE, RAM, and ROM.

storage allocation The assignment of specific programs, program segments, and/or blocks of data to specific portions of a computer's storage. Sometimes called MEMORY ALLOCATION. See PROGRAM STORAGE.

storage block A contiguous area of main storage.

storage capacity The number of items of data that a storage device is capable of containing. Frequently defined in terms of computer bytes (K bytes or M bytes) or words (K words).

storage circuit Refers to a circuit that can be switched into either of two stable states, 0 or 1.

storage device A device used for storing data within a computer system, such as a hard disk, floppy disk, magnetic tape, and RAM.

storage dump A printout of all or part of the contents of the main storage of a computer. The printout is often used to diagnose errors. Also called MEMORY DUMP. See POST MORTEM DUMP and SNAPSHOT DUMP.

storage key An indicator associated with a storage block or blocks; it requires that tasks have a matching protection key to use the blocks. See PRIVILEGED INSTRUCTION and STORAGE PROTECTION.

storage location A position in storage where a character, byte, or word may be stored. Same as CELL.

storage map A diagram that shows where programs and data are stored in the storage units of the computer systems.

storage pool A group of similar storage devices; the disk drives in a computer installation are collectively referred to as the disk pool.

storage protection Protection against unauthorized writing in and/or reading from all or part of a storage device. Generally implemented automatically by hardware facilities, usually in connection with an operating system. Sometimes called MEMORY PROTECTION. See STORAGE KEY.

storage unit See STORAGE DEVICE.

store (1) The British term for storage. (2) To place in storage.

store-and-forward In data communications, the process handling messages used in a message-switching system.

stored-program concept Instructions to a computer as well as data values are stored within the main storage of a computer. The instructions can thus be accessed more quickly and may be more easily modified. This concept was introduced by John von Neumann in 1945. It is the most important characteristic of the digital computer.

straight-line code The repetition of a sequence of instructions by explicitly writing the instructions for each repetition. Generally, straight-line coding will require less execution time and more storage space than equivalent loop coding. The feasibility of straight line coding is limited by the space required as well as by the difficulty of coding a variable number of repetitions. Contrast with LOOP CODE.

strategic plans Overall policies and long-term expectations for an organization.

streamer A tape deck that operates at a continuous high speed rather than starting and stopping between separate blocks of data.

streaming tape drive A device that holds a continuous tape cartridge and is used primarily for backup of hard disk drives.

STRESS An acronym for **STRUCTURAL ENGINEERING SYSTEM SOLVER**. A problem-oriented language used for solving structural engineering problems.

stress testing Ensuring through trial operation that the program or system will continue to perform reliably in spite of data inaccuracies and extraordinary data volumes.

string A connected sequence of characters or bits treated as a single data item. The word "microcomputer" is a string of thirteen characters.

string handling The ability of a programming language to operate on strings of characters.

string length The number of characters in a string.

string manipulation A technique for manipulating strings of characters.

string processing languages Programming languages designed to facilitate the processing of strings of characters, such as LIST, PROLOG and SNOBOL.

string variable A string of alphanumeric string.

stringy floppy A computer storage device that holds a magnetic tape, called a wafer. The enclosed wafer tape is thinner, narrower, and faster than conventional cassette tapes.

strobe A signal that is used to initiate the transfer of data between a peripheral and the computer.

stroke (1) To press a key on the keyboard. (2) In a computer graphics system, textual data stored as a graphical entity rather than as ASCII character symbols.

stroke writer A vector graphics terminal that represents objects on a screen by a series of lines (vectors).

structural design   The overall organization and control logic or processing.

structure   The organization or arrangement of the parts of an entity. The manner in which a program is organized.

structure chart   A design tool for documenting the organization or program modules and the control logic that relates them to one another. A graphic representation of top-down programming.

structured coding   A method of writing programs with a high degree of structure.

structured design   The methodology for designing programs and systems through top-down, hierarchical partitioning and logical control structures.

structured English   An approach to languages that is based on replacing symbols with recognizable English words.

structured flowchart   A method of representing problem solutions in terms of three flowcharting structures: the sequence structure, the selection structure, and the loop structure.

structured programming   A programming technique used in the design and coding of computer programs. The approach assumes the disciplined use of a few basic coding structures and the use of top-down concepts to decompose main functions into lower-level components for modular coding purposes. The technique is concerned with improving the programming process through better organization and programs, and with better programming notation to facilitate correct and clear descriptions of data and control structures. The physical structure of a well-organized program corresponds to the sequence of steps in the algorithm being implemented. Good languages for structured programming must have a carefully thought out assortment of control structures and data-structure definition facilities. Good practices lead to reduced cost of program modification and maintenance as well as original development.

structured walkthroughs   Technical conferences or reviews intended to analyze design, detect errors and exchange knowledge and ideas. All technical members of the project team have their work product technically reviewed with emphasis on error detection.

STRUDL An acronym for **STRUCTURAL DESIGN LANGUAGE**, a programming language used for the design and analysis of structures.

stylus A pen-shaped instrument used with input devices, such as a pen-like device used with a graphics tablet or a light pen.

subdirectory A file that lists the names of other files, and is displayed in a disk directory rather than the name of each file. This system allows files to be classified together to save space in a disk directory.

subprogram A segment of a program that can perform a specific function. Subprograms can reduce programming time when a specific function is required at more than one point in a program. If the required function is handled as a subprogram, the statements for that function can be coded once and executed at the various points in the program. Subroutines and functions may be used to provide subprograms. See FUNCTION and SUBROUTINE.

subroutine A subsidiary routine within which initial execution never starts. It is executed when called by some other program, usually the main program. Also called SUBPROGRAM. See CLOSED SUBROUTINE, NESTED SUBROUTINE, and OPEN SUBROUTINE.

subroutine reentry Initiation of a subroutine by one program before it has finished its response to another program that called for it. This is what may happen when a control program is subjected to a priority interrupt.

subschema A subset or transformation of the logical view of the data base schema that is required by a particular user application program.

subscript (1) The integer value, appended to a variable name, that defines the storage elements composing an array. (2) In noncomputer typefonts, a digit or letter written below and to the right of a symbol to distinguish it from variations of the same symbol, such as R_2 and N_8. Contrast with SUPERSCRIPT.

subscripted variable A symbol whose numeric value can change, denoted by an array name followed by one or more subscripts, such as X(10), R(12,24) or Age(25).

subset A set contained within another set.

substrate In microelectronics, the physical material on which a circuit is fabricated.

substring A portion of a character string.

subsystem A system that is a component of a larger system.

subtrahend The quantity that is subtracted from another quantity. In the subtraction $a - b$, b is the subtrahend and a is the minuend.

subtree A tree that has as its roots the node of another tree.

suite A set or group of closely related programs.

sum The quantity that results from adding two quantities.

summarize To condense a mass of data into a concise, meaningful, usable, and manageable form.

SuperCalc3™ A popular spreadsheet program developed by Sorcim/IUS Corp.

supercomputer The largest, fastest, and most expensive mainframe computer available. Used by businesses and organizations that require extraordinary amounts of computing power. Sometimes called "number crunchers" because they perform hundreds of millions, or even billions, of operations per second. See CRAY.

superconductor An ultra-fast electronic circuit.

superconducting computers High-performance computers whose circuits employ superconductivity to reduce cycle time.

SuperScripsit™ A software package used for word processing on Radio Shack TRS-80 microcomputer systems. It is an advanced version of the Scripsit word processing program. See WORD PROCESSOR.

superscript A letter or digit written above and to the right of a symbol to denote a power or to identify a particular element of a set, such as the 4 in A^4. Contrast with SUBSCRIPT.

supervisory system See OPERATING SYSTEM.

supply company A company that offers a number of supplies that may not be produced and distributed by computer manufacturers, such as printer paper, printer ribbons, and floppy disks.

support The help and verbal advice that a vendor supplies a customer.

support library A library that contains complete programs and subroutines that have already been developed, tested, and documented.

suppress To eliminate leading zeros or other insignificant characters from a computer printout. See ZERO SUPPRESSION.

suppression The elimination of some undesired components of a signal.

surface of revolution Refers to the figure resulting from the rotation of a curve around a fixed axis set at a specified angle.

surge A sudden sharp increase in voltage. Also called a SPIKE.

surging A sudden and momentary changing of voltage or current in a circuit.

surge protector A device that protects electrical equipment from being damaged by short surges of high voltage by filtering them out. A computer or other device is plugged into the surge protector, which is plugged into a standard 110-volt electrical outlet. See LINE SURGE.

suspend Halting a process in a manner that allows resumption.

swapping (1) In virtual storage, bringing a new page into main storage from auxiliary storage and replacing an existing page. (2) In a time-sharing system, bringing the program into main storage or storing it on a storage device. (3) Transferring out a copy of what is in main memory to auxiliary storage while simultaneously transferring to main memory what is in auxiliary storage.

swarm Several program bugs.

swim Describes a situation in which the images displayed on a video display screen move due to some hardware instability or defect. It may be caused by a slow refresh rate. It is an undesirable movement of an image on a video display screen.

switch (1) Physical or electronic means of changing the state of a command or device, such as an on/off toggle switch. (2) In programming, a point at which a program may branch to one or more different program statements depending upon the conditions of specified parameters at that point.

switched line Typically, a telephone line that is connected to the switched telephone network. Synonymous with DIAL-UP LINE.

switched lines Data communication lines that connect through telephone switching centers to a variety of destinations.

switching algebra The name given to Boolean algebra when it is applied to switching theory.

switching circuit A constituent electrical circuit of switching or digital systems. Well-known examples of such systems are digital computers, dial telephone systems, and automatic inventory systems.

switching theory The theory applied to circuits that have two or more discrete states.

symbol (1) A letter, numeral, or mark that represents a numeral, operation, or relation. (2) An element of the computer's character set.

symbolic address An address, expressed in symbols convenient to the program writer, that must be translated into an absolute address (usually by an assembler) before it can be interpreted by a computer.

symbolic coding Coding in which the instructions are written in nonmachine language; that is, coding using symbolic notation for operation codes and operands.

symbolic data Data represented by variables.

symbolic device A name used to indicate an input/output file, such as SYSDSK, to specify a magnetic disk unit.

symbolic editor A system program that helps computer users in the preparation and modification of source language programs by adding, changing, or deleting lines of text.

symbolic I/O assignment A name used to indicate an input/output unit.

symbolic language A pseudolanguage made up of letters, characters, and numbers that are not the internal language of the computer system. See ASSEMBLY LANGUAGE, FABRICATED LANGUAGE, and HIGH-LEVEL LANGUAGE.

symbolic logic The discipline that treats formal logic by means of a formalized artificial language whose purpose is to avoid the ambiguities and logical inadequacies of natural language.

symbolic name See NAME.

symbolic programming Using a symbolic language to prepare computer programs.

symbolic table Table for comparing a set of symbols to another set of symbols or numbers; for example, in an assembler, the symbol table contains the symbolic label address of an assembled object program.

symbol string A string consisting solely of symbols.

symbol table A list of names used in a program with brief descriptions and storage addresses.

Symphony™ A software package, produced by Lotus Development Corporation that provides word processing, data base management, spreadsheet, data communications, and graphics. Symphony, with its emphasis on the spreadsheet, is a number-dominated program that is designed for financial analysts who are chiefly concerned with manipulating numbers in a variety of ways. Many users consider Symphony's word processing and data base management capabilities secondary to its speed, raw power, size, and ability to number-crunch.

sync character A character transmitted to establish character synchronization in synchronous communications.

synchronization Adjustment of the chronological relationships between events, either to cause them to coincide or to maintain a fixed time difference between them.

synchronization check A check that determines whether a particular event or condition occurs at the proper moment.

synchronous communications A method of exchanging data at very high speeds between computers. Involves careful timing and special control codes.

synchronous computer A computer in which each operation starts as a result of a signal generated by a clock. Contrast with ASYNCHRONOUS COMPUTER.

synchronous network A computer network in which all the communications channels are synchronized to a common clock.

synchronous operation The operation of a system under the control of clocked pulses.

synchronous transmission Data transmission in which the bits are transmitted at a fixed rate. The transmitter and receiver both use the same clock signals for synchronization.

synonym Two or more keys that produce the same table address when hashed.

syntax The rules governing the structure of a language and its expressions. All assembly and high-level programming languages possess a formal syntax. See LINGUISTICS.

syntax error The breaking of a rule governing the structure of the programming language being used. For example, typing RIAD A instead of READ A results in the computer failing to understand what is meant. Usually, the computer will respond to such an instruction by displaying an error message such as "syntax error at line 240."

synthesizer An output device that generates and processes sound automatically. Some synthesizers include microprocessors, which are used as controlling devices. A voice synthesizer produces sounds that closely resemble a person speaking, musical instruments, and so on.

SYSGEN An acronym for SYSTEMS GENERATION. The process of modifying the generalized operating system re ceived from the vendor into a tailored system meeting the unique needs of the individual user.

SYSOP Acronym for **SYSTEM OPERATOR**, the person who operates an electronic bulletin board.

system A composite of equipment, skills, techniques, and information capable of performing and/or supporting an operational role in attaining specified management objectives. A complete system includes related facilities, equipment, material, services, personnel, and information required for its operation to the degree that it can be considered a self-sufficient unit in its intended operational and/or support environment.

system analyzer A portable device that can be used as a troubleshooting unit for field service of complex equipment and systems.

system board The main circuit board of a microcomputer. Also called MOTHERBOARD.

system chart A type of flowchart. See SYSTEM FLOWCHART.

system commands Special instruction given to the computer when one operates in the operational time-sharing mode. System commands direct the computer to execute programs (RUN), list them (LIST), save them (SAVE), and do other operations of a similar nature.

system diagnostics A program used to detect overall system malfunctions.

system disk A disk that contains the operating system.

system flowchart A graphic representation of an entire system or portion of a system consisting of one or more computer operations. It is composed of interconnected flowcharting symbols arranged in the sequence that the various system operations are performed. Essentially an overall planning, control, and operational description of a specific application. Contrast with PROGRAM FLOWCHART. See DATAFLOW DIAGRAM, and FLOWCHART.

system follow-up The continuing evaluation and review of the newly installed system to see that it is performing according to plan.

system generation The process of initiating a basic system at a specific installation. Abbreviated SYSGEN.

system implementation The final phase in the creation of a new system. It is during this phase a system is completely debugged, and it is determined whether it is operational and accepted by the users.

system installation The activities by which a new system is placed into operation.

system interrupt A break in the normal execution of a program or routine that is accomplished in such a way that the usual sequence can be resumed from that point.

system loader A supervisory program used to locate programs in the system library and load them into the main storage of the computer.

system maintenance The activity associated with keeping a computer system constantly in tune with the changing demands placed upon it.

system priorities The priorities established to determine the order in which information system projects will be undertaken.

system programmer (1) A programmer who plans, generates, maintains, and controls the use of an operating system with the aim of improving the overall productivity of an installation. (2) A programmer who designs programming systems.

system programming The development of programs that form operating systems for computers. Such programs include assemblers, compilers, control programs, and input/output handlers.

system programs Programs that control the internal operations of the computer system, such as operating systems, compilers, interpreters, assemblers, graphics support programs, and mathematical routines. Contrast with APPLICATION PROGRAMS.

system reset An operation that occurs whenever a computer is fooled into thinking that it was turned off and turned on again.

system resource Any resource of a computer system that is under the control of the operating system.

systems analysis The examination of an activity, procedure, method, technique, or business to determine what must be accomplished and how the necessary operations may best be accomplished by using data processing equipment. The art or science of analyzing a user's information needs and devising aggregates of machines, people, and procedures to meet those needs.

systems analyst One who studies the activities, methods, procedures, and techniques of organizational systems to determine what actions need to be taken and how these actions can best be accomplished. One who does systems analysis.

systems design The specification of the working relationships between all the parts of a system in terms of their characteristic actions.

system security The technical innovations and managerial procedures applied to the hardware and software (programs and data) to protect the privacy of the records of the organization and its customers.

systems engineer One who performs systems analysis, systems design, and/or systems programming functions.

systems house A company that develops hardware and/or software systems to meet user requirements.

systems manual A document containing information on the operation of a system. Sufficient detail is provided so management can determine the dataflow, forms used, reports generated, and controls exercised. Job descriptions are generally provided.

system software Programs that run the computer system and aid the application programmer in doing a task. System software is typically developed by a vendor and sold to a computer user. The vendor who sells system software may be the same vendor who sold the user the computer (still the most common case) or may be an independent software vendor.

system study An investigation to determine the feasibility of installing or replacing a business system. See FEASIBILITY STUDY.

system testing The testing of a series of programs in succession to make sure that all programs, including input and output, are related in the way the systems analyst intended.

T

T An abbreviation for tera, prefix for one trillion.

tab A carriage control that specifies output columns.

table A collection of data in a form suitable for ready reference. The data is frequently stored in consecutive storage locations or written in the form of an array of rows and columns for easy entry. An intersection of labeled rows and columns serves to locate a specific piece of information.

table look-up A procedure for using a known value to locate an unknown value in a table.

tablet An input device that converts graphics and pictorial data into binary inputs for use in a computer. See DIGITIZER and GRAPHICS TABLET.

tabulate (1) To print totals. (2) To form data into a table.

tag A portion of an instruction that carries the number of the index register that affects the address in the instruction.

tail A special data item that locates the end of a list.

tailor-made Refers to a program specially written for one particular task, for one business or set of people. Tailor-made programs are usually commissioned by an individual customer, and not sold to anyone else.

talking computer A computer system that uses a speech synthesizer to produce speech.

tandem computers Two computers connected together and working on the same problem at the same time.

Tandy Corporation A manufacturer of microcomputer systems. Also, the parent company of Radio Shack.

Tandy Model 3000HL™ An IBM Personal Computer XT™ compatible microcomputer sold through Radio Shack retail outlets.

tangible benefit A benefit to which a specific dollar amount can be assigned.

tape A strip of material coated with a magnetically sensitive substance and used for data input, storage, or output. The data are usually stored serially in several channels across the tape, transversely to the reading or writing motion.

tape cartridge See MAGNETIC TAPE CARTRIDGE.

tape cassette A sequential storage medium used in microcomputer systems for digital recording.

tape code See MAGNETIC TAPE CODE.

tape deck See MAGNETIC TAPE UNIT.

tape drive See MAGNETIC TAPE DRIVE.

tape handler See MAGNETIC TAPE UNIT.

tape label Usually the first record on a magnetic tape reel, containing such information as the data the tape was written, identification name or number, and the number of records on the tape.

tape librarian A person responsible for the safekeeping of all computer files. For example, programs and data files on magnetic tapes, disks, and microfilm.

tape library A special room that houses a file of magnetic tape under secure, environmentally controlled conditions.

tape mark A special code used to indicate the end of a tape file.

Tape Operating System (TOS) An operating system in which the operating system programs are stored on magnetic tape.

target disk The disk to which a program or file is copied. See SOURCE DISK.

target language The language into which some other language is to be properly translated. Usually has the same meaning as OBJECT LANGUAGE.

target program Same as OBJECT PROGRAM.

tariff In data communications, the published rate for a specific unit of equipment, facility, or type of service provided by a communications common carrier.

task An element of work that is part of getting the job done, such as the loading of a program into computer storage.

tb Abbreviation for TERABYTE, one trillion bytes; 1,000 gb.

technical writer A professionally trained individual with computer technical experience as well as a satisfactory writing background.

technology The knowledge and methods used to create a product.

technology transfer The application of existing technology to a current problem or situation.

telecommunications The transfer of data from one place to another over communications lines. See DATA COMMUNICATIONS and TELEPROCESSING.

telecommunications specialist A person responsible for the design of data communications networks.

telecommuting Working at home using telecommunications between the office and the home.

teleconference An "electronic meeting" conducted among people at distant locations through telecommunications. Considered an alternative to travel and face-to-face meetings, a teleconference is conducted with two-way video, audio, and, as required, data and facsimile transmission.

telecopying Long-distance copying. Same as FACSIMILE.

Telematics The convergence of telecommunications and automatic information processing.

telemedicine The use of telecommunications, particularly television, for transmitting medical data, such as X-rays or live images of a patient, to a distantly located specialist for consultation.

telemetry Transmission of data from remote measuring instruments by electrical or radio means. For example, data can be telemetered from a spacecraft circling the moon and recorded at a ground station located on Earth.

Telenet A communications network that enables many varieties of user terminals and computers to exchange information.

telephotography The transmission of photographs over electrical communications channels, generally those provided by common carrier communications companies.

teleprocessing The use of telephone lines to transmit data and commands between remote locations and a data processing center, or between two computer systems. The combined use of data communications and data processing equipment. See DATA COMMUNICATIONS and TELECOMMUNICATIONS.

telesoftware Computer programs sent by telephone line or television as part of the teletext signal.

teletext A one-way communications medium. Images, each constituting a single frame of TV data in a special, compressed format, are transmitted in a continuous sequence. Users indicate which frame they would like to see by interaction with the decoding unit in their local TV sets. See VIEWDATA.

television receiver A display device capable of receiving broadcast video signals (such as commercial television) by means of an antenna. Can be used in combination with a radio-frequency modulator as a display device for several microcomputers. See VIDEO MONITOR.

television set See TELEVISION RECEIVER.

telex A telegraph service provided by Western Union.

telpak A service offered by communications common carriers for the leasing of wideband channels between two or more points.

template (1) A plastic guide used in drawing geometric flowcharting symbols. (2) In computer graphics, the pattern of a standard, commonly used component or part that serves as a design aid. Once created, it can be subsequently traced instead of redrawn whenever needed. (3) A set of instructions for relating information within a software development package, usually a spreadsheet. The template instructs the computer to perform certain operations on data contained within the spreadsheet, for example, add 10 percent to shipping charges of those customers who live west of the Mississippi River. The template is stored on disk for future use.

temporary storage In programming, storage locations reserved for intermediate results. Synonymous with WORKING STORAGE.

ten-key pad A separate set of keys numbered 0 through 9 on a keyboard that allow easy entry of numbers. Similar to a calculator keypad.

ten's complement A number used to represent the negative of a given value. A ten's complement number is obtained by subtracting each digit from a number containing all 9s and adding 1; for example, 654 is the ten's complement of 346 and is obtained by performing the computation 999 - 346 + 1.

tera Prefix for one trillion. Abbreviated T.

terabit storage A general term applied to storage devices that can store a trillion (a million million or 10^{12}) bits of information.

terabyte Specifically, 1,009,511,627,776, or 2^{40} bytes. More loosely, one thousand gigabytes, one million megabytes, one billion kilobytes, or one trillion bytes. Used to measure capacities of optical disk mass storage devices. Abbreviated tb.

terminal A keyboard/display or keyboard/printer device used to input programs and data to the computer and to receive output from the computer.

terminal emulation A situation in which special software makes a computer behave as though it were a terminal connected to another computer.

terminal error Error of sufficient consequence that the program cannot continue.

terminal stand A wood or metal stand designed to support computer terminal.

terminal symbol A flowcharting symbol used to indicate the starting point and termination point or points in a procedure. An oval-shaped figure is used to represent this symbol.

ternary (1) Pertaining to a characteristic or property involving a selection, choice, or condition in which there are three possibilities. (2) Pertaining to the numeration system with a radix of 3.

test data Sample data especially created to test the operation of a given program. Usually, one or more hand-calculated results, or otherwise known results, will be associated with test data so the program under test may be validated.

test driver A program that directs the execution of another program against a collection of test data sets.

testing Examination of a program's behavior by executing the program on sample data sets. See DEBUG and SYSTEMS TESTING.

test plan A general description of what testing will involve, including specification of tolerable limits.

test run A run carried out to check that a program is operating correctly. During the run, test data generate results for comparison with previously prepared results.

text Words, letters, and numbers that express the information to be conveyed. Contrasted with graphics, which are shapes, lines, and symbols.

text editing The general term that covers any additions, changes, or deletions made to electronically stored material.

text editor A program that assists in the preparation of text. Used to manipulate text. For example, to erase, insert, change, and move words or groups of words. The text manipulated may be another computer program or any other arrangement of textual information.

text file A file containing information expressed in text form. Same as DATA FILE.

text processing The manipulation of alphabetic data under program control.

text system   A collection of hardware and specially written software used together to manipulate textual information. See WORD PROCESSING.

texture   In computer graphics, any 2-D pattern used to add the appearance complexity to a 3-D surface without actually modeling the complexity. Paintings or digitized photographs are frequently used. Whereas fractals actually add complexity to a 3-D data base, textures do not. The 2-D arrangement of pixels in a computed picture is frequently compared to the warp and woof of textiles, hence the term.

text window   An area on some computer graphics system's display screens within which text is displayed and scrolled.

theorem proving   Two approaches to automated theorem proving are proof-finding and consequence-finding. A proof-finding program attempts to find a proof for a certain given theorem. A consequence-finding program is given specific axioms for which to deduce consequences. Then, "interesting" consequences are selected.

theory of numbers   A branch of mathematics concerned generally with the properties and relationships of integers

thermal printer   A nonimpact printer that produces output on heat-sensitive paper. It uses heat to melt wire particles that contain ink, which are then transferred to paper. Thermal printers have slow speeds, mediocre quality reproduction and use an expensive paper. The device itself, however, i relatively inexpensive, quiet and reliable.

thesaurus   (1) A lexicon, more specifically where words ar grouped by ideas or sets of concepts. (2) A grouping or classification of synonyms or near-synonyms. (3) A set of equivalent classes of terminology.

The Source   See SOURCE, THE.

thimble   A printing element (in the form of a thimble) used for letter-quality printing. Character slugs are arranged around the perimeter of the thimble. As the slug for the character to be printed spins into the correct position, a hammer drives it forward to print the impression on paper.

thimble printer   A printer that uses a type wheel in the shape of a thimble. The thimble rotates, positioning the spokes that the striking device can hit the spoke tip against the ribbon, thus printing the character on paper.

thin film A computer storage made by placing thin spots of magnetic materials on an insulated base (usually a flat plate or wire); an electric current in wires attached to the base is used to magnetize the spot.

thin window display A one-line display used on keyboards, hand-held computers, and so on.

third-generation computers Computers made with integrated circuits.

third-party lease An agreement by which an independent firm buys equipment from the manufacturer and in turn leases it to the end user.

thirty-two-bit chip A CPU chip that processes data thirty-two bits at a time.

thrashing Overhead associated with memory swapping in a virtual memory system. Also called CHURNING.

threaded Pertaining to a program consisting of calls to several separate subprograms.

threaded tree A tree containing additional pointers to assist in the scan of the tree.

three-dimensional (3-D) In computer graphics this refers to the three spatial dimensions stored for each point of a model: height, width, and depth.

three-dimensional array An array that provides a threefold classification: row, column, and layer.

throughput Measure of the total amount of useful processing carried out by a computer system in a given time period.

thumbwheel A device for positioning an input cursor, consists of a rotatable wheel that controls the movement of that cursor in one axis. Normally, thumbwheels are found in pairs, one controlling vertical cursor movement, the other horizontal movement.

Thunderscan™ An inexpensive high-resolution scanner that replaces the ribbon cartridge in an Apple ImageWriter™ printer, and converts photographs and printed images into data that can be stored on a disk. Developed by Thunderware, Inc.

thyristor A bistable device comprising three or more junctions. See SCR.

tick mark A marking along a scale to indicate values. Can be used to denote points between identified numerical values.

tie-breaker Refers to circuitry that resolves the conflict that occurs when two central processing units try to use a peripheral device at the same time.

tie line A leased communications channel.

tightly coupled Pertaining to computers that are dependent upon one another.

tilting screen A video display screen that can be angled back and forth from top to bottom for easier viewing.

time-division multiplexing The merging of several bit streams of lower bit rates into a composite signal for transmission over a communication channel of higher bit-rate capacity. Abbreviated TDM.

time log A logging of how the computer system was used during a specified time period, such as 24 hours.

time quantum In a time-sharing system, a unit of time allotted to each user.

timer The computer's internal clock.

time-sharing A method of operation in which a computer facility is shared by several users for different purposes at (apparently) the same time. Although the computer actually services each user in sequence, the high speed of the computer makes it appear as though the users are all handled simultaneously.

time slice A unit of time.

time slicing The allotment of a portion of processing time to each program in a multiprogramming system to prevent the monopolization of the central processing unit by any one program.

toggle Pertaining to any device having two stable states. Synonymous with FLIP-FLOP.

token **(1)** A symbol representing a name or entity in a programming langue. **(2)** A group of bits, such as eight 1s, used in some bus networks to signal network access by a particular station.

token-passing A scheme that secures network access through a circulating electronic tag (a group of bits) called a token.

tone In computer graphics, the degree of tint and shade in color.

tool In some computer systems, an applications program.

toolkit software Refers to a software package that allows users to develop their own special applications more easily than by writing an entire program themselves. Examples are electronic spreadsheets, data base management systems, graphic systems, and word processing.

top-down development **(1)** An architectural discipline for computer program development wherein the high-level functions are coded and tested in an outline form early in the development process. Lower-level detail is added and tested progressively. **(2)** A program development method that gives order to the implementation of a software system. From specifications and interfaces the complete package is constructed beginning with the highest levels of control, such as job-control languages and operating system services, progressing to program control modules and extending to successively more detailed levels of program modules in a hierarchically descending structure. The effect of this approach is twofold. First, the actual system integration effort occurs simultaneously with the development; and second, an increasingly capable operational system is in use during development. See MODULAR PROGRAMMING and STRUCTURED PROGRAMMING.

top-down programming A programming method that begins with the most general statement of a program and divides it into increasingly detailed sets of routines.

top-level management Management personnel at the head of the organization who make key strategic decisions.

topology The physical layout of a computer network. The interconnection of devices and communication channels into a network configuration.

TOS An abbreviation for **TAPE OPERATING SYSTEM**. An operating system in which the operating system programs are stored on magnetic tape.

touch-sensitive panel See TOUCH-SENSITIVE TABLET.

touch-sensitive screen (1) A display screen on which the user can enter commands by pressing designated areas with a finger or other object. (2) A specialized type of video display that usually incorporates a clear plastic sheet in front of a video tube. The screen can detect the position where the screen is touched, and the computer can perform the function indicated.

touch-sensitive tablet An input device that converts graphics and pictorial data into numerical form for use by a computer. Graphic data can be generated by pressing the tablet with a stylus or finger.

touch-tone telephone A push-button telephone used in teleprocessing systems.

TPI An abbreviation for **TRACKS PER INCH**, a measure of storage density in magnetic disks.

trace (1) The scanning path of the beam in a raster display (2) An electrical pathway on circuit boards that connects electronic components

tracing routine A routine that provides a time history of the contents of the computer operational registers during the execution of a program. A complete tracing routine would reveal the status of all registers and locations affected by each instruction each time the instruction was executed.

track (1) A path along which data is recorded on a continuou or rotational medium, such as magnetic tape or magneti disk. (2) To follow or record the moving position of a vide display cursor, stylus, mouse, or other input device.

track ball A device used to move the cursor around on a com puter display screen. It consists of a mounting, usually box, in which is set a ball. As the user spins the ball, th cursor moves at the speed and in the direction of the ball's motion. Compare MOUSE.

tracking Moving a cursor or predefined symbol across the surface of the visual display screen with a light pen, electronic pen, mouse, or track ball.

tracking symbol The small symbol on a video display screen that represents the position of the cursor.

Tracks Per Inch (TPI) A measure of storage density in magnetic disks.

tractor fed printer A printer through which paper with holes along its edges is fed by sprocket wheels within the device.

tractor feed mechanism A pair of pin-studded belts that rotate in unison and pull paper, punched with marginal holes, into a printer.

tradeoff The balancing of factors in a computer system.

traffic The volume and flow of messages being transmitted in a computer system.

traffic intensity The ratio of the insertion rate to the deletion rate of a queue.

trailer record A record that follows a group of records and contains data pertinent to the group.

training manual A manual designed as a reference tool for learning to use a computer system or program.

transaction An act of doing business.

transaction code One or more characters that form part of a record and signify the type of transaction represented by the record.

transaction file A file containing relatively transient data to be processed in combination with a master file. For example, in a payroll application, a transaction file indicating hours worked might be processed with a master file containing employee name and rate of pay.

transaction-oriented processing Activities related to the processing of transactions as they occur.

transactions Business or other activities such as sales, expenditures, shipments, reservations, and inquiries.

transaction trailing In data base management systems, the creation of an auxiliary file that traces all file updates.

transborder Pertaining to communications between computer systems located across national borders.

transcribe To copy from one auxiliary storage medium to another. The process may involve conversion.

transducer Any device or element that converts an input signal into an output signal of a different form.

transfer (1) To move data form one location to another. (2) To change program control. See BRANCH, CONDITIONAL TRANSFER, JUMP, and UNCONDITIONAL TRANSFER.

transfer address See ENTRY POINT.

transfer rate The speed at which accessed data can be moved from one device to another. See ACCESS TIME and SEEK TIME.

transform To change from one form to another.

transformation In computer graphics, one of the modifications that can be made to the placement or size of an on-screen image. The three basic transformations are translation, scaling, and rotation.

transformer An alternating current (AC) device used in computer power supplies to reduce 115 volts 60 Hertz to a lower, more suitable voltage usable by computer equipment.

transient (1) Pertaining to a phenomenon caused in a system by a sudden change in conditions and that persists for a relatively short time after the change. (2) Pertaining to a momentary surge on a signal or power line. It may produce false signals and cause component failures. (3) Glitch.

transient program Program that does not reside in the computer system's main memory. When needed, the computer reads the program from a disk or tape. See RESIDENT PROGRAM.

transient suppressors Devices that smooth out minor voltage errors and usually provide constant, stable current flow

Most suppressors usually protect equipment from short-term high voltage conditions (spikes).

transistor A semiconductor device for controlling the flow of current between two terminals, the emitter and the collector, by means of variations in the current flow between a third terminal, the base, and one of the other two. It was developed at Bell Laboratories by William Shockley, Walter Brattain, and John Bardeen.

transistor-transistor logic A family of integrated circuits characterized by relatively high speed and low power consumption. Abbreviated TTL.

transit error A type of error that occurs only once and cannot be made to repeat itself.

translate To change data from one form of representation to another without significantly affecting the meaning. See LANGUAGE TRANSLATION.

translation (1) The translation of a program from one language into another language, such as BASIC to machine code. (2) In computer graphics, the movement of an image to a new position on the screen. Under translation, every point in the image moves in the same direction with the same speed at any given instant.

translator A program that converts a program written in one language to another language. See ASSEMBLER, COMPILER, and INTERPRETER.

transmission The sending of data from one location and the receiving of data in another location, usually leaving the source data unchanged. See DATA TRANSMISSION.

transmission facility The communications link between remote terminals and computers, such as communication lines, microwave transmission lines, communications satellites, lasers, telephone lines, fiber optics, and waveguides.

transmit To send data from one location and to receive the data at another location.

transparent Pertaining to a process that is not visible to the user or to other devices. Transparent memory refresh is an example. It describes a computer operation that does not require user intervention and so is transparent to the user.

transponder An amplifier located on a satellite that receives signals from an Earth station and reflects them to a receiving station.

transportable computer A small, portable computer, usually weighing less than 20 pounds.

transpose To interchange two items of data.

transversal The execution of each statement of a program for debugging purposes.

trap (1) A programmed conditional jump to a known location, is automatically executed when program execution reaches the location where the trap is set. (2) Loosely defined, an interrupt.

trapdoor A breach created intentionally in an information processing system for the purpose of later collecting, altering, or destroying information.

trapping A hardware provision for interrupting the normal flow of control of a program while transfer to a known location is made. See INTERRUPT.

tree A data structure similar to a linked list, except that each element carries with it the address of two or more other elements, rather than just one. Trees are an efficient way of storing items that must be searched for and retrieved quickly.

tree diagram A pictorial representation of the logical structure of a program or system.

tree sort A sort that exchanges items treated as nodes of a tree. When an item reaches the root NODE, it is exchanged with the lowest LEAF node. Also called HEAD SORT.

tree structure Another term for hierarchical structure, a form of data base organization.

tree traversal Visiting all the nodes in a tree in a particular order.

trend line A calculated extension of a data series for the purpose of predicting trends beyond known data.

triad A group of three, such as three bits, bytes, or characters.

trichromatic Three-colored. In computer graphics, trichromatic generally refers to the three primary colors (red, green, and blue) combined to create all others.

trigger The button, usually on a joystick, used in video games to initiate an event such as firing a missile or leapfrogging a hazard.

trigonometry A field of mathematics dealing with the measurement of curves and angles. These measuring techniques are employed in a number of scientific calculations.

triple precision The retention of three times as many digits of a quantity as the computer normally uses.

tristimulus values Relative amounts of three primary colors combined to create other colors.

Trojan horse Pertaining to a crime in which a computer criminal places instructions in someone else's program that will allow the program to function normally but also to perform illegitimate functions.

tron A popular high-tech suffix, such as datatron and cyclotron.

troubleshoot A term applied to the task of finding a malfunction in a hardware unit or a mistake in a computer program. Synonymous with debug. See BUG, DEBUGGING AIDS, and TEST DATA.

TRSDOS An acronym for TANDY-RADIO SHACK DISK OPERATING SYSTEM, the operating system for Radio Shack TRS-80™ microcomputers.

TRS-80™ microcomputer The tradename of several microcomputer systems manufactured by Radio Shack, a division of the Tandy Corporation. See HOME COMPUTER, MICROCOMPUTER, and PERSONAL COMPUTER.

True BASIC A version of the BASIC programming language that includes facilities for graphics, subroutines, trigonometric functions and handy control structures like SELECT-CASE, DO-WHILE, and DO-UNTIL. It makes structured programming easier, and requires no line numbers. True BASIC is compiled rather than interpreted, so it produces compact, fast-running code (and gives error messages before it begins to execute the program). See BASIC.

true complement Synonymous with TEN'S COMPLEMENT and TWO'S COMPLEMENT.

truncate **(1)** To reject the final digits in a number, thus lessening precision. For example, 3.14159 truncates the series for π, which could conceivably be extended indefinitely. **(2)** To cut off any characters that will not fit into an allotted space such as an eight-character name field on a printed report in which windsurfing would appear as windsurf.

truncation error An error due to truncation. Contrast with ROUND-OFF ERROR.

trunk The direct line between two telephone switching centers.

truth table A systematic tabulation of all the possible input/output combinations produced by a binary circuit.

TTL An acronym for TRANSISTOR-TRANSISTOR LOGIC. Logic circuits based on bipolar devices, usually low-power Schottky circuits that are fast but expensive because gold-plated Schottky diodes are required on every TTL bus input.

tunnel diode An electronic device with switching speeds of fractional billionths of seconds. Used in high-speed computer circuitry and memories.

Turbo Pascal A popular implementation of the Pascal programming language, developed by Philippe Kahn at Borland International Inc. Turbo Pascal is the leading Pascal compiler for the IBM Personal Computer™ series and is available for other microcomputers including the Macintosh™ and Apple II™ family of microcomputers. Turbo Pascal compiles Pascal programs much faster than conventional compilers, and includes a built-in full-screen editor for writing programs. See PASCAL.

Turbo PROLOG An implementation of the PROLOG programming language, developed by Borland International Inc., for use on the IBM Personal Computer™, Apple Macintosh™ and other microcomputers. See PROLOG.

TURING programming language A programming language developed in 1982 by R. C. Holt and J. R. Cordy, of the University of Toronto, whose primary design goal was to eliminate some of the inadequacies of the Pascal programming language. The language runs under the Unix operating system.

Turing's test Developed by British mathematician Alan Turing, this is a game to determine whether a computer might be considered to possess intelligence. Participants in the game include two respondents (a computer and a human) and a human examiner who tries to determine which of the unseen respondents is the human. According to this test, intelligence and the ability to think would be demonstrated by the computer's success in fooling the examiner.

turnaround To reverse some process.

turnaround form An output document that serves as an input medium during a subsequent phase of processing.

turnaround time The time it takes for a job to travel from the user to the computing center, to be run on the computer, and for the program results to be returned to the user.

turnkey system A prepackaged, ready-to-use computer system containing all the hardware, software, training, and maintenance support needed to perform a given application.

turn off The act of turning off (powering down) a computer system.

turn on The act of turning on (powering up) a computer system.

turtle A small, triangular shape that is displayed on a screen in the use of turtle graphics with the LOGO language. Shows the direction of lines for graphics. For example, if an instruction says "move south," the turtle moves toward the bottom of the screen.

turtle graphics Graphics accomplished by a simulated robot that have been incorporated into LOGO and other computer languages. Turtle graphics is used to teach geometry and computer graphics concepts.

tutorial A hardware or software training manual. It can be a printed document or recorded in magnetic form on a disk or tape.

tutorial program A computer program that explains new material and then tests the user's retention.

TV AN abbreviation for TELEVISION.

TVT An abbreviation for TELEVISION TYPEWRITER, a keyboard and electronics specially designed to covert a television into a computer terminal. A video terminal.

TV terminal A common television set used as a computer output device. See VIDEO MONITOR and TELEVISION RECEIVER.

tweak To fine-tune or adjust a piece of equipment. To enhance.

twinkle box An input device consisting of optical sensors, lenses, and a rotating disk, and capable of determining the three-dimensional position of a light-emitting object by angular light sensing.

twisted wire A data communications medium that consists of pairs of wires, twisted together, and bound into a cable.

two-dimensional Describes graphical information presented with visual aspects representing two physical extends: height and width.

two-dimensional array An arrangement consisting of rows and columns. See MATRIX.

two pass Pertaining to an operation or program that has to manipulate its data twice. It partially accomplishes its purpose on the first pass through the data. The operation is completed in the second pass through the data.

two's complement A method of representing negative numbers. A positive or negative binary number is changed to the opposite sign by changing all 1s to 0s and all 0s to 1s, then binarily adding 1. Synonymous with TRUE COMPLEMENT.

type ahead In word processing, a feature that prevents the loss of characters when the operator is typing faster than the computer can display characters on the screen.

typeball A typewriter striking element that contains all the usable characters. It looks like a golf ball with raised characters set around the surface. It is mounted on a movable axis and acts as a hammer, striking the ribbon against the paper to produce the character image.

typeface A collection of letters, numbers, and symbols that share a distinctive appearance.

type font A complete set of characters in a consistent and unique typeface.

typematic Any keyboard character that repeats for as long as it is pressed.

typeover The ability of an impact printer to strike a character more than once to produce a boldface effect on the printed copy.

typesize The size of type, and type fonts, which are given and measured in points. A point is about 1/72 of an inch. Points give an approximate measure of the vertical size of type.

typewriter An input/output device (a standard typewriter with computer interface circuitry) capable of being connected to a computer and used for communications purposes.

U

u A substitute for the symbol μ, the Greek letter mu, which stands for micro.

UART An acronym for **U**NIVERSAL **A**SYNCHRONOUS RE-CEIVER/TRANSMITTER. A device that converts parallel data into serial form for transmission along a serial interface, and vice versa.

uC An abbreviation for **MICRO**COMPUTER.

UCSD Pascal A high-level programming languge, developed largely by the Institute for Information Science at the University of California, San Diego, under the direction of Kenneth L. Bowles. It contains a number of extensions to Standard Pascal particularly ones that handle graphics and character strings. See APPLE PASCAL, PASCAL and STANDARD PASCAL.

UCSP p-system A program development system created by Kenneth Bowles at the UNIVERSITY OF CALIFORNIA AT SAN DIEGO (UCSD). It includes an operating system, a text editor and compilers for several languages including FOR-

TRAN, Microsoft BASIC, and Pascal. The p refers to "pseu-docomputer." The system compilers produce a very com-pact p-code, which runs on a pseudocomputer. An interpreter converts the p-code into acceptable code for the actual computer on which the program is run, making the system very portable. Only a very small interpreter need be written for each computer on which the p-system runs.

ULSI See ULTRA LARGE SCALE INTEGRATION.

ultrafiche A microfiche holding images reduced a hundredfold or more.

ultra large scale integration The process of placing the equiv-alent of one million or more components on one chip. See INTEGRATED CIRCUIT.

ultrasonic Above the human audio range, that is, above 20 kilohertz.

ultraviolet light Light with rays shorter than those of visible light but longer than X-rays. Used to erase data or instruc-tions stored in an Erasable PROM (EPROM). Once the EPROM has been erased, it can be reprogrammed by using a PROM programmer. See EPROM and PROM PROGRAM-MER.

unary See MONADIC.

unattended operation Data transmission and/or reception without an operator.

unbundled Pertaining to the services, programs, training, and so on sold independently of computer hardware by the hardware manufacturer. Contrast with BUNDLED.

unconditional transfer In program control, an instruction that always causes a branch away from the normal sequence of executing instructions. Contrast with CONDITIONAL TRANSFER.

uncontrolled loop A program loop that does not reach a log-ical end.

underflow (1) The condition that arises when a computer com-putation yields a result smaller than the smallest possible quantity the computer is capable of storing. (2) A condition in which the exponent plus the excess become negative in a floating point arithmetic operation.

undo A word processing command that undoes the effect of previous commands and puts the text back the way it was.

unibus A high-speed data communications bus structure shared by the CPU, main memory, and peripherals.

uninterruptable power supply A battery operated device that supplies a computer with electricity in the event of a brown-out or blackout.

union The joining or combining of two or more things.

unipolar Refers to having one pole. See BIPOLAR.

UNISYS A large manufacturer of computer equipment. The company was formed by a merger of Burroughs Corporation and Sperry Corporation.

unit A device having a special function, such as arithmetic-logic unit, central processing unit, or visual display unit.

unit position The extreme right position of a field.

universal asynchronous receiver/transmitter An integrated circuit device that receives serial data and converts it into parallel form for transmission, and vice versa.

universal identifier A standard multidigit number assigned to an individual to be used in verifying his or her identity.

universal language A programming language available on many computers, such as BASIC, Pascal and LOGO. Same as COMMON LANGUAGE.

universal product code A ten-digit computer readable code used in labeling retail products. The code includes a 5-digit manufacturer identification number and 5-digit product code number.

UNIX An easy-to-use operating system developed by Ken Thompson, Dennis Ritchie and coworkers at Bell Laboratories. Since the UNIX operating system is very easy to use, its design concept had a great influence on operating systems for microcomputers. UNIX is widely used on a great variety of computers, from mainframes to microcomputers. It is a powerful operating system that has many high-level utility programs, and it is capable of running a number of jobs at once. It has many applications including office automation, network control, and control of numerically controlled machinery. Since it also has superior capabilities as a program development system, UNIX should become even more widely used in the future.

unordered tree   A tree composed of nodes arranged in a seemingly random order.

unpack   To separate short units of data that have previously been packed. Opposite of PACK.

unpopulated board   A circuit board whose components must be supplied by the purchaser. Contrast with POPULATED BOARD.

unset   To change the value of a bit (or a group of bits) to binary 0.

uP   An abbreviation for **MICRO**PROCESSOR.

up   Designating a computer, a component of a computer system, or a software system, that is operating correctly and so is available for use. Contrast with DOWN.

up-and-running   Used to indicate that a computer system or peripheral device has just been put into operation and is working properly. Restored to full operation.

UPC   An abbreviation for **UNIVERSAL PRODUCT CODE**. Developed by the supermarket industry for identifying products and manufacturers on product tags. A variety of manufacturers produce printers to print the 10-digit bar symbol and optical scanning devices to read the codes during supermarket checkout.

update   (1) To make data files more current by adding, changing, or deleting data. (2) To change a software system to reflect changes, new editions, or new information.

upgrade   To reconfigure a computer system to increase its computing power.

upload   To transfer data from a user's system to a remote computer system. Opposite of DOWNLOAD.

upper case   Capital letters.

---

uptime The period of time that equipment is working without failure.

upward compatible A term used to indicate that a computer system or peripheral device can do everything that the previous model could do, plus some additional functions. See compatibility.

usability The worth of a system as evaluated by the person who must use it.

US An abbreviation for microsecond, one millionth of a second.

USEC An abbreviation for microsecond, one millionth of a second.

user (1) Anyone who owns or utilizes a computer for problem solving or data manipulation. (2) Anyone who requires the services of a computer system.

user-defined function A function that has been defined by the user.

user-defined key A computer keyboard key that has a predefined function or whose function can be changed by a program. The function is performed by the computer whenever the key is depressed.

user-friendly A term applied to hardware or software that allows a user to operate the equipment or software with little or no instruction. Another way of saying "easy to use."

user group A group of computer users who share the knowledge they have gained and the programs they have developed on a computer or class of computers of a specific manufacturer. The group usually meets to exchange information, share programs, and trade equipment. It provides a valuable opportunity to get and give advice on computer hardware, software and applications. Often a member can talk to someone who used a product he or she is considering buying or using. User-group newsletters also offer useful information.

user-oriented language See PROBLEM-ORIENTED LANGUAGE and PROCEDURE-ORIENTED LANGUAGE.

user profile Refers to the information used as a part of a security system such as the user's job function, areas of knowledge, access privileges and supervisor.

user's manual A document describing how to use a hardware device, a software product, or a system.

user terminal See TERMINAL.

utility A program that helps the user run, enhance, create, or analyze other programs, programming languages, operating systems, and equipment.

utility programs Computer programs that provide commonly needed services, such as transferring data from one medium to another (disk to tape) and character conversion. Vendors of large computer systems commonly supply a set of utilities with their systems. Utilities are designed to facilitate or aid the operation and use of the computer for a number of different applications and uses. Examples of utilities are memory dump programs, program debugging aids, file-handling programs, mathematical routines, sorting programs, and text editors.

utilization statistics Refers to a measure of a computer's performance based on the time log.

V

VAB An acronym for VOICE ANSWER BACK, an audio response device that can link a computer system to a telephone network, thus providing voice response to inquiries made from telephone terminals.

vacuum tube Device for controlling flow of electrical current. The dominant electronic element found in computers prior to the advent of the transistor. Those computers using vacuum tubes are referred to as FIRST-GENERATION COMPUTERS.

validation The examination of data for correctness against certain criteria, such as format (patterns of numbers, spaces and letters), ranges (upper- and lower-value limits), check digits, and equivalent entries on a master file.

value (1) A constant or quantity stored in a computer's memory. (2) A number entered into a spreadsheet cell.

value-added network A system in which a carrier leases communication lines from a common carrier, enhances them by adding improvements, such as error detection and faster response time, and then leases them to a third party.

value parameter The variable in a subprogram that takes on a value that is passed to the subprogram.

variable A quantity that can assume any of a given set of values. For example, in the BASIC statement PRINT A, B, C, the variables A, B, and C represent the actual values that will be printed. See SUBSCRIPTED VARIABLE.

variable-length record Record in a file in which records are not uniform in length. Contrast with FIXED-LENGTH RECORD.

variable name An alphanumeric term that identifies a data value in a program. The term can assume any of a set of values.

variable word length Pertaining to a machine word or operand that may consist of a variable number of bits, bytes, or characters. Contrast with FIXED WORD LENGTH.

VAX A designation for large minicomputer systems manufactured by Digital Equipment Corporation.

VDL An abbreviation for VIENNA DEFINITION LANGUAGE, a language for defining the syntax and semantics of programming languages.

VDT An abbreviation for VIDEO DISPLAY TERMINAL, an input/output device consisting of a display screen and an input keyboard.

VDU An abbreviation for VISUAL DISPLAY UNIT, a peripheral device on which data is displayed on some type of screen.

vector (1) A list of numbers, all of which are expressed on the same line, such as a single column or row. (2) A quantity having magnitude and direction. (3) In computer science, a data structure that permits the location of any item by the use of a single index or subscript. (4) Type of cathode-ray tube on which graphic data is represented by lines drawn from point to point rather than by illumination of a series of contiguous positions, as on a raster display device. **(5)** In plotting, an element of a line connecting two points.

vector display A cathode-ray tube that moves the electron beam randomly to trace figures on the screen. Contrast with RASTER DISPLAY.

vector pair The data points that make up the opposite ends of a vector.

vector processor See ARRAY PROCESSOR.

Vectra PC™ A microcomputer compatible with the IBM Personal Computer AT™, manufactured by Hewlett-Packard.

vendee A person or business that purchases a hardware or software system.

vendor **(1)** A company or business entity that sells computers, peripheral devices, time-sharing service, or computer services. **(2)** A supplier.

Venn diagram A diagram that uses circles and ellipses to give a graphic representation of logic relationships.

Ventura™ A desktop publishing software package that may be used to construct charts, newsletters and most jobs requiring little graphics. Developed by Xerox.

verify To determine whether a data processing operation has been accomplished accurately, such as to check data validity.

version A specific release of a software product of a specific hardware model. Usually numbered in ascending order. For example, DOS 3.3 is a later version of a disk operating system than DOS 3.1 or DOS 1.0.

vertex A point where two sides of an angle meet.

vertical recording A technology that strives to stand magnetic bits of information on end instead of side by side on a disk as they are today. Using this technology, several billion bytes of information could be stored on one disk.

vertical scrolling The ability of a system to move up and down through a page or more of data displayed on the video screen.

Very Large Data Base (VLDB) A data base distributed among multiple computers with different data base management systems.

very large scale integration The process of placing a large number (usually between 1,000 and 1 million) of components on one chip. Abbreviated VLSI. See INTEGRATED CIRCUIT.

vetting The process of making a background investigation of a person to reduce security risks.

VHSIC program VERY HIGH SPEED INTEGRATED CIRCUIT program, a joint government-private industry effort, the purpose of which is to provide the Department of Defense with advanced integrated circuits for use in future weapons and armaments.

video A visual display.

video digitizer An input device that converts the signal from a video camera into digital form and stores it in computer storage, where it can be analyzed or modified by the computer.

videodisk A plastic platter resembling a phonograph record that uses low-intensity laser beams to store visual materials that will appear on a display screen. Many videodisk units can be controlled by a computer.

video display terminal A device for entering information into a computer and displaying it on a screen. A keyboard is used to enter information. Abbreviated VDT.

video game An interactive game of skill and strategy in which the player operates a picking device, such as a joystick or paddle, while observing the graphics of the action on the display screen. A popular activity on personal computers and in amusement arcades.

video game machine A microprocessor-controlled machine designed principally for running commercially produced cartridges that contain games and educational programs.

video generator A device that generates the signals that control a television display.

video monitor A device functionally identical to a television set, except that it has no channel selector. It receives its picture signal from an external source, such as a video terminal board. See TELEVISION RECEIVER.

video signal An electronic signal containing information specifying the location and brightness of each point on a CRT screen, along with timing signals to place the image properly on the screen.

video terminal A device for entering information into a computer system and displaying it on a screen. A typewriter-like keyboard is used to enter information. See CATHODE-RAY TUBE, DISPLAY, and SCREEN.

videotex The generic term for electronic home information delivery systems. Within this broad term, there are two specific approaches, called viewdata and teletext. See TELETEXT and VIEWDATA.

vidicon The tube inside a TV camera that converts the image of a scene into an electrical signal.

view A way of presenting the contents of a data base to the user, not necessarily the same as the way the fields and records are stored in the data base. Different users or programs that call upon the data base for information may have unique views of the data.

viewdata A home information delivery system through which users can access a central data base interactively from their local TV. Users may request specific frames of information. More important, they can directly access what they want, meaning quicker response time and a more structured usage of the medium. Users can communicate with other users via the system (electronic mail). They can also utilize transactional services, including shopping or banking based on information provided by the system. Also called videotext. See TELETEXT.

viewport A process that allows a user to place any selected picture in a chosen location on a video display screen. Compare WINDOW.

virtual Appearing to be, rather than *actually* being.

virtual address In virtual storage systems, an address that refers to virtual storage and must, therefore, be translated into a real STORAGE address when it is used.

virtual machine The illusion of having many copies of the existing computer running simultaneously.

virtual memory See VIRTUAL STORAGE.

virtual storage A technique for managing a limited amount of main storage and a (generally) much larger amount of lower-speed storage in such a way that the distinction is largely transparent to a computer user. The technique entails some means of swapping segments of the program and data from the lower-speed storage (which would commonly be a disk) into the main storage, where it would be interpreted as instructions or operated upon as data. The unit of program or data swapped back and forth is called a page. The high-speed storage from which instructions are executed is called real storage; the lower-speed storage (disk) is called virtual storage.

Virtual Storage Operating System (VSOS) An operating system that uses a computer system's virtual storage capability.

VisiCalc™ A popular electronic spreadsheet program. The name is derived from **VISI**BLE **CALC**ULATION. VisiCalc displays information on a screen as an electronic sheet or grid. Locations within the grid are treated as variables. To manipulate a variable, the user applies an operation to the variable's location in the grid. VisiCalc, the first electronic spreadsheet package, was originally developed for the Apple II™ microcomputer.

vision recognition A method for processing pictorial information by computer. For example, an AI (artificial intelligence) computer can recognize a TV image of a horse and say (or print out), "It is a horse." Recognizing images is a very complex process for machines. See IMAGE PROCESSING.

visual display A visual representation of data, such as a picture or diagram drawn on a display screen or a diagram produced by a plotter or graphics printer.

visual page A visual representation consisting of one or more stored screen display files.

visual scanner See OPTICAL CHARACTER READER.

VLDB An abbreviation for VERY LARGE DATA BASE. A data base distributed among multiple computers with different data base management systems.

VLSI An abbreviation for VERY LARGE SCALE INTEGRATION. Usually means chips that contain between 1,000 and 1 million components. See INTEGRATED CIRCUIT.

VM/SP An abbreviation for VIRTUAL MACHINE/SYSTEM PRODUCT, an operating system for large IBM mainframe computers.

vocabulary Codes or instructions that can be used to write a program for a particular computer.

voder A speech synthesizer.

Voice Answer Back (VAB) An audio response device that can link a computer system to a telephone network, thus providing voice response to inquiries made from telephone terminals.

voice communications The transmission of sound in the human hearing range. Voice or audio sound can be transmitted either as analog or digital signals.

voice grade channel Pertaining to computer-to-computer links that employ the lines used in normal telephone communications. Essential to most telecommunications, these lines permit data transmission at frequencies from 300 to 3,000 Hz and at rates up to 9600 baud.

voice input An input device that permits a human voice to be used as input to a computer.

voice mail Messages spoken into a telephone, converted into digital form, and stored in the computer's memory until recalled, at which time they are reconverted into voice form.

voice output An audio response device that permits the computer to deliver output by the spoken word.

voice recognition Direct conversation of spoken data into electronic form suitable for entry into a computer system.

This technique allows a computer to respond to a set of instructions spoken by a human voice.

voice response Computer output in spoken form.

voice synthesis The ability of a computer to use stored patterns of sounds within its memory to assemble words that can be played through a loudspeaker.

volatile storage A storage medium whose contents are lost if power is turned off. Contrast with NONVOLATILE STORAGE.

voltage Electrical pressure. High voltage in a computer circuit is represented by "1"; low (or zero) voltage is represented by "0."

voltage regulator A circuit that holds an output voltage at a predetermined value or causes it to vary according to a predetermined plan, regardless of normal input-voltage change or changes in the load IMPEDANCE.

voltage surge protector A device that protects electrical equipment from being damaged by short surges of high voltage. A computer or other device is plugged into the surge protector, which itself is plugged into a standard 110-volt electrical outlet. See LINE SURGE.

volume A physical unit of a storage medium, such as a floppy disk capable of having data recorded on it and subsequently read.

VS An abbreviation for VIRTUAL STORAGE.

VSOS An abbreviation for VIRTUAL STORAGE OPERATING SYSTEM, that uses a computer system's virtual storage capability.

vulnerability Weaknesses in a computer system that pose security hazards.

W

wafer A three or four inch thin, circular disk on which many integrated circuits are fabricated and subsequently diced up into individual chips.

wait state A condition in which the central processing unit is idle, not executing instructions.

wait time The time during which a program or a computer waits for the completion of other activities.

walkthrough A review session in which a phase of system or program development is reviewed by peers to identify errors.

wand A hand-held optical device that can read and identify coded labels, bar codes, and characters.

Wang Laboratories A manufacturer of word processors and microcomputers.

warm boot The process of fooling the computer into thinking that its power has been turned off although power is still on.

warming message A diagnostic message produced by a compiler to alert the user to an error.

warm start Same as WARM BOOT.

warm-up time The interval between the energizing of a device and the beginning of the application of its output characteristics.

warranty A guarantee.

WATFIV An acronym for WATERLOO FORTRAN IV, a FORTRAN compiler developed for teaching purposes at the University of Waterloo, Ontario, Canada.

WATFOR An acronym for WATERLOO FORTRAN, a version of FORTRAN developed at the University of Waterloo in Ontario, Canada.

WATS An acronym for WIDE AREA TELEPHONE SERVICE. A service that permits an unlimited number of calls from one point to any location in a large area. The United States is divided into six WATS zones.

WCCE See WORLD CONFERENCE ON COMPUTERS IN EDUCATION.

weed To discard currently undesirable or needless items from a file.

weighted code A code in which each bit position of the code has a weighted value. In the 8-4-2-1 weighted code system, the decimal numeral 529 would be 0101 0010 1001.

West Coast Computer Faire A major microcomputer trade show held annually in San Francisco.

wetzel A picture element added to the image on a visual display terminal to improve the sharpness of the display.

What if? The premise on which most electronic spreadsheet programs operate. New values may be substituted to determine the resultant effect on other values.

wheel printer A printer with a printing mechanism that contains the printing characters on metal wheels.

white noise Continuous noise produced over all audible frequencies to "fill-in-the-gaps" between discontinuous office distractions such as printers, keyboards and footsteps.

whole number A number without a fractional part, such as 92 or 64.0.

Wide Area Telephone Service A service provided by telephone companies that permits a customer, by use of an access line called a WATS line, to make data communications in a specific zone on a dial basis for a flat monthly charge. The U.S. is divided into six WATS zones.

wideband In data communications, a channel wider in bandwidth than a voice-grade channel.

widow The first line of a paragraph sitting alone at the bottom of a page of text. Considered undesirable in all forms of printing. Compare with ORPHAN.

wild card A method that permits an operating system to perform utility functions on multiple files with related names, without the programmer or user having to specify each file by its full, unique name. For example, if a word processor is directed to search for "Don," it might locate "Donald" as well as "Donna" if both were present in the file.

Winchester disk drive A fast auxiliary storage device. A type of hard disk that is sealed in an air-tight, dust-free container.

window A portion of the video display area dedicated to some specific purpose. Special software allows the screen to be divided into multiple "windows" that can be moved around and made bigger or smaller. Windows allow the user to treat the computer display screen like a desktop where various files can remain open simultaneously.

windowing   The act of displaying two or more files or disparate portions of the same file on the screen simultaneously.

wire wrap   A type of circuit board construction. Electrical connections are made through wires connected to the posts that correspond to the proper component lead.

wizard   An experienced hacker.

word   A logical unit of information. A group of bits, characters, or bytes considered as an entity and capable of being stored in one storage location.

WORD   See MICROSOFT WORD.

word length   The number of bits in a word, usually 8, 16, or 32.

WordPerfect™   A fast, full-featured word processor offered in several versions, depending on the intended computer. Developed by WordPerfect Corporation.

word processing   A software system that lets you write, revise, manipulate, format, and print text for letters, reports, manuscripts, and other printed matter. Word processing is the most common use for personal computers in business and the home.

word processing center   A central facility that contains the word processing equipment and personnel that prepares written communications for an organization.

word processing operator   An individual who operates word processing equipment.

word processing program   Software that guides the computer system in writing, editing, and formatting text. Same as WORD PROCESSOR.

Word Processing Society (WPS)   An organization that encourages word processing educational programs in schools to promote word processing as a profession.

word processing supervisor   The person who oversees the work performed in a word processing center.

word processing system An information processing system that relies on automated and computerized typing, copying, filing, dictation, and document retrieval. Increasingly used in modern offices.

word processor A computer program that provides for manipulation of text. It can be used for writing documents, inserting or changing words, paragraphs, or pages, and printing documents.

WordStar™ A popular word processing program that includes a spelling checker and mail merge features, developed by MicroPro International Corporation. Several versions of WordStar are available.

word wrap A feature that automatically moves a word to the beginning of the next line if it will not fit at the end of the original line. A feature found in word processing systems.

workbench A programming environment in which hardware and software items are shared by several users.

work breakdown structure A comprehensive listing of the work elements and dependencies required to complete a given project; a tool for the project planner, serving as a predefinition to speed up the planning process.

working storage Same as TEMPORARY STORAGE.

worksheet Same as SPREADSHEET.

workspace A loosely defined term that usually refers to the amount of main storage available for programs and data and allocated for working storage.

workstation A configuration of computer equipment designed for use by one person at a time. This may have a terminal connected to a computer, or it may be a stand-alone system with local processing capability. Examples of workstations are a stand-alone graphics system and a word processor.

work year The effort expended by one person for one year. This term is used to estimate the personnel resources needed to complete a specific task.

World Conference on Computers in Education (WCCE) An international computer education conference sponsored by the International Federation for Information Processing (IFIP) and the American Federation of Information Processing Societies (AFIPS). The conference is held every four years in a different country.

WP An abbreviation for **WORD PROCESSING**. Involves the use of computerized equipment and systems to facilitate the handling of words and text.

WPM An abbreviation for **WORDS PER MINUTE**. A measure of data transmission speed.

WPS An abbreviation for **WORD PROCESSING SOCIETY**. This organization encourages word processing educational programs in school to promote word processing as a profession.

wraparound The continuation of an operation, such as a change in the storage location from the largest addressable location to the first addressable location; or a visual display cursor movement from the last character position to the first position.

write **(1)** The process of transferring information from the computer to an output medium. **(2)** To copy data, usually from internal storage to auxiliary storage devices. **(3)** Contrast with READ.

write-enable ring A plastic ring that must be placed on a tape reel before information can be recorded on the tape.

write head A magnetic head designed to write data onto the media. Contrast with READ HEAD.

write-inhibit ring A plastic ring used to prevent data from being written over on magnetic tapes.

write protect A procedure for preventing a disk or tape from being written to.

write-protect notch Floppy disks (diskettes) may be protected from the possibility of undesired recording of data by application of a gummed tab over the "write-protect notch." An uncovered write protect notch will allow writing to the diskette. See FILE PROTECTION.

write-protect ring A plastic ring that prevents writing on the tape when it is removed from the back of a tape reel.

WYSIWYG An abbreviation for **WHAT YOU SEE IS WHAT YOU GET**. Refers to word processors that generate screen images that are identical in position and type appearance to the final document, as opposed to those that show the formatting or special type requested only when the document is printed. The advantages are twofold: planning a visually pleasing final product is easier, and errors in the printed document can be found instantly when the document file is reloaded into the word processor.

XYZ

x-axis On a coordinate plane, the horizontal axis.

XENIX A variation of the UNIX operating system created by Microsoft Corporation for use on microcomputers.

xerographic printer A device for printing an optical image on paper in which light and dark areas are represented by electrostatically charged areas on the paper. A powdered ink dusted on the paper adheres to the charged areas and is melted into the paper by heat.

XOR An acronym for **EXCLUSIVE OR**.

X-Y chart A form that allows plotting of one data series against another, without a time axis. Often used to determine if there is a correlation between two series, with the direction, slope, and curvature of the line showing the relationship.

X-Y plotter An output device that draws points, lines, or curves on a sheet of paper based on X and Y coordinates from a computer. See PLOTTER.

y-axis On a coordinate plane, the vertical axis.

yoke The part of the electron beam deflection system used for addressing a video display.

zap (1) A command in many electronic spreadsheet programs that irretrievably erases all information on the spreadsheet. (2) To delete a file or clear a screen accidentally.

z-axis On a coordinate plane, the axis that represents depth.

zero A numeral normally denoting lack of magnitude. In many computers, there are distinct representations for plus and minus zero.

zero flag A FLIP-FLOP that goes to logic 1 if the result of an instruction has the value of zero.

zeroize To initialize a program with zeros. To fill spaces in storage with zeros.

zero suppression The suppression (elimination) of nonsignificant zeros in a numeral, usually before or during a printing operation. For example, the numeral 00004763, with zero suppression, would be printed as 4763.

zone bits Special bits used along with numeric bits to represent alphanumeric characters in ASCII and EBCDIC codes.

zooming The changing of a view on a graphics display by either moving in on successively smaller portions of the currently visible picture or moving out until the window encloses the entire scene. A capability that proportionally enlarges or reduces a figure displayed on a visual display screen.

Zulu time The international point of reference for the time of day. Greenwich Meridian Time.

Z-80 An 8-bit microprocessor chip used as a base for microcomputers.

CONVERSION TABLES

DECIMAL	BINARY	HEXADECIMAL	OCTAL
0	0000	0	0
1	0001	1	1
2	0010	2	2
3	0011	3	3
4	0100	4	4
5	0101	5	5
6	0110	6	6
7	0111	7	7
8	1000	8	10
9	1001	9	11
10	1010	A	12
11	1011	B	13
12	1100	C	14
13	1101	D	15
14	1110	E	16
15	1111	F	17
16	1 0000	10	20
17	1 0001	11	21
18	1 0010	12	22
19	1 0011	13	23
20	1 0100	14	24
21	1 0101	15	25
22	1 0110	16	26
23	1 0111	17	27
24	1 1000	18	30
25	1 1001	19	31
26	1 1010	1A	32
27	1 1011	1B	33
28	1 1100	1C	34
29	1 1101	1D	35
30	1 1110	1E	36
40	10 1000	28	50
50	11 0010	32	62

HEXADECIMAL AND DECIMAL CONVERSION

HEXADECIMAL COLUMNS

6		5		4		3		2		1	
hex	dec	hex	dec	hex	dec	hex	dec	hex	dec	hex	dec
0	0	0	0	0	0	0	0	0	0	0	0
1	1,048,576	1	65,536	1	4,096	1	256	1	16	1	1
2	2,097,152	2	131,072	2	8,192	2	512	2	32	2	2
3	3,145,728	3	196,608	3	12,288	3	768	3	48	3	3
4	4,194,304	4	262,144	4	16,384	4	1,024	4	64	4	4
5	5,242,880	5	327,680	5	20,480	5	1,280	5	80	5	5
6	6,291,456	6	393,216	6	24,576	6	1,536	6	96	6	6
7	7,340,032	7	458,752	7	28,672	7	1,792	7	112	7	7
8	8,388,608	8	524,288	8	32,768	8	2,048	8	128	8	8
9	9,437,184	9	589,824	9	36,864	9	2,304	9	144	9	9
A	10,485,760	A	655,360	A	40,960	A	2,560	A	160	A	10
B	11,534,336	B	720,896	B	45,056	B	2,816	B	176	B	11
C	12,582,912	C	786,432	C	49,152	C	3,072	C	192	C	12
D	13,631,488	D	851,968	D	53,248	D	3,328	D	208	D	13
E	14,680,064	E	917,504	E	57,344	E	3,584	E	224	E	14
F	15,728,640	F	983,040	F	61,440	F	3,840	F	240	F	15

FROM HEXADECIMAL TO DECIMAL:

– Find each hexadecimal digit in the correct column position.

– Record corresponding decimal value for the digits in each position.

– Add the decimal values together to find the final decimal number.

For example, to find the decimal equivalent of the hexadecimal number A4BC, find the hexadecimal number A in the fourth column and record the decimal equivalent of 40,960; find the hexadecimal number 4 in the third column and record the decimal equivalent of 1,024; find the hexadecimal number B in the second column and record the decimal equivalent of 176; find the hexadecimal number C in the first column and record the decimal equivalent of 12. Adding the decimal numbers together results in a total of 42,172—the decimal equivalent of A4BC.

FROM DECIMAL TO HEXADECIMAL:

– Find the largest decimal number in the table that is less than the number to be converted.

– Record its hexadecimal equivalent.

– Subtract the number found in the table from the number to be converted.

– Repeat the process until there is no remainder.

For example, to find the hexadecimal equivalent of the decimal number 41,540, find in the table the number closest to but not exceeding 41,540, which is 40,960. Record the corresponding hexadecimal digit of A. Subtract 40,960 from 41,540. Find in the table the closest number to the remainder 580 that does not exceed 580, which is 512. Record the corresponding hexadecimal digit of 2. Subtract 512 from 580. Look in the table again for the remainder of 68. Find 64 in the table, record the hexadecimal digit 4, and subtract 64 from 68. Look in the last column for the remainder of 4 and record the hexadecimal digit 4. Arranging the digits in order from left to right results in the hexadecimal number A244, which is the hexadecimal equivalent of 41,540.

POWERS OF TWO TABLE

n	2^n
0	1
1	2
2	4
3	8
4	16
5	32
6	64
7	128
8	256
9	512
10	1 024
11	2 048
12	4 096
13	8 192
14	16 384
15	32 768

POWERS OF SIXTEEN TABLE

n	16^n
0	1
1	16
2	256
3	4 096
4	65 536
5	1 048 576
6	16 777 216
7	268 435 456
8	4 294 967 296
9	68 719 476 736
10	1 099 511 627 776
11	17 592 186 044 416
12	281 474 976 710 656
13	4 503 599 627 370 496
14	72 057 594 037 927 936
15	1 152 921 504 606 846 976

THE EBCDIC CHARACTER SET

CHARACTER	BINARY		HEX
LETTERS:			
A	1100	0001	C1
B	1100	0010	C2
C	1100	0011	C3
D	1100	0100	C4
E	1100	0101	C5
F	1100	0110	C6
G	1100	0111	C7
H	1100	1000	C8
I	1100	1001	C9
J	1101	0001	D1
K	1101	0010	D2
L	1101	0011	D3
M	1101	0100	D4
N	1101	0101	D5
O	1101	0110	D6
P	1101	0111	D7
Q	1101	1000	D8
R	1101	1001	D9
S	1110	0010	E2
T	1110	0011	E3
U	1110	0100	E4
V	1110	0101	E5
W	1110	0110	E6
X	1110	0111	E7
Y	1110	1000	E8
Z	1110	1001	E9
DIGITS:			
0	1111	0000	F0
1	1111	0001	F1
2	1111	0010	F2
3	1111	0011	F3
4	1111	0100	F4
5	1111	0101	F5
6	1111	0110	F6
7	1111	0111	F7
8	1111	1000	F8
9	1111	1001	F9

THE EBCDIC CHARACTER SET
(continued)

CHARACTER	BINARY		HEX
SPECIAL SYMBOLS:			
,	0110	1011	6B
=	0111	1110	7E
(	0100	1101	4D
)	0101	1101	5D
−	0110	0000	60
.	0100	1011	4B
/	0110	0001	61
'	0111	1101	7D
<	0100	1100	4C
>	0110	1110	6E
$	0101	1011	5B
¢	0100	1010	4A
%	0110	1100	6C
+	0100	1110	4E
:	0111	1010	7A
;	0101	1110	5E
*	0101	1100	5C
"	0111	1111	7F
‾	0110	1101	6D
@	0111	1100	7C
¬	0101	1111	5F
&	0101	0000	50
#	0111	1011	7B
!	0101	1010	5A
?	0110	1111	6F
|	0100	1111	4F

THE ASCII CHARACTER SET

	CHARACTER	BINARY		HEX
LETTERS:	A	0100	0001	41
	B	0100	0010	42
	C	0100	0011	43
	D	0100	0100	44
	E	0100	0101	45
	F	0100	0110	46
	G	0100	0111	47
	H	0100	1000	48
	I	0100	1001	49
	J	0100	1010	4A
	K	0100	1011	4B
	L	0100	1100	4C
	M	0100	1101	4D
	N	0100	1110	4E
	O	0100	1111	4F
	P	0101	0000	50
	Q	0101	0001	51
	R	0101	0010	52
	S	0101	0011	53
	T	0101	0100	54
	U	0101	0101	55
	V	0101	0110	56
	W	0101	0111	57
	X	0101	1000	58
	Y	0101	1001	59
	Z	0101	1010	5A
DIGITS:	0	0011	0000	30
	1	0011	0001	31
	2	0011	0010	32
	3	0011	0011	33
	4	0011	0100	34
	5	0011	0101	35
	6	0011	0110	36
	7	0011	0111	37
	8	0011	1000	38
	9	0011	1001	39

THE ASCII CHARACTER SET
(continued)

	CHARACTER	BINARY		HEX
SPECIAL SYMBOLS:	,	0010	1100	2C
	=	0011	1101	3D
	(	0010	1000	28
	)	0010	1001	29
	–	0010	1101	2D
	.	0010	1110	2E
	/	0010	1111	2F
	'	0010	0111	27
	<	0011	1100	3C
	>	0011	1110	3E
	$	0010	0100	24
	%	0010	0101	25
	+	0010	1011	2B
	:	0011	1010	3A
	;	0011	1011	3B
	*	0010	1010	2A
	"	0010	0010	22
	_	0101	1111	5F
	@	0100	0000	40
	⌐	0101	1110	5E
	&	0010	0110	26
	#	0010	0011	23
	!	0010	0001	21
	?	0011	1111	3F
	|	0010	0001	21